the Unofficial Guide™ to Power Managing

Alan Weiss, Ph.D.

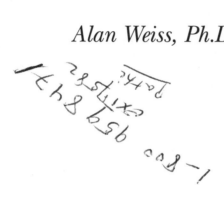

IDG Books Worldwide, Inc.
An International Data Group Company
Foster City, CA • Chicago, IL • Indianapolis, IN
• New York, NY

IDG Books Worldwide, Inc.
An International Data Group Company
919 E. Hillsdale Boulevard
Suite 400
Foster City, CA 94404

This publication contains the opinions and ideas of its author and is designed to provide useful advice to the reader on the subject matter covered. Any references to any products or services do not constitute or imply an endorsement or recommendation. The publisher and the author specifically disclaim any responsibility for any liability, loss, or risk (financial, personal or otherwise) which may be claimed or incurred as a consequence, directly or indirectly, of the use and/or application of any of the contents of this publication.

Certain terms mentioned in this book which are known or claimed to be trademarks or service marks have been capitalized.

IDG Books Worldwide, Inc., does not attest to the validity, accuracy, or completeness of this information. Use of a term in this book should not be regarded as affecting the validity of any trademark or service mark.

Unofficial Guides are a trademark of IDG Books Worldwide, Inc.

For general information on IDG Books Worldwide's books in the U.S., please call our Consumer Customer Service department at 800-762-2974. For reseller information, including discounts and previous sales, please call our Reseller Customer Service department at 800-434-3422.

ISBN: 0-02863749-6

Manufactured in the United States of America

10 9 8 7 6 5 4 3 2 1

First edition

To my kids, Danielle and Jason, who say I do not mention them enough. There.
And to my high school sweetheart and wife of 31 years, amazingly the same person.

Acknowledgments

My thanks to my agent, Jeff Herman, for encouraging me to pursue this opportunity, and to Randy Gil-Ladenheim, my editor, for her flexibility in arranging for it to happen. I am indebted to the clients of Summit Consulting Group, Inc., who, over the past 15 years, have helped me to learn and grow and have trusted me with some aspect of their well-being and their futures. Over the past year I'd be remiss in not singling out Doris Meister, Chairman and CEO of Merrill Lynch Trust Co.; Mary DeLoache Green, Senior Vice President at Fleet Private Clients Group; and Greg Zlevor, manager of internal training at Arthur Andersen; for their kindness and support. Thanks, too, to the members of my private roster mentoring program who have added so much to my understanding of consulting approaches and dynamics, and who allowed me to play a small role in their success.

Finally, but importantly, to Phoebe Weiss for her constant encouragement and support, and to my great partner, L. T. Weiss, now with me through 12 books, and a constant source of inspiration, determination, and intelligence.

Contents

The *Unofficial Guide* Reader's Bill of Rights xiii

The *Unofficial Guide* Panel of Experts xix

Introduction..xxi

I Influencing and Changing Behavior 1

1 Leveraging Our Impact Through Others........3
Fear Is a Mover, Not a Motivator 5
The "In Crowd" Really Isn't...........................7
The Role of Enlightened Self-interest 10
The Role of Influence 13
The Reciprocity of Interests 16
Destinations Are Safe, Journeys Are
Frightening 19
Force People to Let Go *22*
Choose and Support Exemplars *23*
Use Very Bright Lights *23*
Just the Facts 24

2 Empowerment As a Management Tool........27
Empowerment Is an Effective
Management Tool 28
The Rules for Empowerment........................34
What Leverage Really Means 37
The Cycle of Motivation and Self-esteem.......40
Just the Facts 45

3 Resolving Conflict Without Bloodshed.......47
The Two Forms of Conflict...........................48
Defusing the Hostility...............................52
The Truth About Personality Conflicts...........55
The "It's Not Me" Personality Disorder *56*
The Neurotic *57*

The Politician *59*
The Egoist *60*
The Psychotic *62*
The Depressed *63*

How to Pass the Impasse............................64
 Keep the Conflict Nonemotional and
  Never About Personal Qualities *65*
 Separate Fact from Assumption *66*
 Maintain Frequent Communications
  Channels *66*
 Test with Third Parties *67*
 Move the Accountability for Resolution
  to Those in Conflict *68*

Just the Facts 69

II Evaluating Performance and Providing Feedback 71

4 Dealing with Poor Performance.................73

Avoiding Psychobabble and Focusing on
Behavior 76

Coaching and Counseling As Systematic
Processes 80
 The Coaching Process *81*
 The Process of Counseling *83*

Effective Performance Evaluation 89

Just the Facts 94

5 Evaluating Behavior...............................97

The Difference Between Skills
and Behaviors...99

Why We Promote the Wrong People 100

The Four Basic Behavioral Measures...........104
 Assertiveness *104*
 Persuasiveness *105*
 Tolerance for Repetition *105*
 Attention to Detail *105*

The Case for Behavioral Interviewing..........110

Assessing and Adjusting Your Own
Behavior 112

Just the Facts 115

6 Communicating Under Any Circumstances at Any Time 117

Preventing Environmental Interference 119
Restaurants and Cafeterias 119
Hallways and Parking Lots 119
Rest Rooms 120

Preventing Cognitive Interference 121
Testing Incoming Communication 121
Testing Outgoing Communication 123

Allowing for Differences: Virtually
No One Is Like You 124

The Lost Art of Listening 126

The Four Techniques to Make the
Other Person Talk....................................127
Provocative Questioning 128
Reflective Listening 129
Turn-around Questions 131
The Bounce-back Technique 132

Just the Facts 134

III Resolving the Four Common Management Issues 137

7 Raising the Bar Instead of Fixing Problems..139

Why Innovation Is an Underappreciated
Skill...139

The 10 Sources of Innovation 143
Unexpected Success 143
Unexpected Failure 144
Process Weakness 145
Unexpected Events 147
*Changes in Industry and/or
    Market Structure* 148
High Growth 149
Converging Technologies 151
Demographic Changes 153
Perception Change 155
New Knowledge 156

The Checklist 158

Just the Facts 158

8 Finding Cause, Not Blame........................161

Finding Cause and Not Blame 163
*Identification: State the Actual
    Deviation from Standard....................165*
*Identification: Describe the
    Parameters 167*
*Hypothesis: Identify Distinctions of
    the Problem Area 169*
*Hypothesis: Identify Changes Affecting
    Those Distinctions 170*
*Hypothesis: Develop Possible Causes
    from the Changes 173*
*Validation: Test the Probable Causes
    on Paper 173*
*Validation: Test the most Probable
    Cause in Reality 175*

Solving the Toughest Problems—People
Problems 175

Day 1 Problems 177

The Art of Problem Solving 178

Just the Facts 181

9 Making Sound Decisions.........................183

Avoiding and Escaping from the Decision
Traps 184
Following the Rut 184
Listening to the Last or Loudest Voice 185
*Permitting a Single Factor to Turn the
    Tide 185*
Lousing Up the Timing 186
Failing to Stay the Course 187

The Decision Chain 187
Establishing Objectives 190
*Identifying Resource Restraints and
    Expected Results 191*
Establishing "Musts" and "Wants" 193
Generating and Evaluating Alternatives ...196
Generating Alternatives 196
Evaluating Alternatives 198
Assessing Risk 200
Best Balanced Choice 202

Just the Facts 203

10 Protecting Any Plan 205

Identifying Steps in the Plan 206

Identifying What May Go Wrong...............208
Generate Potential Problems 208
Identifying Likely Causes 209

Establishing Protective Actions...................210

Contingent Actions for the Effects Should
the Problem Occur 213

Monitoring the Progress of the Plan 214
Triggers and Mileposts..........................215
Permanent and Interim Actions 218

Knowing When to Act and Setting
Priorities: Situation Appraisal.....................220
Beware of Feeding the Wrong Concerns ...221
The Separation Technique 223

Just the Facts 226

IV The Secrets of Leadership.............227

**11 Choosing Among an Array of
Leadership Styles 229**

Why the Only "Perfect" Style Is
for Despots...230

The Key Factors in Leadership Decision
Making..234

The Range of Leadership Styles...................236
Autocratic...236
Inquiring...237
One-on-One...237
Group..238
Consensus..239

The Dynamics of Style 240

The Seven Leadership Decision Variables 243

Just the Facts 252

**12 How to Negotiate Successfully Without
Resorting to Weapons 253**

Determining the Negotable and the
Nonnegotiable...254

How to Conduct Effective Negotiations 258

Handling the Tough Issues of Our Times......261

Negotiating Tough Responses 264

Negotiating with Customers 265

*Do Not Focus on Features and Benefits,
but on Results and Outcomes 266*

*Take Easy-to-Accommodate Issues
"Off the Table" 267*

Always Provide a "Choice of Yeses" 267

*Never Discuss Costs—Always Discuss
Value 269*

*Never Lower a Price or Reduce a Fee
Without Commensurate Decrease
in Value 270*

The Negotiation Flow 270

Just the Facts 273

**13 Setting Strategy That People
Can Actually Use 275**

The Surprising Difference Between
Strategy and Tactics................................276

The Manager's Role in Strategy 281

Values 281

Vision 282

Strategy formulation 282

Strategy Implementation 283

Aligning Corporate Objectives with
Individual Objectives................................287

Just the Facts 293

V Speaking, Presenting, Facilitating ...295

14 Presenting Like a Pro..............................297

Prepare Thoroughly and Well in Advance 298

Maintain a Poised, Enthusiastic, and
Controlled Demeanor 307

Smile...308

Use Eye Contact Continually....................308

Move Around the Front of the Room 309

Use Gestures 310

Use the Power of Your Voice......................311

Audience Involvement...............................313

Handling Questions................................314

Using Visual Aids 316

End on Time..317

Expect the Unexpected 318

Just the Facts 320

15 Running Meetings (Instead of Meetings Running You) 321

Making Sure the Meeting Makes Sense 321

Results-oriented Agendas..........................326
    Troubles of the Agenda 327

Running the Meeting with Firmness............329

Power Meeting Techniques 331
    Stopping Road Hogs 331
    Ending Circular Discussions 332
    Resolving Conflict Quickly 333
    Overcoming Cultural Barriers 334
    Maintaining High Energy 334

How to Avoid Meetings That Are Weighing You Down..336

How to Get the Most Out of Participation....338
    Arrive a Bit early, and Bring Some Work ..338
    Read Through and Highlight Any Pre-session Work of Importance 339
    Bring Equipment You'll Need 339
    Be Prepared to Present 339
    Determine What You'll "Volunteer" For 340
    Make an Early Excuse to Leave 340
    Plan to Be Involved 340

Just the Facts 342

VI How to Be A Memorable Manager and Role Model..343

16 The "Complete" Manager for the Routine and the Crises..........................345

Serves As a Positive Role Model for Others..346

Integrates Ethics and Values into Business Goals 348

Subordinates Ego to Organizational Needs 349

Shares Credit but Accepts Personal Accountability and Blame 350

Innovates and Attempts to Raise
Standards 352

Sees People as Assets, Not Expenses, and
Develops Subordinates.............................353

Takes Prudent Risks; Looks at Return, Not
Just Investment 355

Strong Communication and Interpersonal
Abilities 356

Views the Customer As the Primary
Focus..359

Lives a Complete Life, with Work As
Simply One Component.............................361

Taming the Crises 363

Just the Facts 367

17 Post-heroic Management and
Self-actualization 369

Why Questions Are More Important Than
Answers 372

Focusing on Results 376

Extending Your Talents Outward 379
    *Teaching Formally Within the
        Organization* *380*
    Informally Teach As a Mentor *381*
    Teach in an Educational Institution *383*
    *Teach in an Informal Community
        Program* *385*

Educating Yourself 385

Self-actualization 388

A Resources for Power Managers 391

B Annotated Books for the Power
Manager..393

Index..397

The *Unofficial Guide* Reader's Bill of Rights

We Give You More Than the Official Line

Welcome to the *Unofficial Guide* series of Lifestyle titles—books that deliver critical, unbiased information that other books can't or won't reveal—*the inside scoop.* Our goal is to provide you with the *most accessible, useful* information and advice possible. The recommendations we offer in these pages are not influenced by the corporate line of any organization or industry; we give you the hard facts, whether those institutions like them or not. If something is ill-advised or will cause a loss of time or money, we'll give you ample warning. And if it is a worthwhile option, we'll let you know that, too.

Armed and Ready

Our handpicked authors confidently and critically report on a wide range of topics that matter to smart readers like you. Our authors are passionate about their subjects, but have distanced themselves enough from them to help you be armed and protected, and help make you educated decisions as you go through the process. It is our intent that, from having read this book, you will avoid the pitfalls everyone else falls into and get it right the first time.

Don't be fooled by cheap imitations; this is the genuine article *Unofficial Guide* series from IDG Books. You may be familiar with our proven track record with the travel *Unofficial Guides,* which have more than three million copies in print. Each year thousands of travelers—new and old—are armed with a brand-new, fully updated edition of the flagship *Unofficial Guide to Walt Disney World,* by Bob Sehlinger. It is our intention here to provide you with the same level of objective authority that Mr. Sehlinger does in his brainchild.

The Unofficial Panel of Experts

Every work in the Lifestyle *Unofficial Guides* is intensively inspected by a team of three top professionals in their fields. These experts review the manuscript for factual accuracy, comprehensiveness, and an insider's determination as to whether the manuscript fulfills the credo in our Reader's Bill of Rights. In other words, our panel ensures that you are, in fact, getting "the inside scoop."

Our Pledge

The authors, the editorial staff, and the *Unofficial Guide* Panel of Experts assembled for *Unofficial Guides* are determined to lay out the most valuable alternatives available for our readers. This dictum means that our writers must be explicit, prescriptive, and above all, direct. We strive to be thorough and complete, but our goal is not necessarily to have the "most" or "all" of the information on a topic; this is not, after all, an encyclopedia. Our objective is to help you narrow down your options to the best of what is available, unbiased by affiliation with any industry or organization.

In each *Unofficial Guide* we give you:

- Comprehensive coverage of necessary and vital information

- Authoritative, rigidly fact-checked data

- The most up-to-date insights into trends

- Savvy, sophisticated writing that's also readable

- Sensible, applicable facts and secrets that only an insider knows

Special Features

Every book in our series offers the following six special sidebars in the margins that were devised to help you get things done cheaply, efficiently, and intelligently.

1. "Timesaver"—tips and shortcuts that save you time

2. "Moneysaver"—tips and shortcuts that save you money

3. "Watch Out!"—more serious cautions and warnings

4. "Bright Idea"—general tips and shortcuts to help you find an easier or smarter way to do something

5. "Quote"—statements from real people that are intended to be prescriptive and valuable to you

6. "Unofficially…"—an insider's fact or anecdote

We also recognize your need to have quick information at your fingertips, and have thus provided the following comprehensive sections at the back of the book:

1. Resources for Power Managers—lists of relevant agencies, associations, institutions, Web sites, and so on

2. Annotated Books for the Power Manager— suggested titles that can help you get more in-depth information on related topics

Letters, Comments, Questions from Readers

We strive to continually improve the *Unofficial* series, and input from our readers is a valuable way for us to do that.

Many of those who have used the *Unofficial Guide* travel books write to the authors to ask questions, make comments, or share their own discoveries and lessons. For Lifestyle *Unofficial Guides,* we would also appreciate all such correspondence—both positive and critical—and we will make our best effort to incorporate appropriate readers' feedback and comments in revised editions of this work.

How to write us:

Unofficial Guides
Lifestyle Guides
IDG Books
1633 Broadway
New York, NY 10019

Attention: Reader's Comments

About the Author

Alan Weiss, Ph.D., is one of those rare people who can say he is a consultant, author, and professional speaker, and actually mean it. He has consulted with organizations such as Mercedes-Benz, GE, Merck, Fleet Bank, and Arthur Andersen. He has published 12 books (including *Million Dollar Consulting, Managing for Peak Performance,* and *"Good Enough" Isn't Enough . . .*), five booklets, three cassette albums, and two videos. He delivers about 50 keynotes a year as one of the most popular management speakers on the lecture circuit, on topics that include performance, productivity, motivation, and empowerment. *Success Magazine* cited him in an editorial devoted to his work as "a worldwide expert in executive education."

Dr. Weiss resides in East Greenwich, Rhode Island, with his wife, Maria.

The *Unofficial Guide* Panel of Experts

T he *Unofficial* editorial team recognizes that you've purchased this book with the expectation of getting the most authoritative, carefully inspected information currently available. Toward that end, on each and every title in this series, we have selected a minimum of two "official" experts comprising the Unofficial Panel who painstakingly review the manuscript to ensure the following: factual accuracy of all data; inclusion of the most up-to-date and relevant information; and that, from an insider's perspective, the authors have armed you with all the necessary facts you need— but that the institutions don't want you to know.

For *The Unofficial Guide to Power Management*, we are proud to introduce the following panel of experts:

Robert Melstein is a producer at Entrepreneurs Only, a CNN Financial News (CNNfn) show that profiles start-up companies and the managers that run them. He has a B.S. in Business Management from Binghamton University in New York.

Alan Menikoff, MSW, MBA is a management consultant and university lecturer based in New York City. His teaching assignments and his management practice focus on helping organizations make the best use of their "intellectual property"—the brains of that most valuable resource, employees! He has designed and implemented a number of successful management-by-objective (MBO) programs. To support these information systems, he has supervised the installation of several computer networks, "rolled out" a large customer-based database product, and has written a number of database programs. Among his teaching assignments he lists a course on Total Quality Management (TQM) taught at the Fordham University Graduate School of Social Services. Mr. Menikoff's most recent publication is *Psychiatric Home Care: Clinical and Economic Dimensions* (NY: Academic Press, 1999).

Sara Jane Radin is an Organization Effectiveness Strategist who partners with domestic and international executives to build comprehensive customer-focused infrastructures to improve business performance. In 1985, Ms. Radin founded Performance Advantage Systems, consulting to Fortune 500 corporations, start-ups, and small companies in a range of industries. Ms. Radin received her B.A. in Psychology from New York University, her M.A. in Psychology from Columbia University, and continued her learning in Finance and Marketing at The Wharton School.

Introduction

Up until the past decade, management power had typically been derived from two sources: control of people and control of information. The long-term, successful corporate manager tried to maximize the number of people within his or her purview, and then carefully doled out enough precious information to enable them to perform under the manager's direction. Usually, the manager had done the jobs of the subordinates prior to being promoted.

That dynamic changed abruptly in the recent past, thanks to technological acceleration and global competition. Today, information is readily available on everyone's desktop, laptop, and palmtop computer, and people have been downsized, right-sized, laid-off, and just plain fired in an attempt to both operate more cost-effectively and compensate for egregious mistakes in the executive suite. The long-term manager, stolidly working up the organization hierarchy until retirement, is an extinct creature, and there's no longer any reason to expect that a manager would need to know how to perform all of the increasingly complex, technological, and distanced jobs within his or her accountability.

Introduction

Yet, many executives and most managers are trying to be successful at the millennium by applying post–World War II skills and continuing to believe in those disappeared dynamics. The key to tomorrow's success is in *leveraging* the talents and abilities of one's self and subordinates to attain a greater, synergistic set of results. That set of skills—a guide to "Power Management," and all of the speed and impact that the phrase implies—is the subject of this book.

I've taken the primary management responsibilities of the coming decade and provided the means to quickly assess, decide, and implement actions which will provide the fastest, most profound results for managers who are literally communicating and making decisions at unprecedented speeds. I've used my experiences watching some of the great managers at the superb organizations in the world apply their skills, often unconsciously, to move unimpeded toward their goals. Within these chapters, I've "decoded" and articulated the processes they use so that the skill sets can be applied immediately—tomorrow—by any manager with the energy and urgency to do so.

There are generally three reasons why managers fail to improve their results or meet their accountabilities:

1. They don't know what they don't know, and proceed in blissful ignorance.

2. They don't have the skill sets to make changes, and don't know how to acquire them.

3. They lack the behavior and the discipline to take action.

You've already overcome the third obstacle by reading this far. I hope you'll now allow me to assist you in overcoming the first two. Managers are not obsolete, but the old management practices based on hierarchy, control, and politics, are. Join me on the pages ahead to become an "insider" on the power of your own future.

Alan Weiss, Ph.D.
East Greenwich, Rhode Island
August 1999

Influencing and Changing Behavior

GET THE SCOOP ON...
Helping others motivate themselves ▪ Helping
others to see things your way ▪
Establishing a reciprocity of interests ▪ Why the
"in crowd" isn't an effective means of influence

PART I

Leveraging Our Impact Through Others

Chapter 1

The "carrot and stick" approach has been ridiculed as primitive and brutal in the management of people. Yet it is often the sole philosophic principle of any sort underlying most managers' approaches to managing others. The more scientific amongst us might label this "good or bad" reward and punishment system as Pavlovian: Provide something of value only when the performer acts in a manner desirable to you, provide nothing (or punish) when that performance is not forthcoming.

Pavlov was able to get dogs to salivate in this manner. You're more likely simply to make people froth at the mouth.

Early in his career building Microsoft, Bill Gates was supposedly asked during an interview what methods he used to keep talented people performing at arduous tasks for long hours. "Leave them alone in a room," he reportedly replied, "and occasionally open the door and throw in some raw

3

Bright Idea
Think about things that have caused you to "go the extra nine yards," to sacrifice for some other cause, and to work harder and smarter than ever before. They will most often not be strictly financial, nor will they be for other people.

meat." Similarly, I once had a Pulitzer Prize–winning reporter stand up in one of my audiences to announce that motivational attempts with employees were nonsense. "Simply throw some money at them, and you'll get whatever behavior you want," he informed us.

The facts, however, are these:

- People are truly motivated by a wide variety of factors, even when they are doing exactly the same jobs in the same manner as others.

- Money is not a motivator, although the absence of money is a demotivator.

- The complexities and sophistication of today's world and today's workplace preclude simple attempts to create large numbers of motivated people.

- Motivation is intrinsic. It comes from within and cannot be created for one person by another person.

- Natural enthusiasm and a positive world view are far superior to any attempts to create a motivated performer where these traits don't exist.

In other words, the carrot and stick, reward and punishment, "shower them with money" approaches are simply not valid. If you have an employee who is unhappy about lack of opportunity, harassment, private difficulties, or similar issues, and you give them more money in an attempt to help them "overcome this unhappiness," what you will have is a *wealthier* unhappy employee.

In this chapter you will learn how to help others to motivate themselves and, in doing so, how to influence people to help meet your goals, tactically, as a manager, and the corporation's goals, strategically.

These are not manipulative techniques, since manipulation is dependent on intent. The techniques themselves are neutral. So long as your intent is to further the legitimate goals of the organization and your specific business objectives, while helping people meet their own personal objectives, the approaches are ethical, objective, and highly effective.

But, first, you have to abandon the carrot and the big stick.

Fear is a mover, not a motivator

The "big stick" approach has its origins lost in the millennia. The Greek Hoplite formations, popularized by the Spartans, were a configuration that ensured vicious fighting by the men in the front ranks because 16 or so other ranks of armed fighters were bearing down on the front rank from behind. The Roman Legion approach to warfare was often characterized as a fighter holding two spears to the backs of the two men marching in front of him, with a spear pressed to his own back by the man marching to his rear.

Fear has long been used as a "mover," and it's an effective one. To save lives, to save fortunes, to save honor, people have been moved to undertake actions which they otherwise would never consider.

In modern management, fear has been used as a mover because it's easy to apply. The "spear in the back" today is often financial pressure, job assignment, overtime threats, making partner, vesting in the retirement plan, and obtaining various perks or latitude of action. Managers in positions of hierarchical authority don't need permission, extensive education, or focused training to apply these brutish techniques. They are not difficult to master and employ. Nor are they very effective.

❝
God pardons the coerced.
— ancient Jewish proverb
❞

When you use the "big stick" approach to try to "motivate" someone to perform in a certain manner, all you've really created is movement. Movement is externally generated, and can be successfully employed *only as long as the big stick is present*. In fact, it has these singular drawbacks:

- The "stick" must be visible. The performer has to recognize the fear-based instrument. The threat must be made tangible, e.g., "If you don't accept the transfer to Memphis, your career here will be over," or "If you do not accept overtime I will give you a sub-standard performance rating."

- The stick must be constantly applied. The desired movement will weaken and even disappear if the perceived threat is not present. "The boss isn't here today, so there's no way he'll know whether we worked through lunch or took the afternoon off." "There's no way she'll be back here in the next 2 hours, and I'm simply not answering a single phone until she's back. Let them ring, no one will know."

- The stick has to be the biggest stick around. Employees don't like to be beaten, and they're quite capable of finding protection. For example, if a manager blindly insists on overtime rather than finding less onerous methods to handle workloads, the employees may just find a champion in human resources or at a superior hierarchical level who takes on the offender: "You've got to stop demanding overtime from these people. They're dead tired in the morning, and customers are complaining about poor responsiveness over the phone. Find another solution."

- The wielder has to be willing to use the stick or the threat evaporates. If the bluff is called, others realize that either the stick has no power or the person holding it doesn't have the courage to use it. "Don't listen to him. He keeps threatening our evaluations, but Gloria ignored him and still got the same evaluation as the rest of us: 'exceeds expectations.' It's an empty threat."

- There has to be an absence of effective relief and remediation for the stick to work. In some environments, attempts at overt force and punishment are quickly countered by institutionalized protective devices. These have proliferated and received greater respect due to publicity and legal precedent. "If you ask me again if I intend to get married and have children when interviewing me about the promotion, I'll go directly to human resources. Those questions are discriminatory and, if it's determined that those facts played any part in your decision not to promote me, you can be terminated and the company can be sued."

For these reasons, the big stick can be a short-term, albeit powerful weapon. Through the application of fear and force, managers have been able to force unethical behavior, illegal practices, sexual favors, and other horrible work behaviors we read about on the front pages. Eventually, however, it's exposed for what it is: a poor substitute for trying to achieve motivation.

The "in crowd" really isn't

Another attempt at changing people's behavior can be found in what I call the "in crowd" approach. The psychologists call it "normative pressure." Colloquially, we call it "peer pressure."

Unofficially... Managers who resort to brute force or appeals to peer pressure are almost always reflecting their own role models, meaning that they have to be reeducated. They usually believe that they're doing the right thing because that's what was done to them.

When I began my career at Prudential Insurance in Newark, New Jersey, I was making very little money. My wife and I would struggle to make ends meet, and we did so without a penny left over. One day, my boss came to me and asked how much I'd like to contribute to the annual savings bond campaign.

ME: Actually, I can't contribute anything. I barely make enough now to pay my bills.

BOSS: Well, that's the position that most of us are probably in. But we all stretch a bit to make this campaign successful because the company has committed to it. Surely you can spare something.

ME: I can't spare a thing, but I'm sure that in another year or so, I'll be able to contribute. I've only been here for 6 months, right out of school.

(A very long pause.)

BOSS: So, you're willing to be the only manager who prevents us from 100 percent participation, which we've had every year for the past five years?

(An even longer pause.)

ME: Ah, I guess not. What's the least expensive bond I can sign up for?

I found out later that my boss told the same thing to all of his subordinates, and that the "100 percent participation" was simply so much mythology. The company had about 75 percent of its managers participating, and many of us dropped out as soon as we realized that the boss said the same thing to all of us. Peer pressure is fickle. The "in crowd" might not be headed in the direction the individual—or the organization—is traveling.

Motivation can't be achieved through appeals to lemminglike, mass mentality. People have become too individualistic, too smart, and too pragmatically selfish. Communication, via e-mail, voice mail, fax, and FedEx, has become so instantaneous that it's relatively simple to validate trends, rumors, fads, and nuances. It's one thing to say, "All the sophisticated people back east are doing this" when the fastest communication source is a stagecoach. It's quite another to claim that "this is the mood in headquarters" when you can personally validate or invalidate that claim by e-mailing friends in the home office in the next 90 seconds.

Both fear and peer pressure are movers, not motivators. They may, temporarily, achieve a change in behavior through forced, external means. But since that behavioral change is not internally driven, it is subject to rapid reversal as soon as the threat or perceived peer pressure disappears or abates. Moreover, while these techniques may generate approximate movement, they will seldom if ever produce prolonged, self-perpetuating, high-quality, long-term behavior change.

I remember when I was forced to work overtime at a factory, while working my way through school. Saturdays were precious, and when the boss forced me to work on some of them, I would loaf with my colleagues in self-righteous indignation over our fate. The boss seldom worked on Saturdays and it was unlikely he'd come in to check on us. So, although we were physically present, the work that actually was performed was minimal. The company wound up paying us time and a half for a tiny bit of productivity.

Contrast that to running my own firm, where I think nothing of putting together a proposal on a Saturday, working late with a client during the week, or skipping lunch to resolve a problem. The difference is that I'm having fun, running my

Watch Out!
Manipulative sales pitches begin with "Don't be the only one to miss . . ." and "Join all of your colleagues who are . . ." Statistics are often made up on the spot. When it's claimed that there's a ground swell, ask around. You might find it's a ground swell of exactly one—the manipulator.

own firm, making my own choices. The quality of this work is very high, because it's work I want to do.

If you are an entrepreneur, or are considering beginning your own business, or are intent upon building a career up the corporate ladder, you must choose a field you are passionate about. The extra time demands and sacrifices will result in high-quality work because you love what you're doing. But don't choose a field simply to make money. Your sacrifices and extra work will result in low-quality results, because you'll see these demands as infringements on your time and freedom, rather than means to your valuable ends. Most entrepreneurial managers fail when they try to find pursuits that will make them rich, and try to grow passionate around them. Most succeed when they find their passion, throw themselves into it, and make money in the process. Motivation, not capital investment, is the real determinant of entrepreneurial success.

You might have found yourself flowing with the "in crowd" at various times, but stopping when your self-interest was no longer met, you became bored, or you found some other "in crowd" of more immediate appeal.

> 66
> In matters of taste, swim with the current. In matters of principle, stand like a rock.
> —Thomas Jefferson
> 99

The role of enlightened self-interest

Motivation can only come from within. I can't motivate you, and you can't motivate me. However, we can try to establish environments that are more conducive to motivation. The route to that goal is the identification of enlightened self-interest. People change behavior when it's in their own best interest to do so. When people change because they want to change—not because they are forced or swept along—we benefit from the following:

- The new behavior does not have to be constantly reinforced externally with expensive and continual attention and rewards.

- Quality of behavior and performance remains high and is self-perpetuating. It can even improve upon itself over time.

- Motivated people create enthusiasm that produces an environment in which more people can realize their own self-interest and become motivated. True motivation can create a "chain reaction" for others.

- Truly motivated people are likely to keep changing their behavior. Unlike the resistance that accrues when constant force is applied, attaining one's goals leads to successes that tend to encourage the performer to consider more behavior change in the future.

We see examples of the effectiveness of appeals to self-interest every day. In the 1920s, the U.S. government passed the Volstead Act, which prohibited the sale of alcoholic beverages and created the era known as Prohibition. During that period, speakeasies flourished, criminals made fortunes from bootlegging illegal booze (it was the heyday of Al Capone, Baby Face Nelson, and the rest of the legendary gangsters), and many people died from "bathtub gin" and other illicit, toxic concoctions produced to circumvent the law.

The Volstead Act was repealed when it became apparent, even to the most radical opponents of alcohol, that the self-interests of the citizenry was to obtain liquor for recreational and social purposes.

Contrast that to the decline in tobacco use in the U.S. (and, increasingly, abroad). Twenty years ago

Watch Out!
Remember those old movies, when you could barely see the actors because of the cigarette smoke? The Hollywood icons demonstrated that sophisticated people smoked. Many died from smoking-related illnesses, as did millions of their fans. Peer pressure can act contrary to self-interest. It's often as deadly for us professionally as it can be personally.

the Surgeon General's office began a methodical campaign, backed by unimpeachable sources and empirical research results, to demonstrate the direct relationship between smoking and various health risks, including heart disease and cancer, two of the highest-morbidity illnesses. Despite occasional anomalies—female, teenage smoking is apparently increasing—use of tobacco in the U.S. decreased substantially over the last two decades. And this occurred despite tobacco being much more addictive than alcohol, despite massive advertising from the tobacco industry, despite tremendous peer pressure, and despite massive legal battles waged by the tobacco industry.

It has been conclusively proven that smoking is inimical to one's self-interests, and smoking has declined as a recreational habit. I am not making a case that liquor should suffer the same fate, but I am pointing out that it has never been effectively demonstrated that alcohol consumption is a detriment to self-interest. So taxing—which is a power technique—and "dry" parties or properties—which are peer pressure techniques—will never be very effective.

In order to encourage those behaviors you desire from employees (e.g., courtesy in answering customer requests) and discouraging behaviors you wish to prevent (e.g., talking to colleagues while customers wait in line) you are best served through appeals to employee self-interest, not threats ("I'm watching you!"), which can't be continually enforced, nor appeals (banners on the wall that state "Our customers come first!"), which aren't embraced.

The role of influence

In fact, whether you are attempting to change employees' behavior, resolve a hostile customer's complaint, influence your boss to take a certain course of action, or generally impact colleagues outside of your direct control, the pursuit of self-interest is the key in obtaining your objectives. "He wields great influence" is a sign of great respect. What's actually occurring, however, is that the wielder is adept at finding the self-interests of others and demonstrating how their objectives will be met by helping to meet his or her objectives.

Example #1:

The president of a bank has an objective to "increase shareholder value." She can't really expect her branch managers to appreciate or respond to that strategic objective. So she determines that the branch managers' self-interest is in helping the customers that they see every day, which is rewarding, gratifying, and immediate. The president identifies those activities that branch managers perform for daily customers (branch managers' self-interest), which also support increasing shareholder value (president's self-interest), and concludes there are four primary examples:

- Creating IRA and retirement investment accounts.
- Providing financing through home equity loans.
- Providing new home mortgages.
- Providing new car loans.

The president begins a campaign to support and accentuate those lines of business, including

Watch Out!
Don't fall victim to the "carrot and stick" idiology that says that lower level people simply respond to financial incentives. The research literature is overwhelmingly supportive of the fact that people at all levels respond best to challenging jobs that utilize—and even stretch— their talents.

recognition for leaders in those categories, stronger home office support, and financial incentives.

Example #2:

The branch managers in the preceding example want to create proactive sales in the four areas. They already have a small stream of customers who come to see them each day for help in such financing and investment, but those customers are the ones who take it upon themselves to do so. The best branch managers decide that the "sales pitch" can best be made at the tellers' stations, since that's where the preponderance of transactions with customers takes place. But how can they help the tellers to become motivated to refer customers to these services and to the branch manager?

It's determined that the tellers are often bored by their high-repetition, confined jobs. In fact, they've often been chastised for chatting with customers and delaying others waiting in line. Also, the tellers have excellent relationships with customers who they see several times each week, and are often asked for help with account problems.

The tellers are provided with brochures for all four product areas at their stations. They are told that the bank's best customers are often unaware of how these services can be helping them, and how grateful customers are to find that they can consolidate debts at lower interest rates, or create more tax-free investments. The tellers' brochures have codes to show which customers have pursued the advice, tellers are given business cards which they encourage customers to take to the branch manager to set up an appointment, and they are provided with incentives based on both referrals and actual sales. All of the tellers receive a brief script to use with customers, and are encouraged to converse if a customer shows interest.

Script:

"You were asking me about rates for certificates of deposit investment options. We actually have much better products for you than those CDs, and we'd be happy to discuss these with you in detail."

Example #3:

The vice president has demanded that no employees make promises to customers about returns or credits without his personal approval. The employees you manage have complained to you and begged you to intercede. The new policy has created tremendous customer hostility, because no decisions can be made on the phone, the customer is forced to call back on phone lines already overburdened, the vice president if often not around to make the approval, and the customer is sometimes forced to wait days for a simple resolution, making three or four phone calls in the bargain.

You determine that the employees are correct after listening to some of the calls yourself. Take a moment to consider. What would you do?

What actually happened was that the manager asked himself what the vice president's self-interest was, and quickly realized that his boss was evaluated on the basis of increased profit, not merely revenue, over the last year. The manager created a spreadsheet showing the increased amount of employee time being consumed by repeated phone calls on what had previously been single call events, how customer ill will was likely to cause a decline in repeat business from current customers (who were the operation's bread and butter), and how increasing employee frustration was causing poorer

Timesaver
The greatest waste of time occurs when you impute malicious motives to someone. It takes much longer to try to bring around a recalcitrant individual than it does to persuade the merely neutral and uncommitted. Don't assume people are against you just because they're not yet for you.

first-time service as well. Confronted with the facts and likelihoods—and by the direct impact on his own self-interest—the vice president reversed the policy within a week.

Few managers will reverse themselves without good reason, because their ego is one of their primary self-interests. However, when you can demonstrate—to a peer, subordinate, or superior— that their own self-interest will be best served by a reversal, agreement, or compromise, there will always be ways to salve an ego.

The reciprocity of interests

Superb managers (and superb organizations) create what I call a "reciprocity of interests," meaning that we serve each other's best interests in the normal course of our work. If I'm leading a sales team, I take the time to determine that one of my sales people appreciates recognition by the team, another responds well to one-on-one mentoring, a third likes tangible goals, a fourth desires freedom in scheduling, and so on. In turn, I need to know about any potential client desertions well before they take place, I need expense reports documented and submitted religiously for expense control requirements, and I'd like promotional offers above a certain level approved in advance to ensure consistency.

The employees understand, respect, and support my interests, as I do theirs, and as all of us do for the company. The key for managers is to understand that self-interest varies from individual to individual, due to:

- Differing values; all valid, but different.

- Differing behavioral predispositions. I place an emphasis on consensus and accommodation, while another manager might stress accomplishment, detail, and task.

■ Differing personal backgrounds, including marital or partner status, indebtedness, children or extended family, friends, civic and social involvement, commuting time, and educational experience.

■ Differing career aspirations.

■ Differing employment experiences (someone got burned for doing that in the past, or this was successful for them in the past).

It's important to try to identify the self-interests of those around you, particularly subordinates, and not expect them to be motivated by the same factors.

Avoid blanket motivational programs like the plague. Any attempt to appeal to diverse employees with a single technique is doomed to failure. Similarly, don't implement "motivational techniques" that create winners and losers, as in many sales contests. Set up approaches where everyone has a chance to "win" (i.e., by improving over last year's performance, not the first one beating some arbitrary number this year), or, even better, where teams can win, so that differing contributions and talents can create a "whole" far greater than the sum of the parts. Otherwise, motivational attempts that are not geared to individual self-interest are not only primed to fail, but they will actually cost money, decrease productivity, and lower morale.

Here is how to establish others' rational self-interest:

■ Ask them. I'm always impressed by executives who pass an employee in the hallway and not

Bright Idea
If you want to try to understand what motivates subordinates, don't equate their goals with your own. Try to put yourself in their position, and in your own career several years ago. Think back to what you wanted then, and you'll be a lot closer to the employees now.

only know their name but also inquire, "How was that trip to Nova Scotia you were planning?" The first step is always in understanding who the person is, what elates them, what their hobbies and off-job interests are, and what's important to them. Managers should have a cordial relationship—not a social relationship, but a professional, cordial relationship—with their direct reports.

- Listen to the examples they use. One employee might make reference to waterskiing, another to volunteering at a hospital, and another to grandchildren. People tend to find metaphors and examples in aspects of their life that they find enjoyable and important to them.

- Watch their behavior. Are they more enthusiastic when managing their own time, or fulfilling your time schedule? Do they enjoy making presentations and being in the limelight, or prefer a backseat and anonymity? Do they prefer to reach out and influence others, or to sit back and be contacted by those in quest of their expertise?

- Analyze their successes and failures. Determine why they achieved their goals in one setting and not another. Try to isolate the factors that might have accounted for superior performance. Are they better managing others or working as individual contributors? Are they better at writing or in front of the prospective customer? Can they compromise well, or do they prefer a set path?

Never confuse others' self-interest with your own. I once worked for a president who loved to spread the contents of his briefcase on the floor, get a brandy, and work, literally, through the night. He was fresh as a daisy the next day, and wondered why the rest of us couldn't get 24 hours of work done by simply refusing to sleep. "It's a great feeling!" he exalted.

I always thought he should have been institutionalized. What motivates us doesn't necessarily motivate others, and this is particularly true when differences in hierarchy, age, gender, background, experience, education, and assignment enter the picture. I love freedom of action and a minimum of constraint and instruction. But not everyone is so enamored with near-anarchy. That's why, as managers, we have to apply the steps above to actively determine what constitutes the enlightened self-interest of others.

One final word, and it's on my deliberate use of "enlightened." Occasionally, self-interest will be illegal, immoral, or unethical, or in other ways antithetical to the organization's best interests. The interest served must always be constructive and positive, and the reason that I call for reciprocity is to ensure that no one gains at the expense of someone else's (or the organization's) loss. So "enlightened" or "rational" self-interest is not meant to imply the analytic over the emotional, because emotional interests are highly valid and even more prone to engender influence than logical ones.

Destinations are safe, journeys are frightening

There is a myth extant that people resist change. That's not accurate in my observation. In fact, the lower you are in the hierarchy, the more resilient

Bright Idea
Hold informal meetings around coffee and donuts or at lunch, and ask employees what could be done to enable them to do their jobs better. You'll find that the responses reflect individual self-interest entwined with performance needs. Don't take notes, just listen. When you hear patterns emerging, you've nailed down self-interest.

you tend to be, because change is thrust at you daily. You're asked to try a new procedure, adjust to a customer demand, fix a quality problem, take part in a new task force, or go on a quick trip to Cleveland.

The higher one is in the management chain, the more calcified things seem to become. Once you have the corner office, covered parking space, executive dining room, private washroom, and personal assistants, you're not exactly anxious to rock the boat. This is as true in leaner, post-downsized organizations as it was in the heyday of "fat" organizations. No one wants to surrender what they have, and the "haves" are the people farthest up the corporate ladder.

And, in fact, all of us face change every day as we have to make our way around unanticipated road closings, dead batteries, leaking clothes washers, kids with scraped knees, and calls from relatives asking for money. We are used to change and inured to change.

So change is not an anathema to employees, and managers don't have to walk on eggs to soft-peddle new ideas and innovative procedures. However, they do have to carefully help people on the journey, because here's what that trip looks like from most employees' viewpoints:

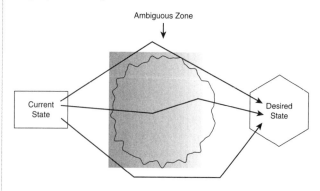

Your employees are familiar with the current state, and have done their best to be comfortable in it. They have "feathered nests," so to speak, and have learned to survive and, perhaps, thrive, in the current system.

The future is understood and attractive. One of the fundamental flaws in dealing with change is the mistaken belief that employees don't understand the future or are afraid of it. Who could really object to fast customer responsiveness, a common e-mail system, more efficient operations, or more rapid sales analyses? These are not the problems, and the future is virtually always depicted with color and clarity by the visionaries (or consulting firms) designing it.

However, the *journey* to the future is almost always seen as perilous. The ambiguity of the path to the future state is never clear, never described with the same level of articulation or certainty, and is often left to be determined (and, in reality, is often not actually understood even by senior management—the general belief is that "we'll get there somehow, because we can't afford not to get there").

Employees don't understand, consequently, what the journey entails, what the pitfalls may be, where the safety net is, and how to pace themselves on the trail. The two largest inducers of stress on the job are:

- Not knowing what will happen tomorrow.

- Believing that you have no control over whatever happens tomorrow.

Both of those conditions prevail when the "ambiguous zone" is between the present and desired state. The result is that employees will tend

Unofficially...
Most change efforts of any sort die in the implementation, not the formulation. Spend more time trying to understand and convey "how" you will achieve something than "what" you will achieve, since the latter is readily understood and the former is always murky.

to buckle down and resist, not because they are afraid of the future, but because they are uncertain about the path. Management exacerbates the difficulty by addressing this problem with still more information about the future state, while continuing to ignore the route to get there (again, because it is still largely vague in their own minds).

Here are the keys to helping employees travel to the future with confidence, mutual-supportiveness, and a minimum of lost productivity.

Force people to let go

When I was a child there was an apparatus in the playground called the "monkey bars." The idea was to swing from one end to the other by grasping the horizontal grips. I would grab the first one, look down at what appeared to be a 40-foot drop, and hold on for my life. Pretty soon my arms cramped, I had to let go, and fell the two feet to the ground.

After dozens of failed attempts, I noticed that my friends were able to traverse the monkey bars by letting go with one hand and reaching out with it to the next bar. It amazed me. The way to move forward was to actually let go. Once I did that, I found that I created my own momentum, and was able to swing from one bar to the next relatively easily.

The same holds true in life: We have to let go to reach out. We can't reach out if we are vigorously holding onto our current positions and possessions. You have to encourage your employees to let go of what's comfortable by:

- Taking it away (Sorry, that system disappears as of next week.)

- Moving it forward (This will only be available on the new computer system, not on the old one any longer.)

Timesaver
Take time out to watch your best employees at work. You can learn a lot for yourself and to transfer to other employees simply by observing the processes and priorities that successful people use in "real time." Ironically, this observation time can be the most productive time of all.

- Providing incentives (The first people to schedule the customer calls will be able to set their own schedules.)

You may have to figuratively pry people's fingers from the bars, but once you do you'll find that they'll be swinging toward the future.

Choose and support exemplars

There are inevitably informal leaders to whom others look for inspiration, examples, and guidance. Choose a few of these people to use as your "point guards," and send them on ahead. Provide them with as much clarity and confidence as you can:

- You will have a key position in the new venture, so we need you to help establish some early parameters.

- I'm expecting you to be a leader in the new organization, so I'd like you to help set the pace now.

- I'd like you to help me to help everyone. Keep your ear to the ground. As you find problems and resistance, let me know so that we can deal with it early and effectively.

People follow informal leadership and people they respect with great loyalty. If a few key people are inquisitive, innovative, and explorative (and not belligerent, resistant, and critical), most others will fall in line quickly. These are the people who can forge paths through the ambiguity.

Use very bright lights

Keep people informed every step of the way. Help them to understand where the safe footing is, and be honest about the possible quicksand. If they know the pros and cons, they will be more apt to make intelligent decisions and follow them.

Watch Out!
When leading people through the ambiguity, always make clear what you know and don't know. If people suspect that you've been holding out on them, or have been blindly groping for answers yourself, they will retreat to their starting point and hold on tighter than ever.

To ensure this:

- Don't make promises you can't keep, but do give whatever assurances you can. (I don't know how many jobs will be needed, but I promise I can tell you within the next 30 days, and we'll design a plan to deal with that intelligently amongst us.)

- Be honest early. (The benefit program after the merger will not be as generous as the one we have today. We were way above the norms, and we're going to be scaled back to more of an industry average.)

- Fight the good fight. (If your own senior management has asked you to march people off a cliff, resist. Explain how long-term commitment will be forever sacrificed to a short-term expedient.)

When you transit the ambiguous zone, remember that there is no royal road, and you might take any number of paths toward the desired state. Make intelligent choices, keep your people informed, and keep them moving. Some teams get lost in the ambiguous zone and are never heard from again.

Just the facts

- Fear is never an effective device, because it only gains temporary movement at best and often causes long-term resistance.

- Peer pressure is fickle and temporary, and often not aligned with organizational goals.

- There are few techniques as powerful as a reciprocity of interests—genuine help for both parties, honestly given and received.

- Manipulation is blazingly transparent, and most people will either ignore it or attempt to undermine it.
- Informal leaders and exemplars are key leverage points for behavioral change in others.

GET THE SCOOP ON...
Why blanket motivation programs always fail ▪
The difference between motivation and move-
ment ▪ The myth of money as a motivator ▪
What to do with people who resist
empowerment ▪ The real road to self-esteem

Empowerment As a Management Tool

Chapter 2

Empowerment has gotten a bad rap. It has become the buzzword of the New Age, touchy-feely gurus whose discipline and advice rarely exceed the whimsical. As its bedfellows, it finds itself connected with "open book management," "open meetings," "left brain/right brain thinking," "stewardship," and all the other bromides of a philosophy destitute of any pragmatism.

However, empowerment actually means something, has a methodical and systematic underpinning, and is one of the greatest weapons in power management.

First, a definition: *Empowerment means that employees can make decisions that influence the outcome of their work.* Decisions about where to place a vending machine or whether or not to offer customers coffee do not affect the outcome (quality/standards/sales/profit/safety, etc.) of the work. But decisions on how to organize overtime, whether or not to hire a job candidate, and how to respond to a customer request certainly do affect work outcomes.

Watch Out!
There is only one
thing worse than
unempowered
employees, and
that is employ-
ees who were
told they were
empowered and
were never
trusted to fulfill
that role. Once
you disempower
people, trust is
extraordinarily
difficult to
rebuild.

TABLE 2.1 EMPOWERED PEOPLE AND DISEMPOWERED PEOPLE ARE EASY TO IDENTIFY

Empowered	Powerless
Self-confident	Insecure
Act ethically	Just follow rules, no matter what the impact
Think "we"	Think "them and us"
Accept accountability	Say "That's not my job"
Achieve results	Perform tasks
Think	Follow rules
Focus on the customer	Focus on themselves
Take prudent risks	Protect themselves at all times
Innovate	Coast

We've all stood in long lines, waited weeks for replies from organizations that dun us if a bill is 2 days overdue, and conformed with silly requests because of bureaucratic, task-oriented employees. And we've all been pleasantly surprised (or swept off our feet) by the quick responses, of a "no questions asked" attitude, and comfortable relationships created by results-oriented, confident employees.

Empowerment is an effective management tool

An empowered organization will:

- Reduce the costs associated with failure work, which is duplicative work necessitated of employees by prior failures caused by uncaring or nonaccountable employees. (Toyota)

- Reduce the costs and delays of decisions constantly sent "upstairs" before resolution. (Nordstrom)

- Create repeat customers through their positive experiences. (Disney)

- Meet its business objectives consistently because employees are aligned behind them, and there is a reciprocity of interests. (FedEx)

- Produce innovative products and services through the "freedom to fail" and prudent risk taking. (3M)

- Have the capacity to rebound from bad times and change customer perception relatively quickly. (Continental Airlines)

- Attract and retain top talent and maintain very low employee attrition. (Microsoft)

- Attract shareholders and investment, even in times of poor financial performance. (amazon.com)

Example #1:

In 1969, on our first wedding anniversary, my wife bought me a Texas Instruments calculator as a gift. It cost $80 and plugged into a wall, but it had a "new" digital display, sat on my desk, and did great work. It moved with us from New Jersey to California, back to New Jersey, and up to Rhode Island. Finally, after 26 years of service, one day I pushed a button and nothing happened.

I wrote a letter to Texas Instruments, and told them that I wished everything I purchased had the reliability of their calculators. I mentioned that I was going right out to buy another one, and I thought they'd like to know that.

One week later I received a letter from Texas Instruments. It was signed by a woman whose title was "administrative assistant," and she thanked me for writing. She told me that the company would like to send me a free calculator, and wanted to know if I had any preferences for functions, and

Watch Out!
Not all employees want to be empowered. If they are "backroom" employees with little customer contact, it might not matter. But if they deal with customers and resist empowerment, they should be moved elsewhere. Powerless employees create powerless customers.

requested that I return the broken calculator so that they could figure out what had gone wrong after more than a quarter of a century.

I sent them the broken calculator, but told them not to send me a free one, since that was not my objective and, besides, I had already purchased their new model TI 500.

One week later I received a second letter from the same woman with a check inside, representing, she thought, about what I had paid at retail for their new calculator. Actually, the check was for a few dollars more than I had spent, but I was afraid that if I returned the change there would be still more letters, stock options, visits from executives . . .

Example #2:

When I moved to Rhode Island, I had to find a bank and deposit a significant amount of money. I walked down Main Street (yes, that's actually its name) in my new hometown, and found several banks. In each one, the manager or assistant manager merely cited the prevailing rates, handed us some brochures, and told us how to give them our money when we were ready. However, in one bank, Fleet, the assistant branch manager asked my wife and I if we would like some coffee, and then proceeded to ask us why we had moved, if we had children, what our financial objectives were, and what our lifestyle entailed.

She then made recommendations for investments, not unlike what the other banks offered. But we chose her (and, therefore, Fleet) to be our bank. Fifteen years later it still is, having made a tidy profit on several house refinancings, an investment portfolio, equity loans, and private banking services.

That's what happens when empowered people compete against disempowered people: They stand out in a crowd, and give the customer a sense of power. They also create long-term profit for the organization. I'm still using Texas Instruments calculators, and I've told that story to over a hundred thousand people in my speeches.

What kinds of employees are you developing? Do they tend to fall on the right side or the left side of the table above?

There are four key steps in developing empowered employees:

1. Create the playing field.

Employees have to know what's "in bounds" and "out of bounds." Empowerment is not abdication, which is probably what scares most people considering the technique. The playing field might have four sides, six sides, or eight sides, and might resemble a soccer field or a hockey rink. (But if it's only the size of a postage stamp, there's not much room to empower!)

One boundary might be "legal constraints," another might be "ethical behavior," a third "financial limits," and a fourth "customer interaction." Whatever the size of the field and the boundaries, the employee must know that *on that field, the employee calls the plays*. The manager sets the boundaries and ensures the performer knows the rules and has the proper equipment, but the employee makes the decisions.

If a decision is to come close to a boundary ("We might go over budget" or "There is no legal precedent"), then the manager should be informed so that the risk can be jointly assessed. No one wants to go out of bounds.

Employees can also negotiate boundaries. "I can't take the customer initiative you desire if my spending limit is only $5,000. Can't we raise it to

Bright Idea
Your employees won't have much of a playing field if you don't have one to share. Analyze your own "freedom of action" and "play calling." If you're not sufficiently empowered to generate the results you're capable of, begin negotiating an expanded playing field with your own boss.

$10,000?" That way, boundaries are never arbitrarily exceeded, but are subject to rational debate. However, no one will know whether a boundary has been exceeded if there is no agreement on where the boundaries are, what the size of the field is, or whether any even exists.

The success of empowerment, ironically, lies in collaboration, not isolation.

2. Develop the skills.

Merely telling someone that he or she is empowered does nothing for that person. The employee must have the requisite skills for the job. If you are empowering someone to work directly with customers and solve their problems at the front line, does that person have interpersonal and problem solving skills? If you are empowering someone to run a profit center, does the person possess the financial skills to do the job?

This is the "can do" aspect of empowerment. The manager is responsible for the skills building required for success. If the employee is incapable of mastering the skills after the best efforts on everyone's part, then that is not the right person for that job.

Not long ago I had to file an insurance claim with a moving company that had transported a piece of office equipment. Four different people in the moving company told me that they sympathized, but did not know how to file a claim. Finally, a distant claims administrator was reached, who faxed me forms and took care of things in 10 minutes. It was a simple procedure. Yet the company had involved four people, their time, their (and my) frustration, simply because no one was empowered to fax a simple form except the "specialist." Multiply that times the thousands of transactions that the company engages in each day, and you begin to see the necessity of providing simple skills to empower people at all levels.

3. Develop the willingness.

This is where our earlier motivation discussions enter the picture. Developing the skills is "can do," but developing the willingness is "want to do." The latter is even more important than the former, *because it represents sustainable, self-perpetuating behavior.*

If the skills are clearly present, but the performer does not accept the accountability, there is a failure in the motivation required to do the job. It may be because the employee feels that accountability is being added without attendant freedom or rewards, or that he or she is simply doing your job at a lower salary level, or that there is far too much risk in failure.

If, despite your best efforts and support, an employee with the requisite skills does not act in an empowered fashion, take them out of a position that calls for empowerment (usually anything demanding customer interaction). Not everyone craves to be empowered. The question then becomes, do you crave nonempowered employees?

While writing this, I had to call an executive at one of my Fortune 100 clients. A woman who answered his phone told me to call back, and she wouldn't pick up, and then I'd get his voice mail. "It's a quick message," I pointed out, "can't I just leave it with you?"

"I'm a temporary employee here and I don't take messages."

"You're an employee who doesn't take messages? Why on earth not?"

She hung up on me. I informed my client the next day. Even temps can be empowered and, if they

Timesaver
If an employee is not performing up to expectations, ask if the employee ever did the existing job satisfactorily. If the answer is "yes," then you know the employee does not have a lack of skill, but rather either a lack of motivation or some obstacle to peformance.

refuse it, they shouldn't be temporary, they should be nonexistent.

4. Create supportive systems and culture.

If I believe I'm empowered, and have the skills and willingness to perform, but coworkers, people in superior positions, and even customers don't believe it, then empowerment is futile.

I once observed an employee strike a deal with a superior from another department. The superior then said, "What's your boss's extension? I'd like to call and confirm her understanding."

"That's not necessary," the employee responded.

"I'm authorized to make these decisions."

"Well, let's just play it safe," said the other, picking up the phone book.

In such environments, empowerment deflates rapidly. The boundaries of the playing field close in until there is no room left to maneuver. However, empowerment will work in "pockets," departments, divisions, and among teams. It needn't be "all or nothing." The key is to create a viable playing field in whatever area you can occupy.

The rules for empowerment

Here are the actions that the manager needs to take in order to empower others effectively.

Enhance self-esteem.

Employees must feel good about themselves in order to feel good about empowerment. Provide positive feedback. Help them to understand that they are competent and supported. Demonstrate examples of how they've performed appropriately in the past. You cannot empower employees who feel inadequate, untalented, or ill suited to the job. Empowerment is not a cure, it's a new level of performance.

Timesaver
Don't launch an "empowerment program" or put banners in the cafeteria. Expand boundaries with those responding well to the freedom and possessing the required talents. Set mutually agreed boundaries. You can empower tomorrow and reap the benefits before the end of the day. Playing fields are always present, but not always used effectively.

Listen.

This, admittedly, is one of the rarest of management skills. By listening to employees you will learn where the boundaries really need to be set. By listening to customers you will understand their perception of responsiveness and ease of doing business. Don't allow your own preconceptions to establish arbitrary limits and boundaries. Make the determination according to the performers, the customers, and the results of their interactions.

Provide constructive feedback.

Don't leave the employee alone on the field. Coach as appropriate from the sidelines. Too often, we wait until a boundary has been violated or a play goes bad, and then we assess blame. Instead, we should be rewarding the desired behaviors and discouraging the undesirable ones. Successful, empowered people are those who receive constant information about their performance.

Surrender the decision-making prerogative.

Employees truly must make the decisions that influence the outcome of their work. You must allow them to do so, even if you fear there will be some errors. Providing a customer with "too much" compensation for a problem will seldom be fatal. Accompanied by the feedback above, however, it's a valuable learning experience. If people can't make real decisions, they will not really be empowered.

Encourage innovation.

Nothing represents empowerment better than encouraging people to continually "raise the bar." When employees aspire to create new standards instead of merely maintaining old ones, they are enjoying empowerment. Conversely, when they are frustrated from trying new approaches because "we've never done that here," they will actually shrink their own playing fields because their freedom has been restricted. As long as the innovation doesn't exceed the boundaries established, support it.

Reward behavior, not just "victories."

> **"**
> The difference between confidence and arrogance is that confident people believe sincerely and deeply that they can help others to learn, while arrogant people believe sincerely and deeply that they have nothing left to learn themselves.
> —Alan Weiss
> **"**

In one of my client companies, we established an award at the annual recognition dinner for "The Best Idea That Didn't Work." Along with the awards for most new clients, best client service, and the like, the president presented the TBITDW award to hearty applause from the crowd. This was his way of demonstrating that innovation and empowerment are important as *behaviors and ways of doing business,* not just when they produce a "win." If people feel that only "victories" justify empowerment and risk-taking, they will become highly conservative, and won't go near the boundaries. Empowered people practice the correct behaviors continually, not conservatively.

Set the overall vision and goals.

The manager's job is to establish, clarify, exemplify, and support the overall direction and goals of the enterprise. Empowerment takes place within that purview. You do not surrender that responsibility. "Customer-driven," for example, is never an end in itself, but a means to an end (for example, "greater market growth" or "greater profitability per transaction"). Make certain that empowered employees are constantly aligned with the organization's strategic objectives.

Subordinate ego.

Yes, you can probably do a great number of things better/faster/cheaper than many of the performers who are empowered first. But that's not the point. Only by doing the job themselves will employees grow into the full potential of empowered contributors. Don't step in unless you see a potentially fatal mistake or a serious customer problem being created. Allow for the "freedom to fail," and don't feel obligated to show how you can do it every time. There is a thin line between coaching and showboating, and the difference is the degree to which the learner learns. Give people some rope. They won't hang themselves, and they won't hang you.

Continually educate yourself and your people.

When empowerment is proceeding well, don't abandon your post. People often fall into the "success trap," believing that they have attained nirvana and that there is nothing left to learn or improve upon. Keep expanding the envelope. Provide new skills, examine the wisdom of moving boundaries, demand new levels of innovation. Among the managers whom I've observed, those best at educating others are also the best at educating themselves.

What leverage really means

In traditional organizational America, managers derived their power through the control of people and the control of information. They gave "marching orders" to others who had to wait for their direction.

In modern organizational America, those two sources of power have disappeared. Everyone has access to information thanks to the communications revolution that has transformed the workplace: cell phones, laptop computers, digital notebooks, the Internet, e-mail, voice mail, teleconferencing, and the like. The numbers of people in companies have declined due to "downsizing," "reengineering," technological improvements in productivity, and outright demands by investors to reduce waste.

Bright Idea
Ask yourself what your job is. If you find that you answer with tasks and inputs (create reports, provide training) then it's likely your people will do the same. Change your orientation before you attempt to change anyone else's.

So the modern, powerful manager has a different source of power: leveraging the talents of others to achieve results that meet or exceed his or her own accountabilities. The employment of techniques that enhance and sustain that leverage are neither manipulative nor inappropriate. They are the hallmarks of intelligent, resourceful, and innovative management.

Old-style managers could manage through fear and threat. Modern managers must use empowerment and influence. Old-style managers could be content in the fact that they could do (and probably did do) every job reporting to them. Modern managers probably can't and shouldn't (excellent coaches needn't be superb athletes). Old-style managers measured and managed tasks. Modern managers evaluate results.

Not long ago I had to place an advertisement for a client in the context of one of my projects. I called *The Wall Street Journal* and *Business Week,* and spoke to two women responsible for ad placements. At *The Wall Street Journal* the conversation went something like this:

HER: That's a very peculiar ad.

ME: I know that. But can you place it?

HER: I don't know. I have to get people together from other departments that I don't control, I'm not sure we can get back to you soon, and I don't know whether we can meet your deadline. It's a real problem. I'm not sure I should even be the one trying to do this.

ME: What's your job there, anyway?

HER: I take advertising insertion orders, and you're not giving me one that I can take very easily, are you?

My fault. Here's the conversation at *Business Week:*

HER: That's a very peculiar ad.

ME: I know that. But can you place it?

HER: Of course. It's a challenge. I'll get some people together right away, and we'll call you back no later than tomorrow morning. Don't worry, we will make this work for you. By the way, would you be open to some suggestions from us on how to improve the potential receptivity to this ad?

ME: Of course. Er, what is your job there, by the way?

HER: My job? Why, it's to improve your business, of course!

Please think about this long and hard. These two women sat at the same desks, received the same salaries, enjoyed the same fringe benefits, and worked the same hours. There wasn't a scintilla of difference between them *except* the first one saw her job as a task or an input: I take advertising insertion orders. The second saw her job as a result or an output: I improve the customer's business.

That is not a difference of capital investment, education, background, skills, or anything else, other than attitude (which was reflected in their behaviors). That's a management difference. The second woman was managed, supported, and reinforced so that the accent was on the customer benefit and the resultant organizational benefit (increased advertising). The first was allowed to simply exist as an order-taker. That's not her fault, it's her manager's fault.

Where are your people spending their time, on input or output? How are you evaluating them? How are you helping them to grow?

For that matter, where are you spending your own time? On input and task, or output and result? Lest you think these are academic and abstract questions, I can't tell you the number of times I walk through organizations and hear sales people tell me that their job is to make sales calls instead of bring in new business, receptionists tell me that their job is to answer the phone rather than direct people to help and answers, and financial people tell me their job is to complete analyses and reports rather than assist line managers in profitably running their businesses.

When I was working with the *Los Angeles Times Mirror* advertising department, I was told by one proud regional manager that his sales team was exceeding the national standards by averaging 10 sales visits per day per person. Yet I knew that this same office was woefully behind its sales and profit goals, averaging a paltry $7,500 per sales agent.

Only one salesperson was in the office, a man named Joe. The manager pointed him out and said that Joe just worked the phones all day, rarely went out, and he was a real "old timer." The manager wanted to know if there was any advice I could provide on how to teach an old dog new tricks, and get Joe out of the office.

"What is Joe's production?" I asked.

"He only averages about five visits a week," explained the exasperated manager.

"No, no, I mean what are his revenue numbers?"

"Oh, he brings in about $25,000 a week most weeks."

"He brings in $25,000 just sitting here?!"

"That's right. Imagine what would happen if I could get him out the door. What would you suggest?"

"Get him a more comfortable chair!"

The cycle of motivation and self-esteem

There is a discernable, manageable, and tangible process to enhancing self-esteem, and it has nothing to do with bromides, "self-affirmations," or other dubious methods of trying to "instill" motivation. Self-esteem must be level, and not subject to the peaks and valleys of past defeats and victories.

Self-Esteem as a Roller Coaster

Constant Self-Esteem

As the graphic depicts, self-esteem is often a "roller coaster" ride, dependent on the last "win" or "loss." Many salespeople will tell you that they fall into "cycles of wins and losses." This means that after losing a deal or two in a row, or receiving several rejections in a row, they actually head into their next meeting expecting to be rejected, behave accordingly (lack of perseverance, easily rebutted, low energy level, etc.), and are then, indeed, rejected. Conversely, when a salesperson makes several sales in a row, he or she enters the next prospect's office with an air of invincibility, which is also manifest in their behavior (confidence, options, rebuttal of objections, relationship-building, etc.), which typically results in still another sale.

People in all occupations fall into the same vicious cycles, often not realizing that they are actually creating their own momentum and inertia,

Bright Idea
Ask employees what skills they need to do their jobs better at the moment. Arrange for whatever is reasonable to be provided, even if it involves one-on-one coaching. You'll find a much better productivity improvement than by applying blanket classroom training.

which means that they can't escape from the failures or can't readily perpetuate the wins past a certain point (or an unexpected rejection).

Self-esteem needs to be constantly high (but less than "manic") throughout one's experiences. You're seldom done in by rejection, and never "home free" through victory. It's consistence that counts.

How do you instill this in office workers and others without clear opportunities to succeed on a daily basis? It's done by learning this sequence:

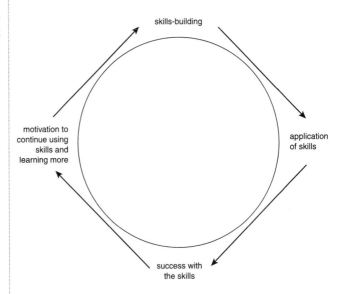

As the steps suggest:

1. People are exposed to skill building. The closer they are to the actual use of those skills, the better. This is what Dewey called "the teachable moment." The more divorced the skills building is from the application of those skills, the less likely it will be applied well (or at

all). If you teach someone customer-response skills, then immediately put them on the phones. This step is learning the skills.

2. The skills are applied on the job with suport. Ideally, this should be done with some monitoring or coaching so that the experience is as successful as possible. Have someone listen in on the call to provide feedback and guidance as they progress. This step is applying the skills.

3. Success and small victories occur. The person monitoring should provide positive feedback or the person performing should have unequivocal evidence of success (for example, quality control approves the application, a story is printed, or a computer program is fixed).

4. The individual, buoyed by these victories, internalizes the skills and becomes "unconsciously competent" in reapplying them as needed (checklists, coaches, and operational aids are no longer needed). The performer is now highly amenable to learning more skills to create more victories. Within this sequence, the occasional setback can be readily tolerated, because the process is known to work. (If too many setbacks occur, then the skills are either inappropriate for the job, the standards are unreasonable, or the skills are being utilized incorrectly.)

Note that this is not a function of evanescent and empty motivational techniques designed to provide temporary solace and positive feelings. Rather, the process is based on the acquisition of tangible and manageable skills that the employee can replicate at will (and teach and convey to others, as well).

Watch Out!
Most contemporary motivational techniques, whether emotionally erupting speakers or outdoor games, are no better than a donut. Once the sugar high is gone, there is no residual nutrition.

Many years ago, I managed a salesman in Texas by the name of Ray. Ray had looked promising at the start of his tenure with us, but for two years had been struggling and, despite training programs, coaching, and a positive work environment, it seemed as though he would have to be let go. Then, just before that decision had to be made, Ray started to sell. In fact, he had the second best year of anyone in the entire western region, and the following year set a sales record for new business acquisition in the U.S.

I asked Ray what the turning point had been: Was it the training finally kicking in, the mentoring, the flexibility in giving him enough time to learn the ropes?

Ray said that he had entered every account worried about his quota and concerned about his job. He kept thinking about his rejections. Then, just when things looked bleakest, he found himself on an airplane sitting next to a salesman from another company.

"All he could talk about," said Ray, "was how much his products helped his customers, how much he loved learning new ways to apply them, and how much he enjoyed the positive customer feedback. He never mentioned his sales quota or production figures once."

"After that, I just decided to try to help each customer, and to equip myself to help the customer, not to help myself. I didn't want a sale, I wanted a happy customer. And pretty soon, I found myself with an awful lot of them."

I learned from that myself. I learned that we had been preparing our people with skills too oriented to meet our goals, and not sufficient to meet the customers' goals. The cycle above is more rewarding when we can see and feel the benefits we're providing others, because the feedback originates externally and not merely within the organization.

Several years ago, while working with the animal health division of Merck & Co., I found myself at my veterinarian picking up some pills for my dog. While waiting, I glanced through a medical book on the counter and found that the pills were, in fact, manufactured by Merck. When I mentioned this to the vet, he actually became quite emotional.

"Those people," he said, meaning Merck, "are responsible for more health and prevention of disease for animals than everyone else combined. That is a great company, and while they're most known for human health products, what they've done for animals has been miraculous."

When I next visited Merck, I told this to one of the animal health division managers. He asked me to wait a moment, assembled his staff, and asked me to repeat what I had told him. After I had done so for the group, there was complete silence.

"What's going on?" I finally asked.

"These people never hear about the good we do here," he said, "and I wanted to share this with them. It will make a big difference for us when we deal with the inevitable complaints about a lost shipment or a price increase."

Just the facts

- Motivation can only originate with the individual; otherwise any change is temporary and not self-perpetuating.

- Money is not a magical motivator, although its absence will tend to demotivate.

Bright Idea
Invite your customers into your organization, or take some of your people on a trip to visit willing customers. Ordinarily, employees hear complaints the great preponderance of the time. Enable them to see and hear the good that they do—this interaction is worth a great deal to both employees and customers.

- Not everyone can be empowered, but if customer interactions are required, empowerment is a must or it's the wrong person for the job.

- Self-esteem is the result of learning skills that lead to ongoing "victories."

- Self-esteem must be constant, and not subject to the last victory or setback.

GET THE SCOOP ON...
Identifying types of conflict ▪ Defusing hostile
environments ▪ Healthy disagreement ▪
Subordinating ego ▪ Finding a third way out ▪
Avoiding transference ▪ Using humor to reduce
tension

Resolving Conflict Without Bloodshed

Chapter 3

We hear about conflict in the workplace all the time. But we hear about it in the most stereotypical of ways. Like any other management problem or opportunity, we can't really deal with it if we don't take the time to understand it. And, like most other management problems, conflict isn't as difficult or messy as we're led to believe. But, first, let's get past the stereotyping.

Here's an exercise: Look at the numbers below, and provide the rational reason that they're in the order chosen. By "rational reason" I mean that this is not my phone number or Social Security number, but rather a sequence that anyone should be able to identify whether they know me or not:

8   5   4   9   1   7   6   3   2   0

An average of one person in 20 discerns the answer within 20 minutes. When I first saw this, I failed to come up with the rational reason. I said that eight minus three is five, minus one is four, but I couldn't explain the nine. So, I started at the other end, but couldn't get past the seven. When my son was a junior in high school, he gave the problem to his math teacher, a brilliant guy, who took two days and surrendered. (My son considered this one of the highlights of his academic career and, looking back, he might have been right.)

Give up? The numbers are in alphabetical order, eight starting with "e," five with "f," down to zero with a "z." If English isn't your first language, you have an excuse, but no one else does. We tend to label this as a "numbers problem" and lock ourselves into a narrow enclosure attempting to solve the "numbers problem." However, there is no numeric solution to this at all. It is an alphabetic problem (or a linguistics problem or a grammar problem). People who do solve this quickly usually explain that they simply let their minds roam freely once they couldn't get a numeric solution, and soon stumbled upon the letter solution.

If we call this a "numbers problem" we will never solve it. Yet, how many areas of conflict at work are we calling a "distribution problem," or a "backroom problem," or the dreaded "communications problem," or even worse, a "chemistry problem." Once we slap the label on, we're much less likely to solve the issue and resolve the conflict.

The two forms of conflict

Conflict is almost always over one of two issues: objectives or alternatives. The mistake we make is to look at the *content* of the situation, or the *personalities* of the situation, or the *history* of the situation. However, it's the *process* that's most important, and people usually disagree over either:

Objectives: The destination or end result to be achieved, or

Alternatives: The means or route used to reach the destination

Timesaver Identifying a conflict rapidly seems also to quickly resolve it: "What do you expect from sales? They never support marketing. It's the typical sales/marketing conflict." In fact, assigning it to a drawer with a label actually delays resolution. It's faster to identify the issue, not origins or personalities.

Case Study #1:

Two employees approach you to act as "referee" and settle their dispute about the annual sales awards conference. Bob thinks that it should be in Bermuda, and that the attendant expense isn't that much considering the morale that's boosted and the gains to be made from the investment in the conference in terms of next year's sales improvement.

Joan believes that morale actually suffers because only about 30 percent of the entire sales force qualifies for the trip, and none of the back-room and support people are ever invited. She believes that sales rely more than ever on teamwork, and the conference doesn't reward teams but just the "point person" who actually gets the contract signed.

Bob points out that Joan has never been a front-line salesperson and can't really understand the motivation of the sales force. Further, he believes that she feels undercompensated and, therefore, opposes the conference.

Joan responds that Bob has never managed any group other than sales, and is woefully ignorant of the dynamics that actually create teamwork and high morale throughout an organization. She also notes that Bob extends his vacation every year around the conference and uses it as a personal benefit.

What would you do?

This conflict, taken from an actual client situation and not at all uncommon, is not about Bob's or Joan's background, nor about competing areas of the company. It is about two people who don't believe in the *objectives* for the conference. As a manager, you have to resolve the underlying issue about its *raison d'être:* Does it serve a constructive purpose

Watch Out!
Immediately
determine
whether the con-
flict is over
objectives or
alternatives.
They require dif-
ferent starting
points. If you
don't do this,
and choose the
incorrect starting
point, you will
extend and
exacerbate the
conflict.

in generating more sales, or is it dysfunctional because it no longer represents the teamwork required for sales in the company's current strategy?

If Bob and Joan had been arguing over whether the conference should be in Bermuda or Chicago, that would have been conflict over alternatives, not the reason for the conference.

Conflict about objectives is characterized by the following:

■ Disagreement over the results or outcomes to be achieved.

■ Questions about the rationale and logic for the decision.

■ Arguments that tend to be "yes" or "no," "do it" or "don't do it."

■ Questions about the validity of the approach.

■ Efforts to change the tried and true, "we've always done it this way."

■ Unwillingness to compromise.

Conflict about alternatives is characterized by the following:

■ The attitude that "my way is better than your way."

■ Argument over inputs: funds, timing, resources, logistics, etc.

■ Personal agendas that will be affected.

■ A tacit acceptance of the worth of the outputs and results.

■ "Politicking" and "back stage" lobbying.

■ A willingness to compromise if an individual's personal, perceived gain from one of the alternatives can be guaranteed and not be lost through the compromise.

The power manager quickly separates conflict into one of its two component causes by asking these kinds of questions of the people involved in the conflict (or of themselves and others involved in the debate):

- Do we agree on the outcomes?
- Do we agree on the intent and reasoning?

If the answers to the above are "yes," then:

- Why do we have differing options and alternatives?
- Is the risk associated with our alternatives different?
- Does one party's alternative succeed at the expense of another?
- Are there personal agendas harmed by others' alternatives?
- Can we combine and alter the current alternative?
- Can we generate a new alternative that satisfies all of us?

If the answers to the above are "no," then:

- What is there about the outcomes or results we disagree about?
- Who "owns" this decision, and is responsible for the results?
- Is the outcome important, and can it be met in other ways?
- Why have we always tried to achieve this?
- Why are we considering trying to achieve something new?
- What is the fit between these outcomes and our overall strategy?

Bright Idea
Never take sides early. Listen carefully and ask questions until you can decide what type of conflict you're facing. When you're forced to reverse yourself after finding out that you incorrectly assessed the conflict, you can make the underlying tensions much worse. In most cases, accuracy trumps speed.

Defusing the hostility

Begin with the notion that there are no evil people, and that the combatants are not innately malicious. (If, factually, this proves not to be true, then remove the malicious parties from your operation.) You have two key questions that can guide you in this:

1. What is the evidence supporting your position?

2. What is the observable behavior I'm experiencing?

Most "personality conflicts" really aren't about personality at all but, astonishingly, they're allowed to take on a life of their own because the manager doesn't wade into the facts and behaviors, but merely brushes away the trouble with the all-encompassing label of "personality conflict" or "poor chemistry." Let's pick up our case study again.

Case Study #2:

MGR: So, Bob, what's your evidence that sales improve each year as a result of the rewards trip? My recollection is that sometimes they've plateaued and, occasionally, declined.

BOB: When there haven't been improvements, it's because of other variables, such as the economy or key accounts closing. When you work with the sales force, like I do, you can tell how motivated they are by the recognition and the trip.

MGR: I recognize you're close to these people. If recognition is the objective, are there other ways to do it, ways that might include the other people contributing to the success?

BOB: I don't know. All I do know is that the trip is an annual event that goes back 10 years and is a part of our tradition. Joan wants to disrupt it for her own personal reasons.

MGR: Let's keep the name-calling and supposition out of this. I just want to examine the facts. You have no right to question Joan's motives. Joan, what's your evidence that the team has taken over from the single salesperson as the key to our acquisition of new business?

JOAN: If you look at the ten largest accounts secured over the past year, on nine of them we had three or more people accompany the salesperson on several calls prior to the signing of the contract, and on all nine the support staff had to generate lengthy comparative reports for the prospect. I'll bet the salesperson didn't even read the report or know what was in it, but just passed it along.

MGR: Do you know that for a fact?

JOAN: No, but I suspect it.

MGR: Then let's just stick with what we do know. What happened with that tenth piece of business?

JOAN: It was a referral that came to us, with no selling really necessary.

MGR: Bob, do these facts sound correct to you, or do you have any additional information to add?

In the course of brief conversations, using intelligent questions to focus on hard facts and evidence and discipline to avoid name-calling and emotional issues, a manager can sort out the conflict relatively quickly. This is a *process* that can be used in any industry, any situation, and at any level.

A problem occurs when the manager inadvertently (or advertently) gets drawn into the middle of the conflict, either defending a point of view or trying to defend against accusations. For example, if someone claims that "The financial people have never been helpful. They simply try to save money and never try to help us meet our goals," there are two ways to react:

Bright Idea
Try to rehearse your opening lines prior to any potential confrontation or negotiation. Make sure that your first statements in particular are firmly rooted in observed behavior and not pop-psychology or past unhappiness with the individual. The opening statements usually set the tone of what follows quite firmly.

Poor:

How can you say that about finance? They care as much as anyone whether we meet our plan. They often feel that line people ignore their very reasonable financial guidelines. You can't blame them all the time.

Even poorer:

Okay, I'll admit that finance has its problems. I've had my share of occasions when I simply did an end run. But let's focus on what we have to do here, whether or not they're on board, because we can't control what they do.

Good:

What evidence to do you have that finance has been a problem in the past? They've been too much of a scapegoat for us. This is about us, not about them.

Even better:

What evidence do you have that finance is a factor of any kind in this particular situation?

Even the best of us get drawn into one side or another in an argument or debate. It's an intellectual challenge, as well as a time-sensitive approach, to try to get beyond an impasse. But it's actually one of the worst things we can do because taking sides early gobbles up still more time before the underlying causes can be identified, and makes it much harder to reverse yourself if you've jumped to the "wrong" side.

There's nothing wrong with informing conflicting parties that "we're going into our conflict resolution mode," and then following a certain methodical set of questions. This will sensitize people to the fact that volume, lobbying, emotionalism, and even threats (no one will work overtime, work flow will

Unofficially...
A powerful reason for approaching conflict in a dispassionate, *process-oriented* manner is avoiding the reputation of listening to those who speak to you last, or favoring a certain argument. If people perceive that you're vulnerable to a particular approach, they'll attempt to manipulate you, making evidence and behavior even more difficult to identify.

slow down, people will leave) are not the way to get their way. It's important to establish a constant, systematic style for handling conflict. Once the subordinates understand the process, they will tend to adhere to it, since it represents their best chance to win their cases.

Moreover, subordinates themselves will begin to ask whether they are arguing over objectives or alternatives, and may well reach some consensus or compromise to present to you, rather than demand that you act as chief umpire. Just bear in mind that compromise about alternatives is almost always safe in the hands of the disputants, subject to budget restraints and other pragmatic issues. But conflict about objectives is not usually safe when purely delegated, *because it is incumbent on the manager to ensure that the objectives reached by the individuals are aligned with and supportive of the organization's objectives.* It does no good to allow employees to reach compromises on objectives that undermine the organization's position.

The truth about personality conflicts

A small but potentially serious form of conflict does arise over true personality problems. When I first entered the workforce, I labored as an assistant manager deep in the bureaucracy of the home office of Prudential Insurance. One morning I was shocked to get a message that one of my employees wouldn't be coming to work that day because she was the victim of a domestic dispute. I reported this to my manager, who was amused at my shock.

The manager walked with me to the window of his office, from which we could see all 400-plus people who worked in his operation. "Son," he said, "take the proportion of alcohol abuse, drug addiction, divorces, income tax cheating, and every other social condition, and simply apply it to this division. If 1 percent of the population has a substance abuse problem, then we probably have four or five in this operation. Get used to it."

I spend the rest of the morning trying to identify those five without success. But I did learn that the workplace doesn't magically erase social and psychological difficulties. So should you.

Here are the major kinds of what I call "non-objective" conflicts that you are likely to encounter among subordinates, peers, and superiors. Bear in mind that these are the vast exception to the conflict noted above over objectives or alternatives, but they will occur on occasion and will not respond to the rational resolutions above.

The "It's not me" personality disorder

An individual with a personality disorder truly believes that "it's always someone else's fault." If the meeting room is lacking a needed overhead projector because this individual neglected to order one, their response will be, "The facilities people should know that an overhead is required for these meetings, and shouldn't have to be told every time," or "The secretary should have asked me what the audio/visual needs are, that's her job." People with personality disorders on this level *never* accept responsibility for a setback, delay, or defeat.

Even in the case of a direct order, this individual will not accept accountability for a less-than-desired outcome. "I know I told you to see the customer before the order arrived, but it never occurred to me that you would still do this even when you learned the order was being changed. You're supposed to use your judgment."

(Some people claim you can always tell the difference between a personality disorder and a neurosis [see below] in this way: Someone with a neurosis will trip over someone who deliberately sticks a leg out and say, "I'm sorry, how could I be so clumsy?" Someone with a personality disorder will trip over nothing more than a chalk line and say, "Who the hell put that there?! I could have killed myself!")

How to resolve conflict with someone with a personality disorder:

Indicators:

- Always blames someone else or "the system."

- Never accepts accountability.

- Finds ways to deny involvement in setbacks.

- Irrationally defensive about abilities and decisions.

Actions:

- Don't make it personal. Focus on the facts and issues.

- Find cause, not blame.

- Don't fall into trap of also blaming others.

- Ask what can be done to avoid the problem in the future.

- Affix clear accountabilities that can't be denied.

- Establish a "buck stops here" mentality and enforce it.

The neurotic

Neuroses are relatively minor psychological impediments (as opposed to psychoses, for example). They are typified by extremes of anxiety, nervousness, and doubts about self-worth. As opposed to a

Timesaver
Never allow someone with a personality disorder to drag you down into the "blame game." Focus on objective facts and issues. Tell them that all of you bear responsibility, especially if you can't fix the problem quickly. Beware of even inadvertently lending your name to support this individual's blaming others.

personality disorder, a neurotic is likely to tell you "it's all my fault," even though the problem was a tornado.

The conflicts caused by neurotics are the result of a combination of poor judgment and conservatism brought on by a lack of confidence and a fear of failing, and an aberrant willingness to accept blame for others' shortcomings. They readily become scapegoats, which not only creates conflict ("What are we supposed to do with him?" "There's no way we're going to meet our goals with her as part of the team."), but also tends to focus attention away from the real causes of the problem.

Among other problems with this personality type is the refusal to question instructions, no matter how incorrect they may be, and an aversion to any kind of innovation, initiative, or improvement.

How to resolve conflict with a neurotic employee:

Indicators:

Watch Out!
Note that you can't and shouldn't *eliminate* stress levels. You want them high enough to achieve some sense of urgency and get the adrenaline to flow, but not so high that they cause fear and paralyze performance.

- Acceptance of blame despite the facts.

- Aversion to risk, self-directed initiative.

- Verbalization of attitude, "I just can't do it right."

- Continual self-blame, anxiety, high stress.

Actions:

- Work with one-on-one, not in front of others.

- Break job into small, conquerable tasks.

- Reward small victories and reinforce good work.

- Help manage stress levels.

- Consider lower-stress positions if nothing else works.

The politician

The politician is someone who is constantly vying for some advantage, either personally, or for their department or operation. These are people who may well be very inconsistent in the issues they support because they perceive a "payoff" for changing sides as things evolve. These are the people engaged in the "backroom" deals, the sidebar meetings, and behind-the-scenes manipulation.

Politicians base their actions on a personal agenda, which may be difficult to ascertain. They are extremely difficult to work for, since their leadership is seldom predicated on the seeming rationale of the issue, but is rather based on a personalized and unseen goal. Consequently, we often see conflicting and incongruous behaviors from the same person on the same issue, as he or she perceives that the winds may be shifting. It's not the issue, but the personal payoff that counts.

Politicians can cause grievous conflict because they are so good at what they do. After all, they practice incessantly, and practice makes perfect. They are at their very best (and everyone else's very worst) when someone attempts to engage them in their own arena. Their conflict undermines initiatives, often reflected in the worst of passive-aggressive behavior: They publicly support you while privately undermining you.

How to deal with the employee who's a politician: Indicators:

- Reports from others that the politician's support is not real.
- Shifting decisions and support made situationally.

- Publicly supportive, never openly hostile.

- Tends to form blocs and groups of supporters.

- May withdraw from agreements at the last minute.

Actions:

- Do not play their game behind the scenes.

- Gain commitment on specifics in public, with witnesses.

- Confront as soon as any deviation is seen. Don't wait.

- Use evidence: "You said this, but did that. Why?"

- Confront repeatedly until behavior stops. Firmness is key.

- If subordinate, use performance evaluation as a tool.

- If superior, get as much as you can in writing.

Unofficially...
Some organizations are politicized, with deals made in halls, not in meeting rooms. This culture does not successfully attract and retain top talent. If you find yourself in such an operation, and you're uncomfortable, don't play the game. Find an organization that values talent more than manipulation.

The egoist

The egoist is out for self-aggrandizement at all cost. Conflicts with this character type are likely and highly damaging: This individual will pursue credit, the limelight, power, reward, and other factors to improve his or her condition at the expense of others, of customers, and of organizational goals. This is the antithesis of the team player.

Egoists are only satisfied through the accomplishment of their personal goals, which are almost always in support of their own narcissism. Consequently, they will claim inordinate credit ("The sales force is over plan not because of sales management, which has been in place for years, but because of the training program I created last year that developed a new approach to business acquisition.") despite their actual involvement (a brief list of points to remember on a sales call that was introduced in the midst of a full-week course developed by sales management). Egoists will use purported histories of success to justify their role in current success. The entire package is illusory, but no less damaging to organizational teamwork, goals, and communication.

We've all seen the egoist. That's the person who, in the midst of a gathering for a photo to celebrate an accomplishment of others, arrives at the last minute to stand right next to the president, then hangs the photo in the office. (We also see another explicit example of the egoist: When occasionally the "record" of success is taken seriously, and the egoist winds up with clear and inescapable accountability for an operation or division, unmitigated disaster ensues. No one can readily explain how "such an important and successful person failed so dismally.")

How to deal with the employee who is an egoist: Indicators:

- Always talks about "I," "me," and "my."

- Never shares credit, never accepts blame.

- Evaluates issues only in terms of personal advancement.

- Creates impressive but unverifiable record of "success."

- Talks much more than listens.

- Heightened and unrealistic sense of self-importance.

Actions:

- Make clear the accountabilities of the team to deal with the individual as the behavior occurs,

Watch Out!
Do not try to apply standard management techniques with serious personality disorders. These latter problems are delineated here to indicate that you ought to get help from human resources or an EAP (employee assistance program) if available for the individual. Anything less than that will tend to exacerbate the problem.

since team members are in the best position to address it.

- Exemplify proper behavior yourself (don't compete).

- Take action privately—don't embarrass publicly.

- Provide small acknowledgements, only if merited.

- Do not allow or provide exceptional treatment.

The psychotic

Psychosis is a serious form of mental illness, most usually typified by periodic (or prolonged) loss of contact with reality. Perhaps half of all admissions to mental hospitals are for some form of psychosis. The neurotic (above) may deny reality, but is not disassociated from it, and can identify his or her own behavior and problems. The psychotic, however, does not identify any problem and cannot control his or her behavior.

Symptoms of psychosis include hearing voices, illusions, hallucinations, and emotional impulsiveness. Such individuals require therapeutic attention. They cannot be helped by management approaches and, in fact, may be further harmed through inattention or neglect. Psychotics can harm people around them.

How to deal with employees who may be psychotic:

Indicators:

- Behavior disassociated with reality (e.g., verbalization).

- Disruptive behaviors.

- Citing of "voices" or "images."

- *Nonsequiturs* and strange conversations.

Actions:

- Do not confront or antagonize.
- Seek assistance through the EAP or other program.
- Alert senior management and human resources.
- Remove the individual from the work environment.

The depressed

Depression is often mistaken for job-related stress or situational emotional problems, and is therefore addressed incorrectly. Clinical depression (as opposed to the colloquial—"I'm depressed about my lousy performance review") is frequently "masked" so that others can't tell what they are dealing with. True depression is caused by a combination of genetic, biochemical, and psycho-social forces. It must be dealt with therapeutically.

Bipolar (often called "manic") depression is characterized by mood swings. In the "up" or "manic" stage, the individual is excitable, talkative, overactive, and restless. There is a surfeit of energy. In the "down" or "depressive" stage, the individual is moody, slow, uninterested, and unresponsive. Severe depression is marked by a loss of interest in the environment, an end to favorite activities, an urge to give away treasured belongings, and suicidal tendencies.

Over the past 3 years, at two different clients where I've been asked to coach highly successful executives who were deemed to be "off their game" or "in a slump," I found bipolar depression to be the cause. No amount of executive coaching, job change,

Bright Idea
Identify someone in the Employee Assistance Program, Human Resources Department, or elsewhere to provide insight and discussion about behavioral problems. Although a minor percentage of conflict, these do represent serious issues for the individual, the manager, and the organization. Don't wait until confronted— have your resources identified in advance.

or skills building would affect that condition. A therapeutic intervention was necessary. Managers can't be psychologists, but they should learn to recognize the signs of serious mental illnesses.

How to deal with the depressed employee: Indicators:

■ Sudden and profound mood swings.

■ A loss of interest in traditional areas of fulfillment.

■ Nonresponsiveness and uncaring.

■ An inability to apply talents to their fullest.

■ Excessive time off work without apparent reason.

■ Fits of energy that seem inappropriate to the issue.

Actions:

■ Arrange for evaluation by appropriate professionals.

■ Engage in conversation. Provide opportunity to talk.

■ Test your observations with trusted others.

■ Do not use traditional coaching and remediation.

How to pass the impasse

The final aspect of successfully resolving conflict on the job is to recognize that it is almost always temporary. With the exception of some of the personality and medical conditions noted above— which constitute a small minority of cases—most conflict is over relatively temporary issues that will eventually disappear. It's important to create an environment in which people can freely "let go."

Vendettas and feuds, such as the fabled Hatfields and McCoys, outlast their origins. That is, after a while, no one can remember what began the whole thing. We often find the same dynamic at work. No one can quite remember why operations and finance have always resented each other, or why underwriting and sales are traditionally at odds. Yet it's tough in many environments for antagonists to readily cede their anger, even if they're no longer sure about the sources of that anger.

The power manager creates a work environment in which it is difficult to maintain "grudges." (The Australians are great at this process. They can disagree with you passionately and loudly during a meeting. Then, when the issue is decided one way or the other, they say, "Well, that's over, mate. Let's have a beer!" It's never personal.)

Here are some techniques to create a rapidly reconciling and healing environment:

Keep the conflict nonemotional and never about personal qualities

Be vigilant in identifying facts, and never let anyone focus on personal attributes. "Our retailers are accustomed to professional and high-quality service, and they are not going to sit still for a woman with just one year's experience on their accounts." That sentence contains a fact about the retailers expectation level, a discriminatory remark about a gender, and a bias that someone can't possess the requisite skills after a year, without testing that sentiment. These "mixed" statements are the most dangerous kind, because they start out from an agreed upon fact before descending into accusation and prejudice.

When conflict is emotional and involves someone's attributes and personal qualities, the bad feelings will linger even if the conflict is successfully decided in your (the manager's) favor. The time to stop this is right at the point of origin, and firmly.

Separate fact from assumption

Just because something is said loudly, for long periods, and with passion, doesn't make it true. Assumptions, when not proved or disproved, linger in the workplace. "We know that our competition will continue to improve their technology, and our technical people are not going to be comfortable in the field with clients. We need more strength in this area." Of course, we don't know what the competition will do, and are we certain that all of our technical people will be such poor performers at the client site?

In these cases, the manager has to literally list the assumptions and ask the group to find ways to validate or invalidate each one. It's dangerous to act on assumptions in any case, and it's important to establish what's true to end lingering feelings of antagonism.

For a long time, even in superb companies, many senior managers made the assumptions that people of Asian descent could not be managers, because they were not "assertive enough" to handle conflict. Consequently, Asians were targeted for research, development, and technical positions that were sole-contributor jobs. This narrowing of career options caused, understandably, tremendous resentment among Asians that has not easily dissipated. This is an example of the long-term damage of unproven and arbitrary assumptions.

Maintain frequent communications channels

Managers who require regular staff meetings, small team and task force meetings, and similar scheduled interactions have a much easier time both in identifying lingering conflict and in reconciling it. If warring parties go back to their own "countries" and don't have to interact frequently, there isn't much opportunity to observe the after-effects of what was deemed to be the resolution of the immediate conflict.

However, if people are forced to interact as a job requirement (and not as a condition of the conflict), you're able to observe and gauge the degree of cooperation and collaboration that exists. Once conflict has occurred, it's never a good idea to separate the formerly warring parties. You should, instead, continue the regular interactions so that you can ensure that the animosity is behind them. This technique works best when the interactions are already in place and are a natural aspect of the work setting. They needn't be long or burdensome. An hour's staff meeting once a week, in which everyone has to contribute and participate, will do the job.

Test with third parties

Use objective, trusted others who weren't part of the conflict and did not take sides or positions to provide feedback on whether the episode is over. These may be colleagues and peers from another department who either send work to your department or receive work from it. Check to see if the quality and quantity of work has declined, if phone responses are slower, or if they hear complaining or encounter finger pointing.

If your environment is sufficiently open and risk-free, you can trust your own subordinates to approach you if the conflicting parties are still causing disruption to the work flow or to those around them. However, keep these inquiries objective: Don't accept "I think they're still trying to give each

Timesaver
Trust your employees to be accountable to resolve conflict at their level, with you as the last resort. Don't allow yourself to be the first resort, or your time will be ruthlessly usurped and your employees will never acquire the requisite skills or responsibilities.

other a hard time." Ask instead, "What evidence do you have that they are still trying to even the score or haven't accepted the decision that was made?"

Move the accountability for resolution to those in conflict

If all else fails, tell the parties involved that they are continuing to disrupt the operation according to the evidence you've obtained. Discuss with them the implications (see the following chapter on confronting poor performance). Tell them that the accountability for permanent resolution of the conflict is now theirs, and that you expect the matter to be settled in the next few days.

Explain that if it is not successfully resolved to your satisfaction, you will take arbitrary action to resolve it, and this action may easily include transfer, loss of position, changed responsibilities, and even termination. Under no circumstances will you allow their behavior to continue to cause disruption, and they will resolve it immediately, or you will.

The key steps:

- Confront them with your evidence of continued conflict.

- Explain why the disruption is intolerable for performance.

- Stipulate what you see as the standard for successful resolution.

- Provide a very brief timetable for that resolution.

- Explain your options if they do not accomplish the resolution.

- Ensure that they understand and end the meeting.

There is no need to fall on your own sword for people in unresolvable feuds and vendettas. When your own boss says, "What's going on in your area? I've heard that there is some terrible antagonism," you know that it's gotten far out of hand.

Conflict itself is unavoidable in the workplace, and is usually quite healthy. A refusal to resolve it and inability to compromise is neither usual nor healthy. It's your job to recognize the difference and to take the appropriate actions.

Just the facts

- Conflict is usually healthy and should be welcomed.

- It's imperative to recognize the type of conflict, since there are different starting points.

- A minority of these conflicts will be emotional or medical (psychological) in nature, and should be referred to experts.

- Ensure that the effects of the conflict do not linger, and that feuds don't arise.

- Keep all efforts focused on facts, verify all assumptions, and do not allow personal attacks—have a zero tolerance for these behaviors.

Evaluating Performance
and Providing Feedback

PART II

Dealing with Poor Performance

Chapter 4

One of the most remarkable aspects of the evolution of modern management has been a gradual withdrawal from providing honest feedback about performance. We've gone from the extreme of the rigors of Taylorism (wherein Frederick Winslow Taylor produced a formalized system for measuring the "perfect" output for virtually any kind of manual worker in the early years of the 20th Century) and his "scientific management," which demanded the optimum pace for the optimum wage, and a certain minimum, measured performance if one was to retain a job, to an era of rubber-stamp evaluations in which everyone is rated as "exceeds expectations" despite their actual performance. Where is Taylor when you need him?

The inability to confront subordinates about poor performance—and the commensurate reluctance to honestly extol excellent performance—have seriously undermined productivity in the workplace. The huge "downsizings" of the last 2 decades are the result of both strategic error at the executive level and tactical inability to improve poor

Moneysaver
Confronting poor performance immediately, no matter how uncomfortable or awkward, costs one-tenth the price of ignoring it until, inevitably, harsh measures are demanded to remove it. Poor performers virtually never improve without outside intervention, and are among the last to accept early retirement or to seek other jobs.

performance at the operational level. In other words, 7,000 productive people were laid-off often because management was unable or unwilling to fire 70 of them for poor performance. The cumulative effect of nonperformers unmolested in the workplace sapped the vitality of many businesses, resulting in overzealous, harsh cuts to make the bottom line appear more respectable.

Unfortunately, there is a myriad of pressures on modern managers to avoid and ignore performance problems. None of them is sufficient to abrogate that responsibility, but nonetheless, each is real and must be acknowledged:

- Legal threat: Both the letter of the law (legislation such as the Americans with Disabilities Act) and the spirit of the law (suits filed against every kind of perceived discrimination) have created a minefield for managers. It's often perceived as easier and less expensive to live with a performance problem than to incur the legal reactions that often result from taking action about it.

- Poor training: Most managers do not go through frequent education about how to conduct employee evaluation interviews, how to confront poor performance, and how to coach and counsel. As in any activity, it's tough to do something well if one doesn't possess the equipment, have the skills, or know the rules.

- Poor system: In many organizations performance evaluations are a once-a-year necessary evil, with poor forms, poor procedures, and little senior management support. No one believes that the process means anything, and they're usually right.

- Fear of confrontation: It's interesting to note that most job interviewers are as afraid of rejection as the interviewee, which explains why they are such lousy interviewers. Similarly, many managers fear the reactions of the person being evaluated, are apprehensive about an argument ensuing, or are simply unsure of their own assessment. Hence, they "soft peddle" the feedback or say one thing while writing another.

- Abuse of the systems: There are countless examples of organizations using the performance evaluation system as a substitute for tangible increases and benefits. This happens most frequently among the administrative ranks with secretaries, but also happens commonly elsewhere. Individuals are is given an "outstanding" rating to salve their egos, but virtually no increase in pay because it's been a bad year, or their performance really wasn't that good, or they're at the top of their pay grade but the manager doesn't want to lose them to a higher level job (no one ever wants to see an excellent secretary move up the ladder, it seems).

- Inadequate human resources oversight: It doesn't take a rocket scientist to tell you that you can't have eighty percent of your employees rated as "outstanding" when your organization has only had an average year! Yet that is exactly what transpires, and human resource departments—the supposed watchdogs and experts—lack the competency, the credibility, and the spine to stand up to executives and tell them that the system is a fiction.

Watch Out!
Inquire in your human resources department as to who the expert is in performance evaluation and feedback. If you find that there isn't one, or that they don't specialize, or that everyone can do it, run for cover. At least you'll know that you can't expect sophisticated help from that resource.

So where does this leave the average manager who wants to excel and leverage the talents of employees to exceed goals? It leaves that manager with the responsibility to develop pragmatic and effective evaluation approaches.

Avoiding psychobabble and focusing on behavior

The underlying key to performance assessment, evaluation, and feedback is to focus on *observable behavior.* Think of it as "evidence" you can cite later that, objectively, the performer and you can agree about without emotion and varied interpretation. This means suspending biases, past experience, and assumptions, and focusing on the specifics of an instance.

Example:

You conduct a staff meeting every Friday morning at 9:00 for 1 hour. You've been doing this for a year for your ten direct reports. People are excused only if they are traveling, which is why you've chosen Friday, seldom used as a travel day. Attendance has been almost perfect, and the meeting is appreciated by your staff.

For the past two Fridays, Joyce had arrived about 20 minutes late. She has never been late before. This morning, she was late for a third consecutive meeting. She has offered no excuse, either at the meeting or after. You've decided that it's time to do something about this, and Joyce is due in your office in the next hour for a scheduled meeting between the two of you on one of her major projects.

Assuming that you will broach the matter of her lateness immediately, what exact words would you use to open the meeting?

There are two basic ways in which a manager could attempt to address this situation:

Approach #1: Joyce, I think we have a problem, and it's time to do something about it. You're not being fair to the team and, frankly, you're not showing much respect for me. You have to share equal responsibilities here, and the way you have begun to casually drop in on our staff meeting exemplifies the wrong kind of attitude. Am I being too critical or unfair?

Probable response: What do you mean by a bad attitude? I'm the one who's always the first to volunteer for work on a weekend when you need someone here. As for teamwork, I've probably led more United Way campaigns and blood drives than anyone else on the staff. Everyone in that room respects my work and contributions. How can you accuse me of such things?

Approach #2: Joyce, my observation is that you've been about 20 minutes late for the staff meeting for the last three Fridays. Is that right?

JOYCE: Yes, that's correct.

MGR: You've never been late before, as far as I know. What's causing it now, and is it likely to continue?

JOYCE: It's the traffic, and I don't see a way to escape it in the immediate future.

MGR: What's changed? The traffic seems no worse than usual, and the rest of us are still getting here on time. Is there something different that affects you?

JOYCE: Actually, there is. My husband has changed jobs, and can no longer take our children to daycare on Friday mornings. Since daycare doesn't open

Unofficially...
If your own superior tends to "get inside your head" and assess blame for presumed faults and flaws, simply and calmly ask, "What behavior or action did you see that led you to that conclusion?" If the boss can't produce any, then you're justified in rejecting the accusation.

until 8:00 and it's in the opposite direction from work, I really can't make it in here much before 9:20 or 9:30.

MGR: Okay, now I understand what's going on. I'll tell you what: Why don't you spend some time today figuring out all the options that would correct this problem, and then, if you need my help, we can talk about it this afternoon? We need you at the meeting, and I'm sure we're all smart enough to resolve this easily.

In the first scenario, the manager has evoked all of the employee's emotional defenses. Once you attack someone's character, all useful communication ends. Defenses are raised and counterattacks begin. Joyce was easily able to cite evidence to the contrary about her supposedly poor attitude, and she would quickly move on to cite instances of the manager's inappropriate decisions regarding teamwork and support, such as not participating in the blood drive himself. Once you attack the person, the conversation is over and any attempts to remediate the problem will fail.

In the second scenario, the manager carefully did two things:

1. He verified the performance deviation with the performer ("Am I right about your being 20 minutes late for three consecutive meetings?") before trying to solve anything. That small technique places the conversation on nonhostile, objective ground.

2. He enlisted the performer to acknowledge the cause (a new schedule, daycare, and traffic) and to try to do something about it (find a new daycare provider closer to the office, have a

relative transport the children). The manager offered further help if needed, and can always provide a solution (reschedule the meeting, exempt Joyce from attending, etc.), but is not in the position of having to do so, or of making decisions that are really about Joyce's personal situation.

The essential steps in dealing with performance deviations are:

1. Identify the problem using observed behavior and objective standards.

2. Embrace the performer in also acknowledging the problem and identifying the likely cause.

3. Enable the performer to develop a solution, while offering your support if the performer cannot do this or needs further help.

Problems that are acknowledged by the performer become objective issues, rather than matters of "blame." Causes that are identified by the performer become changes to implement rather than personal failings. And solutions created by the performer become "owned" and are self-perpetuating rather than unfair management edicts from people who "don't understand me."

Professional psychologists have enough trouble identifying causes of behavior. Don't become an amateur therapist. Don't jump to conclusions about motive, intent, and meaning. And avoid the psychobabble about personality types and profiles if the intent is to simply stereotype and explain away behavior, rather than really trying to understand it. ("What do you expect from an INTJ, anyway?" "He's a 'driver' so he's not going to listen to you." "She's a 'low D' so

Bright Idea
Establish clear standards (e.g., customer response time, work hours, financial responsibilities, travel) that are jointly created by employees. This makes deviations easier to identify, easier to agree upon, and less likely to be viewed as arbitrary management conclusions.

don't expect any bright ideas coming from her area.") These stereotyping tendencies are exacerbated by many of the "profiling" tools in the market, some of which are valid only when used by a trained professional, and many of which have never been validated at all and are simply dangerous to use.

Case Study:

I once had a field manager working for me by the name of Gary. Gary was a nice, likeable guy who virtually never met his plan and failed to meet most of the deadlines that his peers consistently met. Gary always had a common excuse: "No, we didn't hit our plan, but I never really agreed with that plan in the first place." "I don't have the client audits done, but I've always felt that it's not a worthwhile use of our time." "I haven't visited all of my people's key accounts, but I've meant to tell you that I think it isn't needed here." One of my biggest regrets while managing field people was in not firing Gary because he caused so much disruption and provided a poor example for his people. Later on, someone with a clearer focus on standards and less tolerance for excuses did fire him.

Coaching and counseling as systematic processes

All outstanding managers engage in coaching on a daily basis and counseling on an "as needed" basis. We can define the two terms as follows:

Coaching: Coaching is both proactive and reactive support and mentoring provided to employees to improve their performance and to help them when having difficulties. It is mainly focused on maintaining existing, strong performance and improving it still further.

Counseling: Counseling is the reactive, structured approach implemented when an employee is performing below expectations, due to either a skill deficiency or an attitude deficiency. It is mainly focused on restoring performance to a minimally acceptable level or, failing that, removing the employee from that job.

Managers need to be adept at both skills, but also understand that they are discrete and separate endeavors.

All employees should be coached on an ongoing basis. It's a form of mentoring or advising that enables ongoing dialogue between the manager and the subordinate so that feedback on performance doesn't occur only when there is a problem. Moreover, it allows for excellent work to be recognized, supported, exploited, and conveyed to others.

Consequently, power managers spend 10 times more of their efforts and energy on coaching than on counseling. Poor managers confuse the two, don't understand the difference, and usually respond only to problems, meaning that the preponderance of their time is spent on correcting weaknesses rather than supporting strengths.

The coaching process

The strategy for effective coaching should include the following steps:

■ Once a year, the manager creates a developmental plan with each employee that includes areas for improvement. Note that these are not remedial areas that must be improved "or else," but areas that represent continued growth and gratification for the employee, and meaningful additional contributions to the organization.

Bright Idea
Individuals and organizations grow most dramatically and most rapidly by building on strength, not by correcting weakness. Active, frequent coaching enables managers to constantly reinforce strengths. Some form of coaching should be a part of the manager's daily schedule and of the employee's overall developmental program.

- The manager and employee agree on the specific actions required of both of them to meet the goals.

- The manager and employee meet formally once a quarter to review progress and modify the plan as needed.

- The manager builds in to his or her weekly calendar and priorities time for each person in the coaching relationship. That time may be ten minutes to review a given project, or an hour spent on a new technique being implemented. These should not be formal meetings, and they should always be one-on-one.

- The manager also makes it a practice to spontaneously spend a few minutes with employees as conditions merit, for example, praising someone on a nice job, inquiring if help is needed with a difficult customer, or offering a perspective for an unprecedented request.

The most important attributes of a coaching relationship are:

- The dialogue is constant and ongoing, not oriented around a periodic review.

- The feedback is timely, offered at the point where an issue, performance, or problem arises.

- The manager advises but the employee performs. In other words, the manager may provide advice on dealing with a disruptive colleague, but the employee resolves the situation personally.

- Coaching is overwhelmingly positively oriented or neutral. However, the manager does provide negative feedback when there is clear evidence that the employee's judgment was wrong, actions were inappropriate, or performance was below standards.

- The manager is approachable, and the employee feels comfortable initiating conversations and requesting feedback. (A good way to test this is to offer no comment for a week to the employee. If the employee does not initiate a coaching conversation and seems unlikely to do so, then the relationship is too reliant on the manager as the power figure.)
- Employees become coaches themselves. One of the most significant signs of success in coaching is that employees begin coaching others, both subordinates and peers. An organization of coaches is an honest, productive, and synergistic environment.

There is seldom a developmental track for managers on how to coach, yet it is one of the most important daily activities of the power manager.

The process of counseling

Counseling is a progressive sequence of interaction with the employee that results in either restored, acceptable performance, or the performer leaving the job (either to take another position where he or she can perform, or to leave the organization altogether). Counseling is essential to improving organizational performance, yet few managers ever engage in it systematically, and most don't effectively engage in it at all.

Here are the steps in the systematic counseling process:

1. Determine if the poor performance is caused by a lack of skills or a poor attitude (skill deficiency or attitude deficiency).

Moneysaver
Effective and reciprocal coaching at peer level can substantially reduce training costs, since employees will be sharing their own best practices in trusting and mutually rewarding relationships. Time-off-the-job classroom skills building are neither as timely nor as effective.

2. Focus on the behavior and the evidence.

3. Obtain agreement on the standard and the actual performance.

4. Discuss impact of the performance on others or the organization.

5. Discuss manager's available alternatives and the consequences for the employee.

6. Establish action plan for improvement with dates and accountability.

7. Review and monitor progress.

8. Make decision.

Timesaver
Always quickly check to see if there is an obstacle to desired performance inhibiting even skilled and motivated workers. *Example:* If doing the job correctly requires onerous travel, overtime, or risk taking, the performer may opt simply to do the job poorly (e.g., quality assurance) to avoid the "pain."

While this may seem like quite a few steps to improve performance, the sequence actually represents a much faster resolution route than simply attempting to deal with the issue in a casual manner. And, in an age of unprecedented litigiousness, the process lends itself to compliance with legal requirements, as well.

Determine if poor performance is caused by lack of skills or lack of attitude. This step is important because the resultant corrective actions will be quite different. Robert Mager, a member of the Training & Development Hall of Fame, has asked a fascinating question over the years: "Could he do it if his life depended on it?" If the answer to that question is "no," the employee can't perform the job no matter how desperate the situation, then there is a skill problem. However, if the employee could perform the job under duress, but prefers not to otherwise, then there is an attitude problem. The salesperson who chooses not to make calls and prefers to stay in the office because he or she thinks the boss is unfair has an attitude problem. The salesperson who doesn't go on calls because he or she doesn't know how to gain agreement to a meeting over the phone has a skills problem.

Focus on behavior and evidence. Prepare yourself, as discussed in the preceding sections of this chapter, with observable evidence and objective examples of behavior.

Acceptable:

"You sat there while the phone rang and didn't answer it."

"Your client reports are 3 weeks overdue."

"Three customers have complained about your language."

Unacceptable:

"You don't like to talk to people on the phone."

"You're sloppy with documentation."

"You don't take the customers very seriously."

Obtain agreement on the standard and the actual performance. Before you can counsel anyone, there must be agreement about the extent of the deviation. That means that both the standard and the actual performance must be acknowledged by the performer.

Example: Are you aware that our standards are that every employee is responsible for answering the phones, and that no phone should be allowed to ring more than three times? And am I correct that you continued to work while the phone at your desk rang 10 times until it stopped?

Example: Do you acknowledge that client reports are to be turned in within 48 hours of a visit, and that you have not submitted these four client visits for 3 weeks?

Example: I want to show you these customer complaints and play the tapes from those calls. Do you acknowledge that you are the one on the phone,

Watch Out!
When counseling, have all of your options and evidence carefully thought through, and use notes as needed. Difficult employees will make all kinds of claims and promises. Document everything, don't be reluctant to use a "script," and make sure that each step in the counseling sequence is completed before proceeding.

and that you used obscene language, which is clearly against our policy?

Discuss impact of the performance on others and/or the organization. Emphasize to the employee that the negative effects of his or her poor performance are affecting others in the workplace and can't be tolerated.

Make it clear that the performance has an impact that can't be allowed to continue. Many employees will attempt to take the position that "it's just something I'm doing that doesn't concern anyone else." (If that statement is true—for example, that the employee uses the stairs instead of the elevator to go down 20 floors—then you don't have a counseling issue.) It's incumbent on the manager to demonstrate why the organization cannot allow the performance to continue.

Example: The company loses customers when the phones are not picked up within three rings. We've learned this from surveys within the industry. Every time we ignore a phone call we are abandoning a current customer or failing to obtain a new one.

Example: The client reports are used by the service people and the other sales areas to determine how best to coordinate our approaches, so that the client is dealing with "one face," and doesn't believe that we have a disjointed approach. In addition, rapid dissemination of the report on the computer ensures that we're neither duplicating nor contradicting our actions across division lines. Do you see the importance of that?

Example: Obscene language, no matter how difficult or unreasonable the customer may be, is against company policy, against our values, creates a hostile workplace under legal definitions, and is the poorest way of trying to resolve the customer's unhappiness. It will not be tolerated. Is that clear?

- Discuss manager's alternatives available and the consequences for the employee, and
- Establish action plan for improvement with dates and accountability.

Demonstrate to the performer that the manager has limited options, and make it clear what the range is, since the employee's reaction to the counseling sequence will determine which option is taken. The manager can ask the employee, "What options do you think are available to me?" That question may gain more ownership of the solution by the employee. If the employee claims not to know, then make the alternatives apparent. Establish what will happen from this point.

Example: If you're uncomfortable answering the phone, we can provide some training to help you with the typical inquiries. If you don't want to answer the phone, we can search for another job that doesn't require it, but it will be a lower-paying job. If you choose not to undergo the training and respond to the phone as required, we will have to terminate you.

Example: I have to have all outstanding call reports on my desk by tomorrow morning, and every future one input to the computer within the required 48 hours. Is there anything preventing you from doing that, anything I can provide to help you? If so, I'll attend to it. If not, I'll expect compliance beginning tomorrow morning. If you fail to do that, or fall behind again in the future, you will be removed from the sales job and either offered a lower-paying job not requiring this performance, or you will be terminated. Do you understand the options and my expectations? Are you willing to accept these terms?

Example: You have a spotless record, but you are immediately placed on probation. I want you to apologize in writing to each of these customers and take our course in customer responsiveness again when it's offered next week. A supervisor will monitor your calls without notice. If you use such language again, you will be summarily dismissed. If there are no further problems, you will be removed from probation in 6 months. Are you willing to accept this arrangement? If not, you will be given the opportunity to resign immediately.

■ Review and monitor progress, and

■ Make a decision.

Based on the employee's subsequent observed behavior and the evidence you develop, make a decision as to whether additional counseling is needed, the employee can depart from the counseling process and return to normal status, or the employee must be moved to another position or terminated.

In most organizations, the counseling sequence is not invoked with rigor, or it takes much too much time. If a performance problem is caused by a skill deficiency, counseling enables the manager to provide rapid skills development and testing as to whether the employee has the competency to perform the job. If the problem is caused by an attitude deficiency, the manager is able to halt the adverse behavior rapidly by confronting it, clarifying how it must be changed, and creating short-term dates for improvement, thereby minimizing the adverse affects.

Managers are often reluctant to confront poor performance because they have no system for doing so, are fearful of reaction, and are uncertain about legal requirements. Consequently, they spend even less time on supporting strong performers because they "spin their wheels" worrying about poor performance.

Power managers constantly coach strong performance and immediately confront poor performance.

Effective performance evaluation

I am probably called in as a consultant to "fix," change, and otherwise reinvent performance evaluation processes as much as I am for any other assignment. Organizational America's approaches to performance evaluation are akin to owning a race horse, taking it out to the track, and never timing its results. We seem to feel that the mere juxtaposition of the horse, track, and crowd are sufficient.

Performance evaluation is a critical undertaking for the following reasons:

- It demands that standards be created to identify business goals and the performer's role in meeting those goals.
- The performer has an opportunity to contribute to the expectations and contributions that determine his or her own standards for performance.
- The manager and subordinate can objectively discuss progress at any time, informally or formally, and make any appropriate "mid-course" corrections.
- The performer has the ability to be self-directive, and not depend on the manager for daily direction and feedback.

Unofficially...
Is your superior providing coaching, or only critiquing you when something goes wrong? Find someone who can serve as a mentor or advisor, and develop that relationship. Our surveys show that the largest factor in promotions is the support of a strong coach.

- In aggregation, all individual goals can be aligned with and made supportive of the corporate goals.

- The organization has the ability to assess performance and make intelligent selection decisions about promotions, committees, transfers, skills building, and termination.

- All developmental activity can be focused on organizational needs and individual performance needs.

- Performers can be rewarded based on their objective contribution to business goals.

Note that reward comes last. Too often performance evaluation centers around a once-a-year confrontation that is entirely focused on how much money the employee will be able to extract from the organization. This procedure—and the attendant mentality—places the manager in a "no win" position. (In fact, how many times have you or a colleague experienced the squeezed feeling of executives telling you that your merit increase monies are limited, while employees are justifiably telling you that they've met the maximum bonus standards under the current system?)

The steps in establishing a performance evaluation process should look like this:

1. Clarify the results expectations of the job.

These should always be in outputs, not inputs.

Example: The minimum goal for this sales position is $250,000 in business from new customers received during this 12-month period.

Example: The receptionist answers the phone graciously before the fourth ring and routes calls immediately to their proper destination.

Watch Out!
The psychological literature is overwhelming in showing that evaluations attached to awards create adversarial dynamics, change the emphasis from the contribution of the work to the nature of the reward, and demean the process as one that is merely a form of merit increase barometer.

2. Gain agreement with the performer. The goals should be seen as realistic and attainable, and not a fiat handed down from above.

   Example: Does a new division with a new buyer from an existing client count as new business? Shouldn't it, because it's a different location with a different buying point?

   Example: If three lines are ringing at once, I'll either need a backup or the ability to place people on "hold" for a short time, especially between 9:00 and 10:00 in the morning.

3. Agree to the goals in writing. This is to establish the baseline in case individuals or conditions change, and to prevent "memory loss" if actual performance isn't what it should be.

4. Agree on an intelligent measuring scale. Ideally, this should be organization-wide. The typical scales are inappropriate because they imply superior performance is the norm (e.g., "exceeds expectations" is everyone's expectation). A more realistic scale would be:

   ▪ Below expectations: Employee requires development in order to perform the job at acceptable levels. If such development is not successful, employee will be taken out of this position.

   Example: Sales level is not at a rate of $250,000 in new business for the year, and needs significant increase if that goal is to be reached.

   Example: Calls are often not answered until the sixth ring, several callers a day hang up and call back to complain, and departments indicate they are receiving incorrectly routed calls.

■ Meets expectations: Employee is performing as planned and expected.

Example: Sales rate is on target for $250,000 performance by year-end.

Example: Incoming calls are processed with courtesy, speed, and accuracy as agreed upon. Complaints and errors are less than 3 percent.

■ Exceeds expectations: Employee is performing above and beyond plans, and results will exceed original goals.

Example: Sales are already at $225,000 after three quarters, and ultimate results would appear to be in the $300,000 to $325,000 range, given normal fourth quarter volume.

Example: Employee has been able to serve as backup to departmental secretaries and handle overflow word-processing needs while maintaining phone duties without decline in quality. Departments report that many callers comment on rapid response and courtesy at reception.

(Note that the examples are all "mid-course," showing how the system works during ongoing feedback.)

5. Provide feedback at least monthly (or more often) so that there are no surprises and deficiencies can be quickly addressed. This also takes the focus of evaluation off of annual monetary issues and places it on daily performance issues.

6. Document your comments and findings so that there is a record.

At an annual review, merit increase, or potential promotion point, there should be absolutely no surprises about the actual performance or expectations that were or weren't met.

The benefit of this type of flexible yet focused performance evaluation is that education, development, and training can be tightly tied to business requirements, and not become ends in themselves in which a myriad of courses has nothing to do with actual job performance. The sequence might look like this:

Unofficially...
If you're not getting feedback from your boss, seek it. If you receive feedback that you are either above or below expectations, get it in writing or put it in writing yourself. You can then demonstrate how you corrected a problem or document how you performed in an outstanding manner.

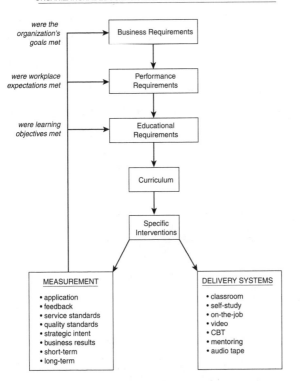

ORGANIZATIONAL EDUCATION TIED TO STRATEGIC BUSINESS GOALS

In the figure, business requirements are the driver. If the organization's goals weren't met, then nothing else really matters (which is why hundreds of "exceeds expectations" ratings simply don't make sense if the organization didn't "exceed expectations").

Individual performance requirements, collectively, determine whether the business goals will be met. Individual educational and developmental needs will support those performance requirements, if they are focused and targeted. Only then can a curriculum of learning, let alone specific interventions, be formulated.

The trouble is that in most cases organizations actually start with arbitrary programs and courses (sales training, first line supervision, time management, etc.) that may or may not actually have anything to do with the individual performance required to attain the business goals. It's incumbent upon managers to look upward and translate downward, otherwise, development and results will be following two independent tracks. By definition, no developmental program can possibly be successful if organizational business goals are not met.

Just the facts

- There is no need to be a "pop" psychologist, and managers should stay away from labeling and quick analyses or personality.
- Coaching needs to be done regularly and informally with all employees.
- Counseling should occur the moment performance deviations become apparent, no matter how awkward or unpleasant.

- The performer should be an integral part of goal setting, ongoing evaluation, and, if needed, improvement actions.
- Performance evaluation is a central process for merging development with business goals.

GET THE SCOOP ON...
The basic difference between skills and behaviors
▪ The fundamental behaviors that drive performance ▪ Why past performance is not a reliable
predictor of future performance ▪ Why promotions are usually based on the wrong factors

Evaluating Behavior

Chapter 5

There is a surfeit of profiling and personality testing tools on the market designed to analyze everything from honesty to tendencies toward violence. Some are quite accurate in that their underlying psychometrics are valid, they have been reviewed in refereed journals, and they are constantly being updated and improved. Others are little more than horoscopes, which stereotype people based on superficial characteristics, and are used more commonly to explain away behaviors than to try to understand them. How much validity does a manager really believe is inherent is a "personality test" that costs $12 a person and provides the vendor with a third of that as commission?

Show me an organization that talks about "high Ds," or "drivers and expressives," or "stage 3 personalities," and I'll show you the nearest door you should run through.

Behaviors, after all, are the result of a complex interaction of several strong variables:

Watch Out!
Do not rely heavily on validated personality tests. Because of the variety of factors influencing behavior, you can understand what is likely to happen in certain situations, but not what will happen. Making hiring, promotional, disciplinary, and other decisions based solely on testing is inaccurate, inappropriate, unethical, and illegal.

1. First, there is the heredity we accept from our forebears. Just as genes play a major role in determining longevity, they also are strong determinants of our propensity to act in certain ways. This is the biochemistry coursing through our bodies every day. It is now believed, for example, that sexual orientation is primarily biological.

2. Second, there is the early nurturing, modeling, and imprinting we receive from our environment. The assertiveness or passivity that we develop is directly related to our parents or other significant family members, our early school experiences, and any traumatic life experiences.

3. Third, there is the environment. We are often "one person" at home, and "another person" at work. ("Be careful, you're not at work now, you know," has been heard in more than one household.) Many people have vastly different sets of behaviors at work, at home, at civic organizations, at social functions, and in other areas of their lives. This explains why two people who each know a third but in differing circumstances, can say, "How can you think he's unapproachable? That's simply not the man I know. He couldn't be more charming." They are probably both right.

4. Fourth and finally, there is the role of the other performer. Even a highly assertive individual will "back off" if he or she meets someone even more assertive. The other performer or performers will always reinforce, modify, or change the behavior of others.

Yet behaviors are important to consider when assigning jobs, communicating, assembling teams, and making selection decisions. And they are different from what we typically regard as "skills."

The difference between skills and behaviors

"Skills" are learned competencies, which can generally be successfully attained regardless of one's behavioral set. In other words, basic math, keyboard proficiency, the ability to learn and explain sales features and benefits, negotiating techniques, and classroom instruction are all skills that can be learned through systematic acquisition of information and practice. Yet we all know that basic teaching skills by themselves don't produce great instructors any more than mastery of sales features and benefits creates successful salespeople. (Yet there are superb teachers who don't have traditional teaching skills, and successful salespeople who "break the traditional rules.")

"Behaviors" are those attributes of our personality and performance which provide for success (or lack of success) in interacting with others. Two salespeople may equally have the skills to explain product features and listen to the prospective customer's needs, but the one with the assertiveness to candidly ask for the business at the right time will tend to be much more successful than the one who is more comfortable waiting for the prospective customer to ask to buy something. Behaviors and skill augment each other, but most organizations spend an inordinate amount of time on skills-building and assign the behaviors to the test instruments, rather than actively using behavioral traits as key indicators of success and input to decisions.

If you can do it, it ain't braggin'.
—Dizzy Dean, Hall of Fame baseball pitcher

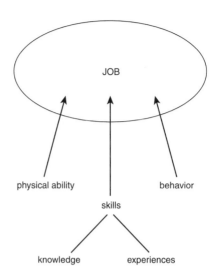

In the graphic, you can see that all jobs have a physical component (reporters must be able to use a keyboard, pilots must use a control wheel), a skills component based on knowledge and experience (reporters must know grammar and have served as an assistant in the newsroom, pilots must know navigation and serve as copilots), and a behavioral component (good reporters are assertive and persuasive in hunting for great stories, pilots must remain calm in emergencies and instill confidence in others). Most of the time we are paying insufficient attention to the behavioral element.

Why we promote the wrong people

Because behaviors are so hard to understand and are relatively unpredictable—at least with any certainty—we tend to rely on past behavior as our crutch. If someone has been successful in the past, and their existing set of behaviors helped them to perform well, we should have a high degree of probability that such behaviors and success will carry forward to the future.

Except, it ain't necessarily so.

When John Scully was cited as a prescient genius and absolute hero at Pepsi-Cola, he took on the job of running the post–Stephen Jobs Apple Computer Company. In fact, he actually helped to oust his one-time advocate, Jobs, once Scully was firmly entrenched as CEO. What ensued was unmitigated disaster, and the beginning of a sequence of inept leadership and failing CEOs at Apple that was only reversed with the return of Stephen Jobs himself.

Did John Scully's skills and behaviors change when he went to Apple? Did his world view or philosophy? Did he undergo some traumatic event or transformation? What exactly happened that could possibly explain this great leader's decline over the course of a year? The answer is blazingly—and frighteningly—simple.

The behaviors that stood John Scully in good stead at staid and low-tech Pepsi were not the behaviors required for success in innovative, combative, and high-tech Apple. Scully couldn't make the change. He was successful at being who he was, but who he was could not be successful outside of Pepsi (or, at least, at Apple). Scully is now a relatively minor player leading a small company. Yet, he is not the exception.

Every day—in fact, as you are reading this— managers are promoting their best salesperson to be sales manager, their best underwriter to be underwriting manager, and their best photographer to be photo editor, all on the basis of past performance. This is probably the worst criterion that can be applied in current-day organizational America. We do it because:

Unofficially...
Among executive recruiters, consultants, and industrial psychologists, the single cause that surfaces most often for executive failure is an inability to adjust behavior and demeanor to the environment. It is seldom, if ever, about skills, knowledge, experience, or physical abilities. It's all about inappropriate behaviors.

- It's always been done that way.

- It's simple and appears to be creating a meritocracy.

- It should be noncontroversial and legally safe.

- It's a vestige of the old apprenticeship systems.

- It's the only safe criterion we believe we have to apply.

- It's fast and painless.

- We don't know how else to do it.

Bright Idea
Understanding the role of behavior in performance is important for one's own career, as well. I've seen countless managers and executives leading miserable lives because they jumped at job assignments and promotions, believing that such moves were essential for their careers. What they found instead were positions that were antithetical to their behavioral predispositions, making them uncomfortable at best and highly stressed at worst.

Very few star ballplayers become star managers or coaches and, conversely, very few of the great coaches and managers were star ballplayers. That's because the behavioral set required to be a star athlete is different from the one required to coach star athletes. Some people may possess both or be capable of acquiring both. Most are not. The same applies in management. When you promote a star salesperson to a sales manager's job, you run the risk of losing a great salesperson and creating a lousy sales manager (who will adversely affect other star salespeople). This is a lose/lose/lose proposition.

Managers shouldn't become pop psychologists. But they should understand the role of behavior in performance, and the particular behaviors that are required for any given position.

Case Study:

An entry level CPA, aside from the financial skills and knowledge required for the job, will find the position requires certain behaviors including attention to detail, patience with repetition, and low assertiveness. If the CPA does well—and practices those behaviors naturally and diligently—a promotion may well ensue to finance manager. In this position, however, the detail orientation will lessen, patience won't be as much of a virtue, and assertiveness will have to improve, especially when handling performance problems or difficulties with other divisions.

If this CPA finance manager does well, however, he or she can expect to be promoted to vice president of finance and, perhaps eventually, chief financial officer. Those positions are "big picture" jobs with details left to subordinates, the need to tackle highly diverse issues such as mergers and acquisitions always a possibility, requiring substantial assertiveness, with executive committee battles and takeover attempts normal occurrences.

How many entry level CPAs can muster that range of behaviors comfortably over the course of a career? How many can even make the first leap to management comfortably? Not many.

We tend to promote the wrong people because we look at the wrong factors. We examine past performance, skills, knowledge, and experiences (if we even do that comprehensive a job), but *we don't look at probability of success in the future job.* Yet, that's really the only important issue.

Probability of success in a future job, whether a new hire, a transfer, a promotion, or a team or task force assignment, is really dependent on:

1. What behaviors are required by the intended job, and how well does the applicant fulfill them?
2. To what extent can the applicant modify behaviors successfully to adjust to the new position, since no fit will ever be perfect?

These questions presuppose that the manager can identify the behaviors necessary for successful completion of a job or assignment, and can find evidence of their presence or lack of in the applicant,

Watch Out!
Some people can "talk a great game." In Texas, this is known as "big hat, no cattle." Most interviewing is based on verbal communication skills and insufficiently on behavioral attributes. Communications skills are important assets, but don't allow them to camouflage actual behaviors. Talking is one thing, performing is another.

as well as information about the applicant's ability to adapt. These issues are not as difficult as they sound, but they do require more work than merely examining past performance.

It's helpful to use just a few indicators of behavior to help understand what's required, what's present, and the extent of the adaptations necessary. After all, we measure job standards and performance. Why shouldn't we measure behavioral standards and performance?

The four basic behavioral measures

There are four basic behavioral measures that are relatively easy to identify in terms of the job requirements and the individual's "comfort zone." There is nothing magical or special about the titles we'll use, but we have to begin with some descriptive measures. Note that these are tendencies, not absolutes, and *that there are no value judgments implied*. That is, high assertiveness is not "better" than low assertiveness. All of these behaviors are healthy and can be successfully employed no matter to what degree they are possessed.

Assertiveness

This is the degree to which an individual is forceful, outspoken, and dynamic. A highly assertive person will pound a table, vocalize, readily demonstrate feelings and opinions about an issue, and will unhesitatingly take public stands to meet goals. A less assertive person will tend to listen more than speak, will be more of a follower than a leader, and will be much more private in either support of or opposition to any given issue. A highly assertive employee will tell you his or her sentiments without being asked, while a less assertive employee will tend to wait to be asked for his or her opinion.

Persuasiveness

This is the degree of social initiating that a person is comfortable undertaking. A highly persuasive individual will tend to openly try to convince others and influence their thinking (not manipulatively, but candidly). This person constantly "reaches out," and will make even strangers feel comfortable. He or she is very approachable. A less persuasive individual is not apt to initiate attempts to influence or to launch appeals to change views. He or she is not comfortable reaching out, and may be seen as "laid back" or detached. A highly persuasive employee will serve as a catalyst for behavior change with colleagues. A less persuasive employee might change his or her behavior without attempting to influence peers.

Tolerance for repetition

This is the degree to which one is comfortable with sameness and identical conditions over time. A high tolerance for repetition is represented by high patience levels, a high boredom threshold, and gratification in getting the same job done in the same way repeatedly. A low tolerance for repetition is represented by rapid boredom (the person who feels "trapped" in regularly scheduled meetings), demand for change and variety, and gratification in the unexpected and breaks from the routine. An employee with a high tolerance for repetition will tend to perform steadily and well as long as there are no surprises. An employee with a low tolerance for repetition will respond well to change and even attempt to create new ways to get things done.

Attention to detail

This is the degree to which an individual focuses on every small aspect of the job with equal attention. A

Moneysaver
Try to match up individual comfort zones with actual job demands as much as possible. In other words, don't hire a nonassertive, nonpersuasive individual to be a sales rep, and don't promote an impatient, low-attention-to-detail person to be on the customer service phones.

high attention to detail means that all the "t's" must be crossed and the "i's" dotted. Such individuals prefer 100 percent completion and quality, and will not allow work to proceed until everything is correct. Low attention to detail means that the bigger picture (forest, not trees) takes precedence over the details, and if 85 percent is sufficient to move on, then let's not wait for the diminishing returns of the final 15 percent. The high-detail employee is the tactician and specialist. The low-detail employee is the big-picture thinker and strategist.

If we view the four vectors of behavior in a graphic manner, we must bear in mind that any behaviors on the continuum are legitimate, high end or low. But if one is "off the chart" to the right of the assertiveness continuum, it means that person is belligerent and bellicose; off the chart to the left would be alienated, depressed, or comatose. So there is a broad acceptable range from low to high, but there are extremes that represent aberrant behavior.

Assertiveness

Persuasiveness

Tolerance for Repetition

Attention to Detail

Ethical Standards

Now, let's select the ideal behavioral set for a sales position, in which the salesperson makes "cold calls," as in insurance sales or telemarketing. We would want someone with high assertiveness (won't

take "no" for an answer too readily), high persuasiveness (influential and socially interactive),
moderate patience (allows the prospect to talk but
is eager to move things along), and relatively low
attention to detail (each call is different and exceptions must be made). (If you don't believe "low
detail," just try to get a salesperson to turn in timely
call reports or expense reports!)

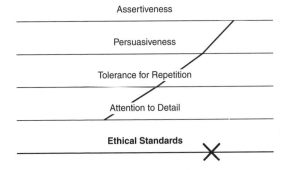

If we know that this is the profile of behaviors for
successful salespeople in our firm or our industry,
then it's simply crazy to place people in those roles
whose behaviors *are markedly different from those normally required.* While each of us can make adjustments, there are limits to both the degree of
adjustment and the amount of time the adjustment
can be maintained.

Think of our ability to change behaviors as being
reliant on our "battery," which is our biological
energy level. We only have a finite amount of energy
to invest in our lives and our jobs. The more adjustments we have to make from our "comfort zones,"
the greater the demand on the battery. The more we
remain in our comfort zones, the more the battery
can sustain us without being depleted.

Unofficially...
Think of the peo-
ple about whom
we're told, "If
you need a deci-
sion, go early in
the day and
never after
lunch." This is
often the sign of
someone whose
battery is burned
out by midday,
affecting quality
and focus. Try to
adjust your
needs to the
comfort zones of
others.

For example, a relatively nonassertive person can raise his or her assertiveness on the continuum in order to run a tough, interactive meeting for an hour a week. But can someone with a very low assertiveness comfort zone raise it to the high end for fifty hours a week as a field sales manager? Not without a toll on stress and health. Similarly, a highly assertive, low patience individual might be able to sit still for a boring, scheduled meeting for an hour a week, but could never do so for several hours every day without inducing high stress (in the individual and/or the surrounding people). It's difficult to change behavior in large degrees, in either direction, on any of the four vectors. When one is forced to make several changes simultaneously, there is tremendous demand on the battery, and the longer the major changes must be sustained, the more the chance for burnout.

When people are forced out of their comfort zones to large degrees, on more than one vector, and for lengthy periods, stress builds. Stress is either internalized, causing illness, or externalized, causing interpersonal strife. This is not a training issue nor, usually, a skills-building issue. It is almost always a behavioral issue, demanding alteration in the work to suit behaviors (provide a low-detail person with an assistant or technological help), modification of behaviors (demonstrating that total quality means 100 percent, not 90 percent, of the job completed), or a change of position (people with low patience levels are never appropriate for customer complaint situations).

Just to provide another view, here is the typical profile for an insurance underwriter:

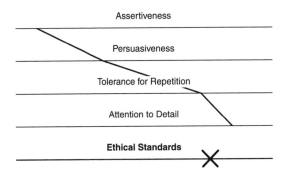

No surprises there, right? The job requires low assertiveness, low persuasiveness, but a high tolerance for repetition and a very high attention to detail. These are positions that don't deal with the public but must ensure absolute compliance to risk standards and actuarial tables.

One final factor, or vector, to consider, is "maturity" or "ethical standards." This dimension strongly influences how the behavioral combinations of the other four will be applied.

For example, a highly assertive person who also has high ethical standards will tend to be forceful, goal oriented, and use power constructively. But that same person with low ethical standards will tend to be seen as dictatorial, insensitive, and self-centered. The highly persuasive person with high ethical standards will be seen as approachable, sincere, helpful, and charismatic. That behavioral set with low ethical standards will produce feelings of manipulation, politics, untrustworthiness, and "lip service."

The degree to which our standards, values, and maturity are manifest impact greatly the effectiveness of our behaviors with others.

In this case, "high" and "low" do have significant value connotations. Vector five is the determinant of

Watch Out!
People in stressful situations either make themselves ill or make others around them ill. My wife tells me that I'm a carrier.

the legitimacy of the first four in terms of impact on others.

The case for behavioral interviewing

How does a manager test for these behaviors? If we're not to be pop psychologists, how can we tell whether an individual has the correct behaviors for the job? There are three key things to do:

Unofficially...
An art form has arisen around "inverting interviews," which means interviewing the interviewer to control the situation and avoid tough questions. If this occurs, tell the interviewee, "We'll get to me later. Right now, I need to ask you some questions and hear from you."

- Make sure the behaviors for the job itself are determined. One good way to do this is to approach it "backwards." Find those people who have been most successful in the job in the past, and determine what their behavioral patterns tend to be. When you have a pattern emerging, you probably have a sound description of the job's needs. Note that this won't be effective for a new position, which hasn't been performed before. In that case, you'll need to make some assumptions, working backwards from the results desired.

- There are some valid tests that can be used judiciously, and only in conjunction with other determinants. Ask your human resource experts for help (if, indeed, they have expertise in this area—not all do). Even better: Inquire of the American Psychological Association or the American Psychological Society what validated testing they recommend for these purposes, and how best to administer it.

- Learn to use behavioral interviewing skills to determine "comfort zones."

Point three is something relatively easy to do that you can begin tomorrow. It simply means that in interview, selection, and similar settings, you use questions designed to reveal behavioral tendencies and not intellectual or rote responses.

Here are some examples of poor interviewing questions in terms of seeking behaviors, because they deal with what someone thinks or allow the individual to tell you what the "right answer" is:

- What do you think you can contribute to this job?
- What are your greatest strengths and weaknesses?
- How would you describe your work ethic?
- What do you think is key to customer satisfaction?
- Where would you like to be in 2 years?

Here are some examples of good, behavioral, interviewing questions that tend to elicit how someone would actually act:

- If you had evidence that your boss was stealing from the company, what would you do?
- Under what circumstances would you lie?
- When and why have you been unsuccessful?
- If an excellent customer asked you to do something—on the threat of going to the competition—clearly forbidden by our policies, what would you do?
- If someone offered you in an interview the confidential business strategy of our closest competitor, what would be your response?

All of these questions are taken from actual interviewing workshops designed for clients. The idea is not to determine perfect or "right answers," but to find out if someone has high ethical standards ("I'd approach my boss, verify what I had found, and either demand that he turn himself in to his superiors or I would myself") or tends to be political and situational ("It would depend on the amount and if

Bright Idea
Don't ask what
they think, ask
what they would
do, which is a
behavioral
response. If the
answer is too
pat, then ask
how they would
handle the con-
sequences: "If
you went to your
boss's superior
and she believed
your boss, you
would have
ended your
career. Wouldn't
that change
things?"

I thought any real harm was being done"). Most interviews are nearly worthless because they don't elicit any behavioral information at all.

On the job, you're able to judge behaviors and comfort zones over time by watching the patterns and gaining evidence through observation. With new people, that isn't possible. There are work-shops, books, and tapes that can be used to help with behavioral interviewing. But it's not rocket sci-ence and can be mastered quickly by the manager who is sensitive to the key roles that behaviors play in job performance.

Assessing and adjusting your own behavior

You can greatly enhance your own productivity by monitoring your behavior, comfort, and discomfort and making appropriate adjustments. This is impor-tant because we all have a limited energy level (the "battery") and we can easily wear it down by engag-ing in behaviors that are high energy drains while at the same time poor productivity enhancers. (One quick example is excess stress, which gobbles up energy output but doesn't provide an appropriate productivity gain on the huge investment.)

Test yourself to see if you are ever experiencing any of the following conditions:

- High nervous energy (especially at meetings) not being channeled, but instead dissipated through physical movement (pacing, knee jerk-ing, exasperated body language).

- Extreme drowsiness caused by ennui and a failure of the immediate issues to sufficiently stimulate you; occasional falling asleep on the job even after a good night's rest.

- Peaks and valleys during the day, during which you sometimes seem capable of tackling any challenge and you sometimes feel that just one more demand will be too much to handle.

- Missing key details that others catch or that undermine a project, no matter how meticulous you thought you were.

- Excessive focus on small matters at the expense of missing the larger picture (you were so focused on setting priority on sales reports that you never suspected the client was going to the competition).

- Overreaction or rude behavior toward otherwise innocuous and harmless questions or feedback.

- Unwillingness to respond to feedback, critique, and even attack, no matter how incorrect or inappropriate it may be.

If these and similar conditions affect you with any frequency at all, you are probably experiencing events which are not in your normal comfort zone and for which you are not making proper adjustments.

For example, if you find yourself "trapped" at meetings and feel desperately bored or frustrated, you can make it clear that your schedule is tight and you have to leave the meeting at a certain time; or you can take some inconspicuous work to do while you're participating; or you can take a break every thirty minutes and visit the rest room or check your voice mail.

Another example: You're having trouble dealing with an individual who is continually demanding and abrasive. You're being worn down trying to be polite and trying to avoid confrontational meetings with him or her. (Interpersonal conflict is among one of the very worst drains on energy.) In this case, you need to raise your assertiveness temporarily, explain the reasons why neither of you is being well served by the current relationship, and mutually explore ways to change it. Merely by taking the initiative in these discussions, you will gain tremendous leverage and alleviate the feelings of powerlessness and frustration that the situation has been causing.

Finally, one of the most important "battery rechargers" is time away from the source of the drain. Ironically, the best and most productive way to deal with heavy job demands, tough deadlines, and huge new projects, is to build-in time off. Most managers make the mistake of becoming martyrs to the cause, working long hours (in an attempt to set the example), taking work home, and sacrificing their personal lives and interests for the sake of temporary work excesses, which somehow always turn out to be more than "temporary." The longer that managers work in oppressive, unrelieved stressful conditions, *the less effective they become, requiring still more effort and longer hours.*

The more managers can responsibly and maturely take time off from a hectic environment, recharge their batteries, and regain a sense of control over their lives, the more they are productive during the normal course of business, and the better the example they establish for subordinates.

I tell all of my clients the same thing when I see people in the office early in the morning or late at night: This is the antithesis of a productive workplace, no matter how many hours are being invested. A job should be able to be performed in about 40 hours a week, or there is something wrong with the person or with the job (or both). Thus, the more time one takes to build energy, the more productive one is on the job. More hours doesn't mean more productivity.

The key to helping others to adjust their behaviors efficiently and constructively is to begin with your own behaviors and your own flexibility. "Necessary evils" are rarely such; they are usually challenges that we simply fail to take the time to resolve. If you find yourself frustrated, drained, and unable to employ your full range of talents, take some time to examine the circumstances and to adjust your behavior.

You will create a tremendous "ROE": Return On Energy.

Just the facts

- Behavior is complex and not easily "profiled" or predicted.

- Behavior change is not accomplished by skills building.

- Past performance is not a certain indicator of future performance.

- You can use behavioral "keys" readily to gather quick information.

- You should become adept at behavioral interviewing.

> 66
> Don't pity the martyrs. They love the work.
> —George Ade
> 99

GET THE SCOOP ON...
Why listening is more important than speaking
■ Preventing interference ■
Providing honest feedback ■ Overcoming ego
needs that undermine understanding ■
Accommodating other styles ■ Communicating
bad news ■ Confronting the boss

Communicating Under Any Circumstances at Any Time

Chapter 6

In every organizational survey I've ever conducted, "communications" emerges as one of the top areas for improvement. The toughest job is convincing executives that this is a *good* thing, since it means that employees crave more information about their jobs and their customers, and better ways to achieve their goals. It's the apathetic employees who don't want to hear anything and don't want to contribute anything, who are the real problems.

Communicating is a simple process based on complex underpinnings. As you can see in the figure on the following page, I mean to say something that I then translate into speech. You hear it and translate it—"get" it—and then mean to say something in response, which you say, I hear, and I "get." The "mean" and "get" are cognitive processes, requiring translation, analysis, and evaluation. The "say" and "hear" are mechanical functions, subject to the surrounding environment.

The problem is that each of us has a set of values, beliefs, background, friends, socialization, education, travel, and a host of other experiences that are unique to us. The probability of those factors being identical for any two communicators is, effectively, nil, and the more communicators in the loop, the more the differences. Advertently or inadvertently, we use these factors as "filters" to help us decipher and assess what we "get" and what we "mean." Usually, we assume that the other person can readily apply similar filters to create similar meaning. Almost always, we are wrong.

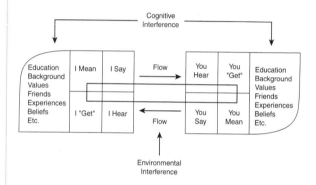

There is also environmental interference caused by distractions, noise, other people, and culture (e.g., "Don't stand around talking, do something!"). We also have our own agendas at work, ranging from wondering whether the car is repaired and how much it will cost, to the perception that the other person has unfairly taken credit for one of your projects.

Rather than being upset that we often communicate poorly, we should be astonished that we're able to communicate at all under these circumstances!

Communication is a function of every role the manager is engaged in, so improvement here results in improvement across the board. A variety of poor performance issues can often be resolved with more attention to fundamental communication skills.

Preventing environmental interference

Aside from random encounters and casual chats in the hall, communication should be planned to be as free of environmental interference as possible. We adhere to that rule pretty well in formal meetings, where we choose a closed conference room, shut the blinds, arrange chairs for optimal interaction, and so forth. Yet we seldom plan as well for one-on-one encounters or small, informal groups. Here are some places that are totally inappropriate for business communication because of the environmental interference:

Restaurants and cafeterias

Juggling food, silverware, and napkins while being interrupted by wait staff, other diners, and bussed tables is not conducive to anything but light, social conversation. While many people love to "close the deal" or "confront a problem" at a restaurant, they don't love it so much when the deal isn't what they thought and the problem doesn't go away.

Hallways and parking lots

High traffic areas present two problems. The first is the obvious interruptions from others stopping by to say "hello" or to find out what's going on. (In my surveys at Merck & Co., the pharmaceutical firm repeatedly cited as one of America's best companies in *Fortune Magazine*'s annual polls, managers complained about being asked by superiors, "What's this about?" every time a few met in a hallway for brief discussions.) The second problem is that this sort of visibility can create rumors, especially if the

Timesaver
It actually takes less time to communicate in a variety of ways than in only one manner. Reinforcing oral communication in a memo or e-mail will, at worst, reinforce, and, at best, clarify what was said. It's difficult to communicate important issues too much.

conversation is heated or animated. This can either artificially dampen or exaggerate reactions.

Rest rooms

This seems as if it's too obvious to mention, but I find it repeatedly. The best example was someone talking to another party behind a closed stall, who turned out to be someone else entirely! I'm told by women that business conversations abound in the rest rooms, and one event planner told me once that I had "passed the ladies' room test," which had involved her deliberately listening in during breaks in the rest room to ascertain from her eavesdropping how well the participants had liked me as the speaker that morning. She told me that the ladies' room conversations were her acid test for speaker effectiveness!

The best way to avoid environmental interference is to have a private conversation in which all participants are comfortable, focused on each other, and committed to the communication. Placing some chairs around a desk, forwarding the phone, turning off beepers, and establishing firm eye contact will go a long way to "isolating" you and your colleague(s) from the surroundings. If you have an office, close the door. (In those firms that have become "cubicle" cities, it's especially important to guarantee privacy from nearby ears. You may ask your colleagues for some "room," which you can reciprocate by vacating your space at times, or you may have to go find a conference room.)

If you have to meet someone quickly or an unexpected, important conversation arises, make some jury-rigged "quiet space" for yourself, even if it means going to the deserted cafeteria for a table, borrowing the office of someone who's out of town, or huddling in a storage room. The ability to establish communication accurately and quickly the first time is one of the greatest timesavers and productivity enhancements available to a manager.

Preventing cognitive interference

The most effective way of ensuring that cognitive interference doesn't occur is by assuming that it's always occurring. Therefore, you should never assume that you've completely understood a message, nor that the other party has completely understood you. The key to this is a technique called "testing for understanding."

Testing incoming communication

Let's assume that you've just been told by a breathless and worried subordinate that one of your key clients has decided not to renew their contract this year because of a slowdown in their sales. Instead of immediately launching into remedial (or crisis) actions, it usually pays to take a few minutes to ask the following questions:

- Do I understand correctly that they have told us they will not renew, and that the decision has come from their buyer to our account executive?

- Do you mean that they will not honor the current contract or that they will not renew it for next year?

- Are you saying that the client is definitely not renewing, or that this is simply a possibility?

The subordinate's frame of reference (beliefs, background, experience, etc.) might indicate that anyone in management at the client can make such a decision, but you know from your frame of

Unofficially...
One of the real indicators of power in modern organizations is control over conference rooms. Secretaries guard the access jealously, and managers maneuver over priorities. This is because the conference rooms guarantee higher quality communication.

reference that only the vice president of advertising can actually decide not to renew. The subordinate may not be familiar with the fact that renewal can be done at any time, and the client may have merely indicated that they won't renew as early as they had the prior year, out of courtesy for your planning. Or the subordinate may be completely accurate and attuned to your understanding, as well. However, you can't be sure of any of that until you test.

This is particularly important with written communication, including e-mail. Since written communication lacks all inflection, tone, body language, volume, and nuance, it can be highly misleading. If your frame of reference is that the sender tends to be sarcastic, you may interpret the written phrase, "You've met your goals exactly—job well done," as a taunt, meaning that you didn't beat your goals at all, while the sender may have been quite sincere in the praise. Since e-mail is such an instantaneous response mechanism, we tend to viscerally read and reply to communication on that medium with particular vigor and not enough patience.

If the e-mail says, "Have all appropriate people at a meeting in my office at 4:40 p.m. to discuss the Figby Contract," you might be incensed that you're being asked to stay late to discuss a contract you are only peripherally involved with. But by clarifying the message with a few testing questions, you may ascertain that the meeting will only be for ten minutes, that your presence isn't required but that you were informed out of courtesy, and/or that you could make your contribution briefly and leave. But you don't know that if you don't ask, and the default position for not asking is almost always that of a negative expectation.

Testing outgoing communication

Few of us go beyond the satisfaction of a subordinate's nodding head or affirmative "Will do!" to ensure ourselves that our directives are understood and are being carried out. But power managers understand that subordinates are always too eager to please and too loath to indicate that they didn't understand something, no matter how perfectly you communicated it.

While traveling across Great Britain I had become tired of rather uninspired English food when, to my pleasant surprise, we found a distant cousin of the American food franchise TGI Friday's. I asked the waitress for the largest cheeseburger available, but everything seemed too easy. Before she left the table I said to her, "You understand that I want a cheeseburger, not a hamburger?"

"Of course, sir," she replied.

"And it should be medium rare?"

"I've made a note," she said, and again turned to leave.

"Oh, one more thing," I yelled, "what kind of cheese comes with that?"

"Why, melted, sir," she said as she walked away.

Whenever you provide a directive, give an order, make a request, or otherwise provide guidance, make sure that you are not victimized by cognitive interference. Test your outgoing message. If you responded to the subordinate above about the contract nonrenewal with this instruction: "Tell the sales team involved to gather whatever information they need and meet me in my office or call in to our conference line in 1 hour," then you can quickly test your message with the questions below:

Bright Idea
Just because you can immediately reply to e-mail doesn't mean you should. Set your e-mail software to "queue" instead of "send immediately" and allow your responses to sit for an hour or so, then reread them before sending. You'll save yourself a lot of grief (and lose fewer friends).

- "Who are you going to notify?"

- "What time will you tell them to meet or call?"

- "What phone number will you provide to them?"

- "What will you do if you can't reach any of them?"

- "What information might be pertinent?"

In this way you'll be able to tell if the subordinate heard and "got" what you meant and said. This is a very simple example. You can imagine the importance of this technique when you're dealing with rumors, innuendo, or crises. At a meeting, after agreeing on actions and giving your marching orders, go around the room quickly and ask what each person is going to do next, what resources they will need, what changes they will make, what obstacles they envision, and so on. You don't have to ask all of those questions, but ask enough to convince yourself that everyone has "got" what you meant.

Allowing for differences: Virtually no one is like you

People communicate best within their own comfort zones. Although these zones may differ and vary, they are seldom fortresses impregnable to outsiders.

I've done a great deal of work in Japan. I was originally told that "Japanese don't like confrontation and will not respond well in interactive meetings. They don't participate like Americans do." The Japanese culture does not support spontaneous contributions, especially when there may be real or implied criticism of the company or of a superior. However, the culture certainly supports critical thinking, efforts for improvement, and team effort.

Timesaver
It actually saves time to take a little more time when you're giving instructions, especially under tight deadlines. Once you've provided a course of action, ask the employee what is the first thing he or she is now going to do. If it fits with your intention, fine, but if it doesn't then you can clarify before any more time is wasted.

Consequently, it's most effective in Japan to break a large group into subgroups, give them information well in advance to consider and analyze, and assign a spokesperson representing the subgroup, which deliberates in private. In this way, no one is singled out for a certain opinion or point of view (it's the group's position and the speaker is merely the representative), and advance information provides for careful diagnosis. This technique is highly effective, and generates as much innovation and healthy critique as do more confrontational and spontaneous American meetings.

Similarly, you can adjust to and accommodate a host of "comfort zones" if you take the time to realize what they are. (This is why personality stereotyping and "profiling" is so detrimental to communication, as discussed in Chapter 5.)

Power managers don't demand that others adjust to them, but rather develop the flexibility to adjust to others. If someone is highly assertive and interpersonal, don't challenge them or become involved in ego competitions. Allow them to express their style, but be firm and don't be cowed. If someone is more amiable and passive, don't attempt to bully them into a position or a challenge. Listen to them, encourage them to speak, and respond honestly.

Here are some guidelines for accommodating differing communications styles:

- Don't use the same style yourself with everyone. Not all people will respond the same way, and flexibility is incumbent on the manager, not the managed.

- Never cut people off or finish a sentence for them.

- When someone is excessively vague or you can't follow them, take the onus on yourself and say, "I'm sorry, but I'm having trouble visualizing that. Can you give me an example?"

- Don't fill silences. Allow the other person some time and see if they will add anything. Uncomfortable silences actually seldom last for more than a few seconds. Artificial attempts to fill them create miscommunication.

- After group communication, talk to people one-on-one when possible. This will reinforce your points and will also serve as a useful testing mechanism.

- Use as many analogies and metaphors as possible. People latch onto examples much more readily than they do the result of interpreting a lot of verbiage. This is also why visual aids are highly recommended for meetings.

- Use a variety of differing techniques for the same message. Support a meeting with handouts, send e-mail reminders after conversations, and leave a voice mail to augment a memo. Different people "get" things better from a variety of inputs.

Moneysaver
Ask your team or staff to make a list of those events and items that were communicated best over the past year, and those that were communicated worst. Then list the distinctions between the two lists. Those distinctions will form the key items for improvement in your communications.

The lost art of listening

I was called by the executive vice president of a major insurance firm to help with the aftermath of a huge merger. He had his staff assembled, and wanted me to suggest the right communications strategy for the company. Apparently, this was the "test" question to help determine which consultant to hire.

"What should we be telling employees, and how?" he asked.

"I wouldn't tell them anything for now," I suggested.

"What?! Shouldn't we be talking to them daily?"

"Well, do you know which offices you'll be closing?"

"No, not yet."

"Do you know what the new benefit plan will look like?"

"We won't know that for at least three months."

"Do you know which company's information technology will be dominant?"

"No, we have consultants working on that."

"Do you know who the key divisional officers will be?"

"We're still in negotiation. It will take at least thirty days."

"Well, you have nothing to tell them. I'd suggest you listen, listen carefully, and then show them that you've listened."

"That's completely counterintuitive," he mulled.

"Yes, and what's your point?" I asked.

I got the job.

There is a great American management myth that's begun to take hold globally, to no one's good fortune. The myth is that we, as managers, are paid to take action. That is completely untrue. Power managers are paid *to get results*. The results, or outcomes, are paramount, and they are often best achieved by *not* taking action. Speaking is considered active, and listening, passive. We have to understand that listening is one of the most powerful tools in a manager's kit.

The four techniques to make the other person talk

Not everyone is an avid talker, of course. Employees—and subordinates, in particular—will often avoid speaking, not because they realize that listening is more important, but because they want

Bright Idea
More than two-thirds of communication is about listening, not speaking. You can't learn while you talk. You can't reflect and allow yourself time to analyze when you're speaking. And you can never get in trouble when your mouth is shut (or at least it's extremely difficult).

to see which way the wind is blowing, allow someone else to take the lead, and ensure that they don't incur your displeasure.

There are four powerful techniques to encourage others to talk. You should master all four and use them as needed.

Provocative questioning

Most people ask "binary" questions, which means the inquiries can be answered with a simple "yes" or "no" type of response. Compare the following:

"Do you think the Bradbury promotional plan will work?"

"Yes."

"What do you think are the biggest potential opportunities and threats for the Bradbury promotional plan?"

"Well, the greatest opportunity is that it will open up a new buyer demographic among older purchasers. But the threat is that our younger purchasers might feel alienated, and we don't want to lose that strong customer base."

Provocative questions, as in the latter case, generate narrative responses which demand some analysis and description. They are useful to force people to commit their *reasoning* and not just their position.

To determine if you tend to be an introvert or an extrovert, psychologists will often ask this question: Would you rather be home with a good book or at a party with strangers? My response is that I'd rather be home with a lousy book I've already read. I abhor small talk, and try to avoid it whenever possible. I am an introvert. At a cocktail party, sitting happily alone on the couch with a drink, I noticed the hostess headed right for me, feeling it her responsibility not to allow me to be alone. As soon as she sat down, I asked her two questions that saved my life.

"What do you do for a living, Dale?"

"I'm an emergency room nurse."

"Can you describe your average day?"

She spoke for nearly an hour before her husband took her away to mingle with other guests. When we left that night, Dale told my wife at the door, "You know, your husband is a brilliant conversationalist."

The sound that most people love most is that of their own voice. Get them to use it by asking questions that demand explanation, reasoning, description, and opinion. This works extremely well with customers—particularly irate ones—as well as peers and superiors.

Provocative questions and follow-up questions might include:

- What do you think of . . . ?
- Why do you think we should do this?
- What reasons can you give me not to do this?
- If you were to implement this, what would concern you most?
- What are the three greatest priorities in this situation?
- If I told you to focus on one area, what would it be and why?

Reflective listening

This is a common psychological approach, often known colloquially as "active listening." It is a method of staying in the conversation minimally enough to show interest and involvement, but allowing the other party to dominate and express his or her views.

When I was consulting with Merck, they asked me to meet with the newly appointed president of their subsidiary, Calgon. I was warned that he had already been through several consultants quickly,

Bright Idea
To get someone talking, ease the way: Ask about something of interest to them, such as a hobby or recent trip. It will get them "warmed up," and they'll respond much more easily on the ensuing topics. "How are your kids doing?" or "How's your dog?" often do the trick.

and that the budget and the choice of a consultant were his, although Merck would provide the introduction.

When I arrived in Pittsburgh I met with the president, who was a charming guy who loved to express his views. He spoke to me for 45 minutes continuously about the past of Calgon, the present of Calgon, the future of Calgon, and his plans for Calgon. He was enthusiastic and passionate. Every 90 seconds or so, I'd simply interject, "Really?" or "Is that right?" or "In other words . . ." or even "Hmmmnn."

At the end of 45 minutes the president ran out of steam, but I sat silently. He looked at me and said, "You are the first consultant who has sat in my office who really understands this business."

I received the assignment, and what amounted to $500,000 in business over the next several years.

The other consultants had consistently broken into the president's stream of talk, trying to impress him with how good they were, what they would do in certain situations, and how they had experienced similar conditions. None of that was important. The crucial element was to allow the president to talk unimpeded, but to demonstrate "presence" through occasional comments of interest. This is not a manipulative technique. It's a technique to allow the other person to express their thinking.

Don't be quick to perform the "upsmanship" that can quiet another person. Every 90 seconds to 2 minutes, insert a brief comment like:

- Interesting.
- How many did you say? (Ask for a repetition of a fact.)
- You're kidding!

- What was your reaction to that?

- I've never heard of that happening before.

- In other words . . . (short paraphrase or summary)

Turn-around questions

One of the reasons that we speak so much is that we feel cornered (often by a superior or a customer, but sometimes even by a subordinate). We hear these types of questions, and feel that we must respond in detail:

- "What can you do for me?"

- "How much will this cost us?"

- "Why should we choose you?"

- "How will this affect us on the job?"

- "How long will this take?"

- "Why has this gone wrong?"

We have the feeling of being cornered, and forced to fight our way out with logic, excuses, explanations, details, and fancy footwork. Actually, we usually don't have to do any of that.

There are two key philosophies for turning a defensive situation around:

- You're not omniscient, and are simply not certain yet what the answer or outcome will be.

- The inquirer is as accountable for the outcome as you are.

When a prospect says to me, "What will this cost?" or "What can you do for us?" in a strongly assertive manner, I simply reply, "I don't know." When they then ask, "What do you mean, 'you don't know'?" I tell them that I have to hear more from them about their issues and their expectations

Unofficially...
All techniques are neutral, but their intent determines whether they are legitimate or manipulative. Getting the other person to talk is legitimate, but pretending you've supported their actions when you haven't is manipulative.

Timesaver
Don't get upset with someone who is upset, but don't pretend that the emotion doesn't exist. Simply say, "I can see you're upset and I want to help. Let me have your impressions and observations, and I'll be able to determine what the both of us should do from here.

before we can mutually arrive at a possible solution or working relationship. They then continue talking.

When an irate customer, employee, colleague, or superior approaches you belligerently or aggressively and says, in effect, "What are you going to do about this?!" simply reply that you're immediately willing to listen to everything they have to say so that you can determine what should be done, and what the two of you can do together (or you alone or they alone) to resolve the situation.

Don't feel obligated to act or defend yourself. And don't feel too anxious to immediately resolve the customer's problem, since customers, despite the adage, simply aren't always right (and neither is the boss). By taking the time to get the other party to continue talking and explaining (rather than accusing) and listening dispassionately to the facts, you'll be in an ideal position to determine who should do what to whom before the discussion is over.

Turn-around questions should be nonjudgmental, truly inquisitive, and delivered in an even, reasonable tone. Some examples:

- "I'm not sure, why do you ask?"

- "I believe I can help, but I'll need some more information."

- "What exactly occurred to prompt you to ask this?"

- "Between us, we can take care of this, but what are the key facts that you have and I don't?"

- "Why have you come to me with this?"

The bounce-back technique
The bounce-back approach simply requires that you repeat the last word that the other person has

uttered (but only after you're certain that they haven't merely paused to take a breath). It is an involuntary reaction to a psychological prompt to explain more. This technique is often used in the courtroom, which is why attorneys are always cautioning witnesses never to respond with anything more than what's needed to answer a specific question.

However, what usually happens is this:

"Where were you on the night of June 17th?"

"I was at home."

"Home?"

"Yes, well at least for early evening."

"Evening?"

"Okay, I did go out for a beer at the tavern."

"Tavern?"

"Yes, I was there, and I did see Natalie."

"Natalie?"

"YES!! I was with her, I've hated her since she stole my bike when we were 12, and I killed her at the bar!!!"

This isn't so far-fetched. Try this with your subordinates (or customers) and you may find yourself relieved of having to play the hero and in receipt of a great deal of information that will make your job easier.

"We're in big trouble, and only you can help us with the Ross contract."

"Contract?"

"Yes, we're having trouble getting by the usual pre-pay provisions with legal."

"Legal?"

"The new general counsel, Anderson, doesn't understand the uniqueness of the Ross account. In fact they've never actually met."

"Never met?"

Bright Idea
Don't "step into" silences. They won't kill you or the other party, and trying to fill "dead air" has prompted many managers to utter banalities or trivialities they wish they'd never said. Let the other person talk, or at least take your own time.

"I see where you're going! We could arrange a meeting directly between Anderson and Ross, which should change her mind. Thanks for the insight . . ." I'm only slightly exaggerating! People will respond with little prompting if you give them the chance and aren't speaking yourself.

Listening is a lost art, but not one that can't be reclaimed immediately. We have to discipline ourselves not to speak constantly, and have to master the devices that will enable others to speak readily and comfortably.

Communicating is not an event but a process that is in constant motion. Despite the content—whether we're talking about airplanes, chemicals, insurance, or computers—the process remains the same.

We can practice this at home, at civic events, at social gatherings, and other places, and use it professionally on the job.

Listening carefully actually makes you an object of interest to others. It requires some patience, and the willingness to believe that the other person actually may have something interesting to contribute to you and to the organization.

Just the facts

- Interference in communication can be external or internal.

- An excellent communicator "tests" both incoming and outgoing messages to ensure meaning is accurate.

- There are specific techniques that can be employed immediately to enhance listening skills.

- Communicating is not synonymous with "telling," and it's usually better (and safer) to simply listen.
- Both parties, ideally, must accept accountability for their mutual communication.

Resolving the Four Common Management Issues

PART III

GET THE SCOOP ON...
The ten sources of innovation • Why a focus on
"fixing" is a low-growth strategy •
How to encourage creativity • Prudent risk
taking • The freedom to fail means being
allowed to fail more than a single time

Chapter 7

Raising the Bar Instead of Fixing Problems

There are four common management issues that consume up to 99 percent of a manager's time. While many managers invest an inordinate amount of time and energy in trying to tackle the one percent (which is often unresolvable), power managers ensure that they are adept at the four sets of skills required most of the time. Those four areas are:

- Innovation: raising the bar and improving standards.
- Problem solving: fixing things that go wrong.
- Decision making: choosing among options.
- Planning: protecting future actions.

We'll devote a chapter to each of these areas.

Why innovation is an underappreciated skill

From the time we enter school, we are taught to be problem solvers. Our parents, teachers, and other role models place an emphasis on fixing things that go wrong, whether it be our behavior, the family car, a leaky roof, or a fuzzy television screen. On the job, we're rewarded for resolving customer complaints, reducing defects, solving distribution delays, and ending poor performance of subordinates.

These are important skills, but they are all *focused in the past.* In fact, with rare exception, traditional problem solving is intended to restore prior performance. The roof should stop leaking. Defects should return from an unacceptable 8 percent rate to the standard 4 percent rate. We must return to 100 percent of our sales goals from the current 91 percent. The successful problem solver has, in effect, made things as good as they used to be.

The flow of problem solving might look like this:

Bright Idea
When you encounter a problem and assign your people to fix it, don't ask them to merely restore prior performance. Ask them to investigate whether they can improve upon the old performance. This is how to "co-opt" problem solving resources for innovation.

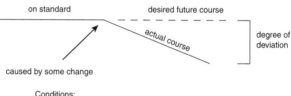

Conditions:
1. Deviation of actual from desired course.
2. Cause is unknown.
3. Deviation is serious enough to concern us.

In the graphic, performance declines. This may be an underwriter's acceptance of prudent risk, a lathe, or a distribution process. The performance might decline gradually or precipitously. Yet at some point, alarms go off. These alarms may be a customer complaint, an unacceptable loss ration, or a sprinkler system, and they alert responsible people that performance had deviated from acceptable norms. The problem solving then begins.

Managers are often judged almost solely on their problem-solving ability. After all, there are tremendous inducements:

■ We know the performance is attainable, because it had been achieved in the past.

■ It is instant gratification.

■ The organizational benefit (and the recognition) are immediate: The complaint ceases, the product is received on time.

■ There is minimum risk.

■ The process is rapid and resources can be committed for such an obvious need.

■ Organizations traditionally reward problem solving.

However, here's another way to view a manager's accountability:

In this case, performance is already acceptable, but the manager takes the initiative to attempt to improve it still further. The manager takes the necessary prudent risk to attempt to create a higher sales close rate than ever achieved, a faster distribution level than customers expect, or fewer incorrect hires than the organization has been prepared to accept historically.

Innovation is more important than ever in a world of rapid change. Unfortunately, it is often associated with technology to the exclusion of more

Bright Idea
When employees request your approval to "fix" some aspect of their job, processes, or equipment, ask them if they've considered improving it rather than merely fixing it. If you do this enough, they'll begin to approach you with innovative ideas rather than just Band-Aids.

traditional areas. But innovation is desperately required every day (and is practiced every day by superb organizations and superb management). There are no "alarms," however. It is up to the power manager to recognize opportunities and initiate prudent actions to try to "raise the bar."

The chief inhibitors to innovation are:

- There can be considerable risk, since the intended level of performance has never been achieved before.

- There is strong inertia, often manifest in "don't rock the boat" mentalities.

- It is difficult to raise support and resources, particularly in the initial stages without any small victories.

- We suffer from the myth that managers are paid to take action, which emphasizes problem solving, and subordinates the real management responsibility that is to get results. Yet the most dramatic results are inevitably the product of innovation, not problem solving.

Fortunately, there is a process and a set of tools to assist managers in innovative pursuits. Keep this in mind throughout: Innovation is the *redeployment* of assets and resources for better yields and better returns. The hotel manager who wants to increase check-in and check-out volume at the front desk can do so by hiring more staff and buying more computers. That's not very innovative, and requires additional investment. However, if that manager accomplished greater volume by cross-training staff to handle both jobs, arranging the waiting lines for faster flow, and allowing for express checkout for frequent guests, that yields a far better return with existing assets.

The 10 sources of innovation

There are ten generic sources of innovative ideas. You may identify six or eight as appropriate for you and your organization, or you may have an eleventh and twelfth to suggest. The key is to use these areas as a "radar array" that you and your subordinates utilize daily to scan the environment for innovative opportunity. Opportunity does not knock but once. It is knocking all the time. The trouble is that we don't recognize the sound because we have no way to identify it.

Unexpected success

When something goes beyond our plan, projection, or expectation, our immediate response is usually, "Let's do more of it!" In the case of a temporary fad (pet rocks), this will quickly end the novelty and the sales. In the case of more pragmatic products (cell phones), the market quickly becomes saturated and price pressures ensue.

The innovative response to unexpected success is to find out how to build on it for other advantages. (And, as in all innovation, the unexpected success may be a competitor's.)

Example: American Airlines was the first to begin a frequent flyer program. Competing airlines immediately launched their own programs because of the success of American's. Then the more innovative organizations began alliance programs (rental cars, hotels), associations with credit cards, interchangeable award points, elite frequent flyer status, and so on. The goal wasn't simply to enlist more and more people (in fact, that was dysfunctional in terms of free seats that would be gobbled up, and many frequent flyers complain that it's too difficult to use their points as it is), but to offer options, flexibility, status and other measures that would increase the loyalty of the most important customers—those who spend the most on travel.

Ask these questions:

- Where have we been successful beyond our expectations, why has it occurred, and where can we use the same approaches elsewhere?
- How can we build on existing success with additional products, additional services, or heightened relationships?
- What new customers, markets, publicity, and other opportunities are available given this new success?

Unexpected failure

You might conclude that any failure is unexpected, but I'm referring to the whopper, where you're sliding downhill so fast that you can't catch your breath. In most of these instances, people are consumed with damage control, desperately trying to right the ship and restore performance to some acceptable norm.

However, while that is going on, there is plenty of room for cooler heads and more innovative minds to create new scenarios, having learned from the debacle.

Example: Post-It Notes were "invented" at 3M after a bench chemist was unsuccessful in creating a longer-lived adhesive, but found that the temporary one he had created from his "failure" was ideal for keeping his place in his church hymnal.

Example: The colossal failure of Ford's Edsel shook the company, but it jolted Lee Iaccoca, then production chief, to realize that consumers were no longer buying cars based on promotion of the name plate, but rather as a lifestyle statement. He launched the Mustang (despite earlier "lifestyle" failures with the early Thunderbird) and it became the largest new model success in automotive history to that time. The unexpected success of Mustang prompted General Motors to launch its own lifestyle product in response, the Camero, in record time.

Example: The product tampering of Tylenol years ago, a failure in packaging that was not anticipated or normal (it was a criminal act), launched the entire "safety packaging" industry, which is now responsible for our inability to get an aspirin out of a new bottle at two in the morning without getting an even worse headache.

Ask yourself these questions:

- In fixing this failure, is there a way to raise the standard beyond former performance?

- Although not what we tried to create, we have created something new and different. Are there other uses or other markets that may be appropriate?

- What have we learned about the *causes* of this unexpected failure that we can use to improve our products, markets, or relationships?

Process weakness

There are often "weak links" in processes that we attempt to shore-up. We may find that sales and manufacturing are performing just fine, but distribution is weak because we have to rely on independent shippers. We correct the inevitable problems by shipping by overnight courier to those customers whose shipments are dangerously late, incurring large costs and eroding profits.

Moneysaver
The place to stop hemorrhaging money is wherever your people are deep into constant corrective and contingency actions. Pull them out of the vicious circle of compensating for weak links and tell them to change the entire approach. No system—or organization—is stronger than its weakest link.

Process weaknesses will forever devour money so long as they're viewed as problems to be solved or accommodated. However, when they're seen as opportunities, they can become the sources of entirely new systems that not only eliminate the problem, but actually catapult performance forward.

Example: Fred Smith founded FedEx based on the postal service's process weakness of unreliability for short-term, accurate delivery. If he were a problem solver, he would have tried to hire better people, or create better optical scanners, or to sort mail more effectively. Instead, he determined that the distribution process had to be changed, and created the hub and spoke methodology: Send a package from New York to Detroit, and it goes through Memphis. This earned him a "C" as a senior thesis from his college professor, and a few billion dollars from the public as a viable consumer service.

Don't accept a process weakness as a "necessary evil." The more weakness we tolerate or attempt to offset with contingent actions (using FedEx, for example to compensate for our own lousy delivery system), the more we erode profits and sap strength.

Questions to ask yourself include:

■ In what areas are we tolerating weakness, and how can we change the process itself?

■ Where are we spending the most in contingent actions to compensate for continual problems, and how do we change the entire approach?

■ Where do we receive the most complaints, and how can we eliminate or alter the entire process?

Unexpected events

Unexpected events, whether internal or external, generally cause people to "hunker down." They resort to bromides: "Let's wait until the dust settles," and generally become quite conservative. Power managers do something else—they try to determine what advantages can be exploited.

By definition, the unexpected requires agility and willingness for quick action. Whether it's an internal reorganization, a competitor's announcement, or geopolitical upheaval, power managers investigate, "What's in it for us?"

Example: Last winter, a power outage in my community occurred at about 7:30 a.m., just when people were beginning their morning regimens and commute. As people already on the road reached their favorite coffee and drive-through donut shops, now powerless, what arrived in the lots but the mobile "canteen" trucks which you normally see servicing factories and construction sites. Some of these entrepreneurs had rescheduled their routes to arrive just where they knew the customers would be congregating!

Example: Unexpected security needs emerging from terrorism—from airplane hijackings to weapons smuggled into courtrooms—have generated new applications for metal detection devices, X-ray technology, and security guards. If you look at the machine names, or at the shoulder patches of guard uniforms, you won't see dozens of competing firms. You'll find that those that have made the transition the fastest also received the predominance of the business. What might have appeared as isolated or unrelated events, were actually opportunities,

Watch Out!
Most people regard unexpected events as harbingers of bad times, and consequently figuratively duck under their desks. You'll stand out in a crowd if you calmly ask, "How can I grasp an opportunity from this unexpected event?" Besides, you're likely to be the only one standing!

with a short window of recognition. This is a prime example of the redeployment of assets and resources we noted at the beginning of the chapter.

In this last example, if you know everything about hiring, training, monitoring, evaluating, and retaining guards, there is very little effort needed to redeploy those abilities to a new focus of application (banks, airports, courtrooms, hospitals, etc.). What are you doing to take advantage, nimbly and quickly, of unexpected events?

Questions to ask:

- How can this event or action be exploited with our existing products and services?
- Are we capable of providing an additional product or service that will fill a need created by this event?
- What is the "up side" to the new configuration that most people will be unaware of at the outset?

Changes in industry and/or market structure

In this case, the very nature of the business or its marketplace is altered. Once rare, this is now an almost common phenomenon, sparked largely by technology and the global economy. Sometimes organizations and management continue to operate at very high standards according to the *old* reality, which means that they are merely efficiently losing ground.

Those that take advantage of market and industry changes can operate fairly inefficiently at first, if they must, because they have been graced with a head start.

Example: The broadcast television industry has changed radically. Cable, satellite, direct access, and other options have broadened consumer choice beyond anyone's dreams. Yet it's not sufficient to simply provide more and more channels (and can be detrimental, if they are repetitive or of low quality). We see innovative management forging ties between traditional networks and cable (MSNBC), new networks with highly targeted demographics (FOX), and combinations of cable access with computer access and phone access (@home).

Among the industries and markets experiencing upheaval are health care, telephone, computer, and recreation. Is your business among those in change or headed in that direction?

Questions to ask:

- How do the changes in the industry affect our customers, and how can we fill new needs?

- How do the events around the changes create opportunities for new products and services?

- What new alliances, collaborations, or relationships now make sense in light of what is emerging?

High growth

We sometimes experience growth that is above and beyond our projections, estimates, quotas, timetables, and expectations. Too often we treat it as simply good fortune, and attempt to do more of the same. In other words, if people are buying this, let's produce a lot more of it. The problem is that such mindless volume often oversaturates the market, creates boredom, or produces disaster when technology, perception, or other factors move buyers away from what is now a dangerous commitment or high inventory level.

Timesaver
If you hold regular staff meetings, use 5 minutes each time to ask subordinates, "What about our business and our business environment has changed since last time?" This will prevent changes from sneaking up, and will send the message that you want people to stay on top of new developments.

High growth is a superb opportunity for innovation, if we use it for leverage and springboarding new ideas and additional products and services, and not solely as an excuse to produce more of the same (which is merely reactive and not innovative).

(This is a good place to point out that the categories are not "process pure," and that "unexpected success" could also lead to high growth and vice versa. These categories are simply meant to be triggers, which may indeed overlap.)

Example: When personal computers were first introduced, people placed them on card tables, counter tops, and empty spaces in the kitchen. The only thing to read about them was the manufacturer's instructions, which were often obtuse.

Today, there is an assortment of ergonomically designed (a term not really used nor understood by the general public prior to computerization) furniture which not only provides platforms for the computers, but can also hide keyboards and printers, be modularly rearranged, and is comfortable. There are also publications devoted to a particular hardware (*MacHome*) and to a particular software (*Word*). Both the furniture and the publications industries were able to take advantage of the high growth of computers. In fact, there are relatively few industries that such growth hasn't affected (General Motors, by dint of the scores of computers built into every single car, is often cited as the largest computer manufacturer in the world).

Managers should look around their operation and determine what areas are growing most dramatically and how they can be exploited. Are increasing numbers using the call response center, is a service feature most requested by retailers, is there a warranty that is almost always purchased? These are tactical measures.

On a more strategic basis, and in contributing to the organization as a whole, what kind of growth is occurring internally, in the environment, or with competitors, that can be utilized to "springboard" the organization's growth and success?

Questions to ask:

- Where are we succeeding beyond our best estimates and plans?

- Where are we forced to scramble in order to catch up to customer demand?

- What growth is occurring externally to the organization that we wish we were a part of?

Converging technologies

When two or more technologies can be combined in various ways to support each other or to make the result more valuable than the individual components, new opportunities are born. This was once a relatively minor source of innovation, but has emerged as a primary one today, in this technological age.

Technologies may be combined in an integrated manner (for example, building wireless communications technology into a palm-sized computer, so that e-mail can be downloaded at any time), or in an informal manner (for example, equipping sales people with cell phones and laptop computers so that they can work all day from the road and not waste time coming to the office to file reports and receive messages).

Example: Using a combination of video, telephonic, computer, satellite access, and other devices, many hotels now offer express check-in,

Unofficially...
Not all growth is automatically good growth. Be cautious about low profit, returns, complaints, high servicing needs, and commensurate losses offset elsewhere in your product line. Some Web sites experience so much growth that they can't adequately service the visitors, who then never return.

video check-out, fax service in the room, first-run movies and sophisticated games on the television screen, remote monitoring and rapid replenishment of mini-bar usage, and so on. It's common in many upscale hotels to check in immediately upon arrival without waiting in line, finding your favorite papers, flowers, or wine in the room, and immediately retrieving your e-mail from the computer "work station." These combinations not only enhance the traveler's productivity and comfort, they also reduce staffing levels.

Airlines, often to traveler's apprehension, have inaugurated electronic tickets, which eliminate paper problems (lost, damaged, stolen) and greatly minimize interactions with reservation agents, gate agents, ticket counter agents, and other personnel, thereby enabling them to reduce staffing levels. In fact, a customer could make a reservation on a personal computer for air, hotel, and rental car, show up directly at the gate with identification, proceed directly to a rental car at the destination with a contract already inside it, and check in automatically at the hotel. The only two people mandatory in that sequence are the gate agent and rental car exit agent.

Questions to ask:

■ What are the technological aids we use most individually, and how might we combine them for even more impact?

■ Where is there a chronic slowdown or delay involving technologies that interface but don't complement each other?

■ What bottlenecks of processing or information flow can be removed through the application of combinations of technology?

Watch Out!
Technology for its own sake is a killer, not an innovator. Focus on the result, not the input side. At a clothing store in Providence which installed an expensive inventory computer system, it now takes twice as long to process a purchase as it did by hand.

Demographic changes

Demographic changes include changes in the age, educational background, income level, ethnicity, geographic dispersal, and other measures of your customer base. Most managers don't realize that demographic changes are as varied and dramatic as technological changes. At the moment, the population of the United States is older, more affluent, better educated, larger, and more diverse than ever before. If your organization is regionally or locally focused, or deals within very narrow market niches, tracking demographic shifts is even more important.

Most people believe that the greatest discretionary buying power today is with youth, or perhaps with baby boomers. In actuality, it is senior citizens (those age 55 to 75) that have the greater buying power. The younger of this group are people for whom the IRA (Individual Retirement Account) legislation has provided unprecedented savings, and who no longer have to worry about raising children, college education, buying homes, or saving for retirement. As a matter of fact, in the early 21st century, maturing IRA accounts will release trillions of dollars into the economy in a very brief time span. No one is certain about the impact of this infusion of capital.

We see today leisure communities, recreation and vacation opportunities for seniors, "eldercare" emulating day care, assisted living, and charitable and grandchildren trusts. We can also see seniors re-entering the work force, not out of financial need, but for stimulation, as consultants, part-time workers, and volunteers, providing a new and reliable labor pool in what are, at present, very low unemployment times.

Example: Clothing manufacturers have made looser-fitting garments, with larger buttons. Appliance manufacturer's have made "power assisted" doors and created extra safety features. Vacation destinations have focused on an elder market (no children allowed). Companies have hired part-timers from this group to gain experienced people at relatively little cost (no large retirement plan expense) to compensate for small labor pools.

Of course, it's not just the elderly who constitute demographic opportunity. There are also increasingly diverse ethnicities, the movement from the suburbs back to the cities (gentrification), increasing numbers of people with at least a community college education, the rise of women in the workforce, declining birthrates and smaller average families, and so on. (For instance, fast-food providers have benefited tremendously from the two-income, no-time-to-cook phenomenon.)

Your customers and employee base will not remain static. Convents have closed because nuns have grown old and not enough new candidates have entered religious orders. Traditional clothing pattern manufacturers were made obsolete when women left homes to work and had little discretionary time left to devote to making their own clothing, a market quickly entered by off-the-shelf and ready-to-wear providers. The largest registered lobby in the United States, by far and away, is the AARP: The American Association of Retired People. The age criterion to join? Anyone age 50 or above can automatically become a member.

Questions to ask:

- How will our customer (and employee) base shift in the next several years in terms of

Timesaver
You don't have to guess about emerging customer needs, nor be concerned that your frame of reference is incorrect. Hire diverse people who mirror your present and future customer base, and use them to tell you what needs to anticipate. Reflect your customer base in your employee base as much as possible.

location, education, income, backgrounds, and so on?

■ What will prospective customers be requiring in terms of their lifestyles and their perceptions *at that time?*

■ What new customer groups will be emerging for whom we do not currently have adequate products and services?

Perception change

This is the only category on our innovation checklist that can be manipulated. We can manage perceptions. The facts may not change, but people's interpretations of them do. The fashion industry has changed opinions (and consequently sold clothing) based on the management of perception and what looks good, or what coat is "in" and what coat is "out," even though both garments might keep you warm in the winter. The advertising industry is geared to the attempt to manage perceptions.

What can you do to effectively change and build on the perceptions of your customers? The move toward "lifestyle" automobiles is largely influenced by perception, as are vacation choices, artworks, and personal accessories. One of the most effective advertising campaigns that I've ever seen was Kodak's, which talked not about film but about memories. After all, it's one thing to buy a box with film in it, but quite another to worry that your daughter's wedding pictures might not be perfect.

Example: When I was a kid, I wore something on my feet called "sneakers." I wore these to play basketball, run down the block, or generally hang around. They cost about $12. Today, we have jogging shoes, cross-training shoes, racquetball shoes, and a myriad of other footwear that all sell for $120

Watch Out!
Manage perceptions aggressively. The rumor mill and the grapevine are the two operations that function smoothly every day. The default positions are always negative. Take the time to assertively communicate and manage interpretations of events.

a pair. Are these shoes really so specialized that they enhance each of those closely related activities? I don't think so, but the footwear industry has done a great job of creating that perception.

Example: Smoking use to be the sophisticated act depicted in movies, and getting drunk was so cool that comics like Foster Brooks and shows like Dean Martin's revolved around that humor. No longer. Today we have programs, patches, and gums to stop smoking. We have Mothers Against Drunk Driving, designated drivers, and nonalcoholic beverages common even in bars.

Perceptions are fickle, and can change on a dime. What are you doing to both monitor customer perceptions and to help shape them? If you are not shaping them, someone else may well be. For that matter, what are you doing to help employee perceptions remain focused and positive?

Questions to ask:

- What general trends about health, well-being, recreation, education, family, and so on, seem to be undergoing changes that relate to our business?

- What should we be doing to test customer and employee perceptions (and to what extent have I been too dependent on my own views of the business and the operation)?

- How can we proactively manage perceptions about our products, services, and relationships, and what is the best means to do so?

New knowledge

Most patents (about 80 percent) in the United States are granted on the basis of new knowledge, but only about 5 percent of them—yes, that's

5 percent—ever reach the market in terms of being a viable product or service. While most managers believe that new breakthroughs and technological creations are the best roads to innovation, they are actually among the rarest. In some respects, there is nothing new under the sun.

However, there are exceptions, and I want to include this category since it can be a source of innovation. And for managers in R&D product development, and other developmental positions, it can be a primary source.

Example: Merck & Co., and other successful pharmaceutical researchers, make their livings from new knowledge about disease control, prevention of illness, and so on. 3M and DuPont are famous for continuing invention, as is Bell Labs. However, these organizations invest huge amounts of money (in Merck's case, over $1 billion annually) in research and development. By definition, there are more failures than success stories.

For the manager, the creativity and invention may best come from a new way to service an account, a creative response to customer need, or an improved product modification or enhancement.

Questions to ask:

- What can we produce and commercialize in the near future that will better serve an existing need or begin to fill a projected need?

- If we ignore all of the ways in which we've accomplished this before, how would we begin today to do this if we had no history?

- If there were no budget or resource constraints, and we wanted to be the leading edge in this pursuit, what would we produce or provide?

Bright Idea
Many people will tell you that there's actually very little new under the sun, and they may be right. But the ability to take tested and true ideas and approaches and make them applicable and relevant in contemporary society is, in itself, a contribution to new knowledge.

The checklist

Here is the checklist or guidelines that may be useful to consult on a regular basis to determine whether your "radar array" is properly calibrated to detect, assess, utilize, and exploit the opportunities that surround you with customers and employees:

- Unexpected success
- Unexpected failure
- Process weakness
- Unexpected events
- Change in industry and/or market structure
- High growth
- Converging technologies
- Demographic change
- Perception change
- New knowledge

Use the list and the commensurate questions, to probe these issues at staff meetings and in performance reviews, as a daily reminder, as a coaching aid, with colleagues, and so on. We need to wean ourselves away from problem solving, and to systematically focus on innovation. Add to the list if you find additional areas relevant for your operation, but try not to delete from the list, no matter how rarely some of the categories might apply. You'll never know when that particular radar unit will detect the next major opportunity.

Just the facts

- Problem solving is important for maintaining standards, but innovation is essential for growth.

- It's the manager's job to proactively "raise the bar" on a regular basis, not as a special event.

- Innovative ideas can arise internally, externally in the environment, or from competitors.

- Innovation is based on improvement and not simply "doing more of what we're good at."

- "Triggers" or a "radar array" are needed to interpret and decipher the opportunities surrounding us every day.

Finding Cause, Not Blame

I n the preceding chapter we discussed innovation, the first major concern of the power manager. The second, third, and fourth major management issues revolve around problem solving, decision making, and planning. Their interrelationship can be easily understood in this fashion:

Timing:	Concern:	Response:
past	something's gone wrong	fix it
present	something must be done	select an action
future	something will be begun	ensure success

An immediate clue for the manager is whether we are to focus on the past, the present, or the future. While all three may be involved at times, *the key is that we have to begin somewhere.* More often, only one element is relevant, and it might be any of the three. For example, a customer complaint has to be fixed, as does a leak in the roof. A choice of conference sites or vendors for new computers requires a selection. The introduction of a new compensation plan or an enhanced service offering demands

161

Chapter 8

Timesaver
When faced with a crisis in which people are shouting out vastly different actions to pursue, calm the storm by quickly deciding what kind of issue you have. Crisis is seldom about planning—you're apt to be facing either a terrible problem or an urgent decision.

planning to ensure success. (Note: Although problem solving approaches have been promulgated since the ancient Greeks created valid techniques, the seminal modern thinkers about these approaches to problem solving have been Charles Kepner and Benjamin Tregoe. See their book, *The Rational Manager*, Princeton Research Press, Princeton, New Jersey, 1981.)

Timing

	Past	Future
Cause	Corrective	Preventive
Effect	Adaptive	Contingent

Factors

These three actions have completely different starting points, which is why the identification of what kind of action is immediately demanded is so important:

■ Problems require that we find their causes so that corrective actions can be implemented.

■ Decisions require that we establish objectives so that alternatives may be evaluated against common criteria.

■ Planning requires that we clarify an implementation plan so that potential problems can be identified and prevented.

In all of these approaches it's important to note the relationship among the actions available to the manager.

Problems have effects, which we see and draw our attention, such as a customer complaint, a fire, a leak, a broken piece of machinery, or a computer glitch. They also have causes which underlie those effects and are seldom immediately seen, such as sloppy inventory control, incorrect fuses, an absence of building maintenance, loose bolts falling into moving parts, and poor software programming. We often assume that a patch on the effect—easing or eradicating the symptom—solves the problem. It doesn't. It merely removes, for the moment, the pain. Only by removing the cause do we remove the problem.

Addressing cause in the past, after the effects are felt, is corrective. Ameliorating the effects we're feeling is adaptive. Anticipating and averting causes from arising in the future is truly preventive. Anticipating and lessening the effects in the future (should the preventive action fail or unforeseen causes develop) is contingent.

A fire marshal checking for unsafe conditions is a preventive measure. Insurance to cover losses if fire occurs anyway is a contingent measure. Finding the cause of the customer's perpetually late shipments so that they don't recur is a corrective measure. Giving the customer free delivery and credit to ease current unhappiness is an adaptive action.

The keys to problem solving involve a rigorous separation of cause and effect.

Finding cause and not blame

The response to being told of a problem is too often, "Who did that?" or "Whose fault is that?" or

Timesaver
There is no greater waste of time than acting precipitously and prematurely. Invest the time to determine what kind of issue you are facing, since starting down the wrong road too fast can be calamitous.

"Who was responsible?" or even, "Heads will roll!"
The weakness with these reactions is that they tend
to freeze and dry up any sources of potential information that may help to solve the problem. Problem
solving is a search for cause, not a hunt for blame.
The more blame is sought—especially early in the
process—the more the true cause will tend to be
hidden and deliberately obscured.

Problems generally appear in this configuration:

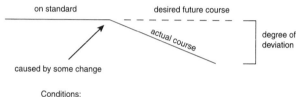

Conditions:
1. Deviation of actual from desired course.
2. Cause is unknown.
3. Deviation is serious enough to concern us.

Sometimes the decline is gradual, sometimes
precipitous. But the immediate concern should be
twofold: ameliorate the current effects and find the
cause in order to remove the problem itself. While
the symptoms may be moderated with adaptive
actions (a bucket under the leak, credit to the customer, hiring a temporary worker), the problem will
remain, with all its attendant expenses, until the
cause is found and removed (hole in the roof, incorrect addresses, insufficient staffing).

These are the steps in effective problem solving
and the successful pursuit of causes:

Identification

■ State the actual deviation from the standard
■ Describe the parameters

Hypothesis
- Identify distinctions of the problem area
- Identify changes affecting those distinctions
- Develop probable causes from the changes

Validation
- Test the probable causes on paper
- Test the most probable cause in reality

It's vitally important to take the time to describe the situation carefully before taking action. Although this seems like a waste of valuable time, it's actually a wise investment since the description prevents inappropriate actions later, which are always expensive and time-consuming, and can't be "undone."

Identification: State the actual deviation from standard

A problem statement should have two basic components, with some modifiers, as needed. The components are the problem and the deviation. For example: Customer shipments are late in the northeast region. The object is "customer shipments," the defect is "late," and we've specified further that it's only in one region that we know of.

The problem statement allows you and your team the luxury of focusing on a common, agreed-upon deviation from standard, without premature guessing as to cause, assessment of blame, or suggestions for arbitrary actions. We may know, for example, that customers are getting free shipping credits and we're sending emergency replacements by overnight courier, but we now have to find out why this is happening so that we can eliminate the problem and the expensive adaptive actions we're forced to take for the moment. (Adaptive and contingent actions are almost always more expensive, unwieldy, and inefficient than corrective and preventive actions.)

Bright Idea
Use inclusive pronouns and phrasing, e.g., "We have a problem, let's work together on it." This will tend to involve everyone in the pursuit, rather than create stonewalling by saying, "I want to know which one of you allowed this to happen."

Unofficially...
Most problems
are actually
made worse by
premature
attempts to jump
to action. Few
problems are
fatal. It's more
important to
locate accurate
information
sources than it is
to try to fix
something you
don't yet under-
stand. This is
particularly true
of "people
problems."

Note that we want to begin with a problem state-ment at the level of unknown cause. In other words, we don't know why shipments are late in the north-east. If the original report said "too many calls on the service lines to handle within standards," and we asked, "Do we know why?" the response would be, "Yes, we are getting customer complaints in higher than normal numbers." If we asked, "Do we know the cause of the complaints?" we'd be told, "Yes, shipments are late reaching customers in the north-east." If we asked, "Do we know why the shipments are late?" we'd be told, "No." We are now at the point where we have to search for cause.

Searching for cause is often a "stair step" method as described above, which may look like this:

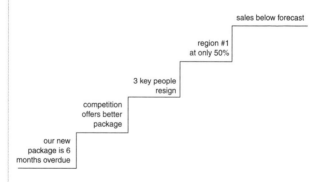

We know the cause down to the point of why our own plan hasn't been finalized and is so late. We have to pursue cause (or action) at that level. It does no good in the long-term to try to raise the quotas of the other regions, or to attempt to lure the three customers back. Similarly, if we knew that late cus-tomer shipments were being caused by a union slowdown in that region, we should take action at that level. But for the sake of our example, we don't know the cause of those late shipments. We do know that some managers have started to suggest that the trucker's union has sabotaged the shipments, others are pointing a finger at the relatively new shipping manager, and still others, who never wanted to change shippers, feel the new one isn't as reliable as the one who lost the contract a few months ago. But we simply don't know who is right, though the union has a reputation of doing such things before.

Identification: Describe the parameters

To quickly get our arms around the problem, we want to describe the conditions under which it is occurring and the conditions under which it is not occurring. This allows us to draw tight boundaries around the problem, enabling us to quickly find distinctions from which we can hypothesize the cause. If the problem is occurring under certain conditions and within certain parameters, then under what conditions and within which parameters might it be occurring but, in fact, is not? The sharper the comparison, the tighter the boundary and the easier it is to isolate causes.

Timesaver
It may be counterintuitive at first glance, but finding out where something is not occurring is just as important in determining the scope of the problem as is delineating where the problem is occurring.

By asking questions in just four areas—almost as a good newspaper reporter or detective might do— we can isolate the problem conditions quickly:

What is the object or person that's below standard?

Customer shipments.

What could be a closely related person or object below standard but is not in this instance?

Customer product quality, service calls, telephone service.

What is the deviation?

Lateness.

What could be the deviation with the shipments, but is not?

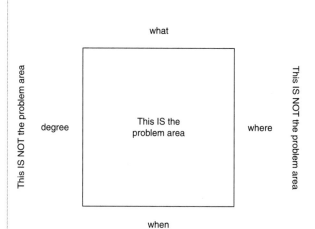

Damaged product, lost product, no shipments at all.

Where is this occurring?

Northeast region.

Where might this also occur but, in fact, is not?

Our other four regions: southeast, central, northwest, southwest.

When was the problem first noticed?

Complaints began coming in at 8 a.m. this morning regarding yesterday's shipments.

When might the problem have been first noticed, but was not?

There were no calls of this nature before 8 a.m. this morning, when the call lines opened, and no late product deliveries prior to yesterday.

What's the degree of lateness?

About two-thirds of all of our retailers in the region are reporting delays ranging from half a day to no delivery at all.

What could be the degree of lateness but is not?

Not all retailers have complained yet, and not all deliveries are late or missing.

What's the trend?

It seems to be growing worse as the morning progresses and more dealers are calling.

What could be the trend but is not at this point?

It's not stabilizing and it's certainly not getting any better.

We have not completed our identification of the problem. The boundary around the "is" and "is not" conditions and parameters is relatively tightly drawn: One region, lateness, but undamaged goods, began with yesterday's deliveries, and is apparently getting worse as more retailers discover the problem. We're not ready to hypothesize about the cause.

Hypothesis: Identify distinctions of the problem area

Since we're able to isolate the problem area from other, related areas, any distinctions about the former are quite relevant in trying to identify the most probable cause of the problem. We are interested only in distinctions about the "is" areas, since distinctions of the "is not" areas are irrelevant and misleading. Note that distinctions must be entirely true of the "is" areas and must be entirely untrue of the "is not" areas. If they "cross the border" at all, they are not true distinctions.

Once again, we'll simply ask a series of questions to find out what, if any, distinctions exist. (Note that distinctions will usually come from nouns, timing, and things, for example, "northeast region" or "yesterday," rather than adjectives and degrees, for example, "more or less," "stable," etc.)

What is distinct about customer shipments versus product quality, telephone response, or service calls?

Unofficially...
The ability to question crisply and rapidly is a key asset for power managers, yet not a skill set necessarily taught in school or on the job. Develop this ability, even if it requires you to make a reference list of important questions for referral.

They involve truck transport.

What is distinct about lateness versus damaged product, lost product, or no shipments at all?

No clear distinctions, just a particular kind of deviation.

What is distinctive about the northeast region compared to the other five regions?

It has much higher levels of truck transport, since it is the most compact area.

It has a much higher percentage of chain stores and fewer independent retailers than other regions, due to population density.

It has the highest volume, normally, of any region.

It has a new distribution manager, on the job for only one month, and hired from a competitor.

What is distinct about 8 a.m. this morning and yesterday, as compared to any prior time?

The call lines open at 8 a.m., so late shipments probably wouldn't have been reported prior to that.

Yesterday was the first time that the truckers' union announced that they may not approve the new contract offer from the company.

Yesterday was the first day that the new computer software was in use for national distribution.

What is distinctive about the degree of lateness or the trends, as compared to what they might be but aren't?

These are merely differences of degree with no clear distinctions.

We have now concluded the first part of our hypotheses by identifying distinctions of the "is" areas. We're now ready to further filter and refine our search for cause.

Hypothesis: Identify changes affecting those distinctions

For something that was operating on standard to have departed from that standard, there must have

Watch Out!
Don't fall prey to "we don't have time for that" as you try to isolate the information relevant to the problem. People will be supporting their "pet" causes (or targets of blame) and have nothing to lose by suggesting actions that you'll have to take responsibility for later.

been some change(s) involved. If nothing had changed, the performance wouldn't have deviated. We have to confine ourselves to relevant changes. We've done this by describing the conditions under which the problem is occurring, and then found distinctions about that area. Now we can focus strictly on those changes that may have some affect on those distinctions.

Let's take another look at our distinctions, and see what, if anything, has changed in or around them. (Note that distinctions will usually come from nouns, timing, and things, for example, "northeast region" or "yesterday," rather than adjectives and degrees, for example, "more or less," "stable," etc. Distinctions in time are also always changes. If something is distinct now as compared to some time ago in chronology, then something has changed, by definition.)

What is distinctive about lateness versus damaged product, lost product, or no shipments at all?

No clear distinctions, just a particular kind of deviation.

Changes: There are no changes to pursue, since there are no clear distinctions.

What is distinctive about the northeast region compared to the other five regions?

It has much higher levels of truck transport, since it is the most compact area.

What has changed in, about, or around that truck transport?

We have a new national shipper that took over 3 months ago.

The shipper's union just announced that it is unhappy with the latest offer.

It has a much higher percentage of chain stores and fewer independent retailers than other regions, due to population density.

What has changed in, around, or about those chain stores?

No known changes.

It has the highest volume, normally, of any region.

What's changed in, around, or about that volume?

No known changes.

Timesaver
These questions are obviously repetitive and the situation may not require all of them every time. They are presented here to show the entire process at work. Use your judgment on the job as to how many are required to get tight descriptions and clear possible causes.

It has a new distribution manager, on the job for only one month, and hired from a competitor.

What has changed in, around, or about that new manager?

That is a change in and of itself. He began only last month.

What is distinct about 8 a.m. this morning and yesterday, as compared to any time prior?

The call lines open at 8 a.m., so late shipments probably wouldn't have been reported prior to that.

What has changed in, around, or about the call lines opening at 8 a.m.?

No known changes.

Yesterday was the first day that the new computer software was in use for national distribution.

What has changed in, around, or about the new computer software?

That is a change, in and of itself.

What has changed in, around, or about the truckers' union announcements?

That is a change in and of itself, as of yesterday. Yesterday was the first time that the truckers' union announced that they may not approve the new contract offer from the company.

What is distinct about the degree of lateness or the trends, as compared to what they might be but aren't?

These are merely differences of degree with no clear distinctions.

Changes: There are no changes to pursue, since there are no clear distinctions.

Hypothesis: Develop possible causes from the changes

It's now time to determine how, if at all, the relevant changes could have caused the problem. Let's list our changes and hypothesize the relationships:

- The new shipper has somehow delayed shipments in not making a smooth transition from our former shipper, or in some other error.
- The new shipper's labor union is trying to make a point by deliberately delaying shipments.
- The new distribution manager made some errors in scheduling or truck allocation, which have resulted in delays.
- The new computer software has a glitch in it associated with the northeast region.

These possible causes—only four in all—are high-quality avenues to pursue because they are based only on relevant change emanating from distinctions about the problem. But to pursue them all would be a waste of time and money, and would inevitably cause interpersonal disasters. So we now want to enter the testing part of the process.

Validation: Test the probable causes on paper

Each possible cause should be constructively tested against our description. That is, we should demand to know how the possible cause can explain why the problem is happening where it is *and* why it is not happening in other areas. Unless it can adequately explain both, with a minimum of assumptions, it can't be considered a probable cause.

Timesaver
When you are legitimately in an urgent situation trying to solve a problem, focus solely on those changes that have taken place immediately prior to the problem's occurrence. Changes that took place subsequently couldn't possibly be the cause of the problem, no matter how much people may claim otherwise.

- The new shipper has somehow delayed shipments in not making a smooth transition from our former shipper, or in some other error.

If this is the cause, then why is the problem only in the northeast? The shipper is used nationwide. And why is it happening now? The shipper has been doing just fine for the first three months after the changeover.

- The new shipper's labor union is trying to make a point by deliberately delaying shipments.

If this is the cause, then why isn't the union doing it all over the country? Why is it a localized action? And how is the union able to react so rapidly? The new offer was just released yesterday. Would they have been able to delay shipments immediately, and in such large numbers?

- The new distribution manager made some errors in scheduling or truck allocation, which have resulted in delays.

If this is the cause, it would explain why the problem is only in his area. But he's been on the job for a month. After operating well for a month, why has he made such a glaring mistake all of a sudden?

- The new computer software has a glitch in it associated with the northeast region.

If this is the cause, it would explain why the problem is limited to the northeast region, and why it occurred yesterday, the first day after the new software was controlling distribution schedules. It would also explain why the complaints are increasing this morning, as the extent of the problem becomes known. It also means that if we don't do something immediately, today's shipments will suffer the same fate.

From this analysis, it would appear that the new computer program is the most probable cause, at least insofar as our paper test is concerned. Now we have to test it in reality as our final step.

Validation: Test the most probable cause in reality

We now get our programmers on the problem to actually run a test of northeast region scheduling. What they find is that a misplaced line of code has pushed all deliveries back by at least 6 hours, meaning that the entire "just in time" philosophy has been compromised. It is easily fixed.

In such cases, the more common response would have been to accuse and threaten the union; to tell the shipper that the delays would be deducted from payments and that the contract was in jeopardy; to tell the distribution manager that he'd better shape up or he'd be back in the accounting office; or to run in circles while trying to deal with angry customers.

The search for information, on a methodical basis, can also lead to areas in which we are missing vital information. For example:

"Where is this occurring?"

"We aren't sure."

"Well, is it localized or national?"

"We haven't sorted that out yet."

"Well, get on it, because that will make a big difference in trying to isolate the relevant changes."

Solving the toughest problems—people problems

The process is effective with people issues, no less than mechanical, process, or procedural problems. However, some adjustments are required in the questioning to accurately reflect information about

Watch Out!
We operate on assumptions rather than information more times than we imagine. Trusted subordinates can often provide ideas and opinions that they pass off as fact and evidence. Learn to ask, "How do you know that?" and "Did you see that yourself?" as a normal response to assumptions.

people rather than about equipment. Those questions would look like this:

- Whose behavior are we concerned about?
- (Whose behavior could we be concerned about, but are not?)
- What is that behavior?
- (What could that behavior be, but is not?)
- Where is the behavior occurring?
- (Where could the behavior be occurring, but is not?)
- When was this behavior first noticed?
- (When could the behavior have been first noticed, but was not?)
- When in this person's job or career was the behavior first noticed?
- (When could the behavior have been first noticed, but was not?)
- What is the degree of the behavior?
- (What could be the degree, but is not?)
- What is the trend of the behavior?
- (What could be the trend, but is not?)

The distinctions, changes, and possible causes follow in sequence. With people, it is exceptionally critical to do as much analysis as possible on paper before confronting or even reacting in the real world. Even mild rebukes or casual comments can create lasting impressions and resentment.

Here's a potentially incendiary inquiry:

"John, was it my imagination, or did your performance decline during the last week when we were under pressure to get the work out?"

Here's a statement made after testing:

"John, my analysis is that you were unable to meet your normal quotas last week because your assistant was pulled away in midweek to help a newer person. Is that accurate?"

By using the structured questioning implicit in this system, you are forced to focus on observed behavior and factual evidence, not emotional reactions and personalities. For example, if three people come to you to complain about their supervisor, what is your reaction? If we use the first question: Whose behavior are we concerned about?, the only legitimate answer is: The three people sitting in your office complaining. After all, the deviation is the complaints (there should be none) and you've got three from the people sitting in front of you. The cause might be the supervisor, or it might be something entirely different, but to immediately pursue the supervisor as the culprit or villain would be inexcusable. The immediate pursuit should be to find out why the three individuals are really complaining— what's the cause—and what can be done about it.

Day 1 problems

Some problems aren't the result of obvious changes, because the problem has existed "from day one." In other words, the process, equipment, or person's performance has never been up to the standard created for it.

In this case, there are two steps:

1. Examine whether or not the standard is realistic to begin with. Ask these questions:

    ■ Was the standard ever reached before, in any other circumstances?

Unofficially...
Many complaints about management are actually the result of "transference." Poor working conditions, problems with equipment, a lack of resources, and other legitimate issues are often lumped together and blamed on poor management, which is sometimes true and sometimes not.

- Did a prototype or pilot reach the standard?
- Has the competition ever hit this standard?
- Were the assumptions that went into the standard validated?
- Have we come closer to the standard at some points than at others?

2. If the standard seems reasonable after step #1, then proceed through the process as normal, except do not pursue changes, because there won't be any, and hypothesize possible causes from the distinctions.

Day 1 deviations often occur in start-up situations, with the implementation of new technology or procedures, and with the introduction of new people. It's important to determine at the outset whether the standard is reasonable or if the performance is at fault. No amount of improved performance will meet unreasonable or unattainable standards.

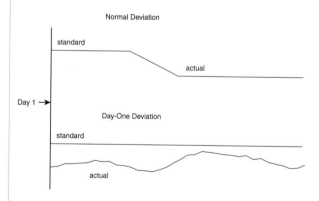

The art of problem solving

Problem solving is not, of course, simply a mechanistic scheme where you plug data into a system and pull out an informed resolution at the other end. As we've shown in the previous chapters, the human element is critical, including skills involving conflict resolution, influence, feedback, and other forms of communication.

However, as in most pursuits, there is both art and science in the act of problem solving, and you ignore either at your own risk. The methodical search for data that can be turned into information and, eventually, useful knowledge, is an interactive process involving your colleagues and subordinates. It's the manager's job to lead the way through opinion, emotions, and hunches to the facts of the case, and to make objective determinations based on those facts.

Every outstanding problem solver I've met has had this basic process at the ready. He or she may not have always been able to articulate it, but when you analyzed what was happening, the results always led in this direction. Those who solve problems "by gut" or "by instinct" were, in actuality, seldom correct much more than 25 percent of the time, which is a very poor efficiency rating.

Here are the overall keys to keep in mind, combining the art and science of problem solving:

- Never take action immediately, except in conditions of grave crisis (a fire is roaring toward volatile chemicals).

- Demand that fact be separated from opinion. ("How do you know that?" "What's the evidence?" "What actual behavior did you, personally, observe?")

- Arrange for two types of people to take part: those with firsthand knowledge and observations, and those who are fine analysts with critical thinking skills. (Sometimes people with great experience simply insist on doing what

Unofficially...
There is nothing wrong with experienced managers having intuition, "gut" reactions, and informed hunches. These should not be ignored or discarded, but should be put through the testing noted above to assure that the intuition can explain the empirical facts.

was done in the past, which may or may not be
relevant now.)

- Make sure you're working at a level of
  unknown cause. (If someone suggests that
  cause at that level is actually known, ask,
  "Would you bet your career on it?")

- Create as tight a description of the problem as
  possible, since all else will rely on that definition, including your testing.

- Make sure distinctions are true only of the
  problem area, and are completely untrue of all
  other areas.

- Find only relevant changes, affecting those distinctions. Changes that occurred subsequent to
  the problem's occurrence cannot possibly be
  relevant.

- Destructively test and destroy causes, until one
  explains the facts with a minimum of assumptions. If none do, go back and generate additional possible causes. If too many do, then
  your description of the problem isn't tight
  enough, because it's allowing almost anything
  to explain the facts.

- Validate on paper and in reality before taking
  action.

- Take adaptive actions to mitigate the effects of
  the problem, and to give you time to solve it.
  But you must find cause if you want to take the
  corrective action required to remove the problem in its entirely. (There may be occasions in
  which you want to make adaptive action permanent, because corrective action is simply too
  expensive or is impossible. If the corrective
  action to remove glare is moving the building

6 feet to the left, you may prefer the adaptive action of placing electronic shades along the western windows.)

Problem solving is a required, daily set of skills in organizational life. In times of increasing complexity, we know we will inevitably face unexpected problems. Consequently, we ought to have a methodology in place to deal with the issues in a timely and efficient manner. The system is available, and the skills readily learnable. What we need is the volition.

Just the facts

- Problem solving has a unique starting point, which is a search for an unknown cause.

- Search for cause and not blame if you want to inspire a free flow of information and ideas.

- The worst thing to do is to jump to immediate action without analyzing the facts.

- Adaptive actions should be used to ameliorate effects and calm unhappy customers, but corrective action is needed for resolution.

- Whenever people are involved—which is usually—act only on observed behavior and factual analysis, because action here cannot be "undone."

Timesaver
Consider organizing a "SWAT" team that is skilled in the methodology of problem solving, and can convene rapidly in cases of serious problems. Others can deal with adaptive actions while this team quickly finds the real cause.

Chapter 9

GET THE SCOOP ON...
Identifying the decision chain ▪ Separating
"musts" from "wants" ▪ Setting objectives
before finding alternatives ▪ Assessing risk
accurately ▪ Making balanced decisions

Making Sound Decisions

The third major management issue is that of making decisions. It is, perhaps, the most common. We make decisions every day, often unaware of the criteria we're applying to make them.

There should be three main components in any decision, and they should occur in this order:

- Objectives: Objectives are the outcomes to be achieved by the decision. If all of our critical objectives are met ("musts") and most of our desirable objectives are met ("wants"), the choice will have been successful. But we can't make that choice without knowing the port to which we're sailing.

- Alternatives: Alternatives are the options available to us to meet our objectives. They may be few or many, and there are usually many more than we suspect (or are ordinarily willing to consider). These are the routes available to reach our port, but they don't all offer the same speed, efficiency, or comfort.

183

■ Risks: Risks are those threats attendant to
   nearly any alternative which may undermine
   the most attractive of options. Few paths are
   risk free. These are the threats posed by the
   conditions surrounding any given alternative,
   some of which are unique to certain paths and
   some of which may occur no matter what path
   is chosen.

The starting point, then, for a decision, is the
realization that we must choose a course of action to
achieve some future result. That could be as minor
as where to place a piece of furniture, or as major as
the selection of the servicing team for our largest
client. It could be as short-term as where to hold a
staffing meeting for the next hour, or as long-term
as whom to promote to manage the field force.
Nevertheless, the decision-making process remains
the same.

Avoiding and escaping from the decision traps

One of the difficulties in effective decision making
is that our parameters for making the decision,
rather than the components listed above, are often
framed by incorrect criteria. We need to recognize
these and to refuse to allow them to dictate our decisions.

Following the rut

We often simply choose what's always been done. In
other words, we order supplies from the same ven-
dor, turn to the same consultant, hold the conference in the same facility, and promote the highest
performer in a function to manager of the function.
We do so simply because those routes have always

worked out pretty well in the past. However, always doing what we've done is guaranteed to never "raise the bar," as described in Chapter 7.

■ The best way to escape this rut is to ask, "Why are we choosing this course of action? Should we step back and at least examine what alternatives are open to us?"

Listening to the last or loudest voice

When we don't fully understand the issues (they may be too technical or too removed from our everyday focus), we tend to rely on others for information and opinion. However, we also may have no strong favorite path and be unable to see a clearly superior alternative. In that case, we may just listen to the last person or the loudest person who captured our attention. This is dangerous because not being intimate with the issue can spell disaster if our choice is based on little more than accident, volume, or sequence.

■ When you're in unfamiliar, uninteresting, or conflicting territory, always talk to all key players at least twice, providing an opportunity to "bounce back" ideas and choices heard subsequent to the first conversation. This allows for more objective feedback and rational decision making. Group meetings with uninhibited feedback are also good approaches.

Permitting a single factor to turn the tide

Some courses of action offer so much value and attractiveness that we find it hard to even consider anything further. We are enticed by the allure of an option that the union will support, costs nothing in capital investment, utilizes existing resources, and

Watch Out!
There is a tendency to automatically accept an alternative proposed by a superior, even if it's clearly an inappropriate course of action. To avoid being "dragged under," suggest that the team explore other alternatives just to ensure that a comprehensive analysis can be demonstrated to other parties.

turns iron into gold in the bargain. Damn the tor-pedoes, full speed ahead. How bad could the conse-quences be?

Conversely, we often run scared immediately when a particular kind of threat appears. No matter how favorable the course of action, having to fight finance, retrain the support staff, or close an office simply can't be entertained. This car may look and run great, but I don't want to have to read the owner's manual.

- In both situations, we need to take a holistic view of the situation. In the first case we have to ask, "What can go wrong? This is simply too good to be true. What may be waiting to thrash us?" In the second case, the response should be, "Why are we so scared of this? Could this be like the *Wizard of Oz?* Maybe we should look behind the curtain."

Lousing up the timing

In both comedy and athletics—two very difficult pursuits—the experts will tell you that "it's all about timing." The same holds true for decisions. Sometimes we feel that we're under pressure to act, or that our very competence will be judged by speed, and we dash to make the decision as rapidly as possible, often without proper information, debate, and analysis. Conversely, we sometimes want to demonstrate that we are truly analytic, not rash in judgment, and we examine every aspect and debate every curve to the point that we move nowhere, or when we do move the original conditions have changed and our analysis and decision are no longer relevant.

- Early in your determination that action is required, estimate the "window of opportunity," and ensure that your decision is made within it. That will probably give you more time than you think you had while still highlighting the date beyond which the decision will go sour.

Failing to stay the course

A decision is simply that: a conceptual agreement to proceed along a certain course. However, decisions entail gaining support for the implementation, putting actions in place to ensure success and to mitigate risk, monitoring progress, checking on assumptions that were made, and validating results. This might not be as important when you're assigning desk space, but it becomes rather vital when you're assigning customer support personnel. Most decisions do not fail in their conceptualization; they fail in their implementation.

- As you proceed in the decision-making process, assign accountability—to yourself as well as to others—for each key component of the decision and its implementation. If you have to retrain staff, determine who in human resources or among your own staff will be responsible, when it will happen, and who will monitor it. Accountability has a wonderful way of making decisions highly tangible.

The decision chain

Decisions are seldom made in splendid isolation. They tend to come in "chains," meaning that the decision you're now making is the result of some prior one, and that subsequent ones will be made as a result of this one. We're not talking about implementation steps here, but rather a true sequence of linear decisions.

Timesaver
If your staff meetings regularly make decisions, have a format preprinted on the easel or in the agenda, so that objectives, alternatives, and risk must all be properly examined every time. Don't allow the decision-making process to deviate, and you won't have to revisit all of those poorly made decisions later.

In the graphic below, our "chain" starts with a generalized need for transportation, and winds up with a specific list of sports cars. Although some of the intermittent stops may have been assumed, those decisions were nonetheless made, either implicitly or explicitly. Note that the lower we go in the decision chain, the more limited the options (Porsches and Ferraris), while the higher we go in the chain, the broader the options (trains, planes, bikes).

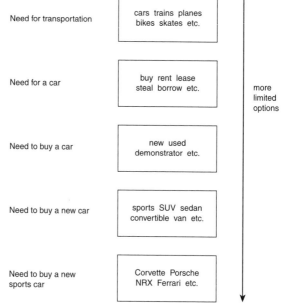

Watch Out!
You will not always be at the appropriate level of the decision, although you may assume so. Most people who complain that "We had to make the best of a bad situation," are actually failing to raise the level of the decision to a point where they have a fair chance of success.

We seldom enter a decision chain at the beginning or at the end, and it's important to understand where we are because we may choose to consciously raise or lower the level of the decision.

Here's the decision chain in a typical business setting:

In this actual client example, accounting had asked line management to choose the rental car company for the next fiscal year, so that the best financial deal could be arranged. The accounting department negotiated a favorable corporate rate, and the company chosen (Avis, for the past 2 years) provided generous frequent flyer points for the airline affiliations of key company employees.

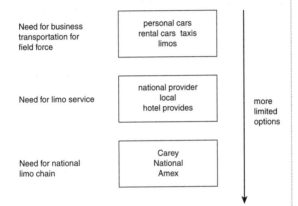

In the best years, management put a team together to quickly choose among Hertz, Avis, and National, using parameters such as the number of sites, insurance provisions, variety of vehicles, and avoidance of lines and delays at airports. However, one year a new manager asked an interesting question: "Why are we making this decision?" He reasoned that, if the need were for field force transportation in major cities, there would be alternatives other than rental cars—which were a major cost, no matter how favorable the rates—that ought to be at least considered.

The chain you see above was what resulted, and it turned out that Carey Limousine could pick field personnel up at airports, deliver them to

Bright Idea
Examine all of your "routine" decisions (for example, handling overtime, responding to customer complaints, choosing a task force) and ask yourself if you're stuck at the wrong level. In at least some cases, you may be able to take a fresh, new look in the future.

appointments, and either wait or return later for pickup at cheaper rates than massive rental car use. Moreover, the field people no longer had to worry about getting lost, parking, flat tires, or the extra airport time required to pick up and return rental cars to increasingly more remote lots. There was actually a huge productivity gain, not to mention the morale gain from allowing key people to be chauffeured, during which time they could safely call for messages from their cell phones, take notes, rearrange their schedules, and even work on their computers.

These types of savings, efficiencies, and improvements are readily available if we're willing to consciously examine where we are in the decision chain. In general, we should raise the level of the decision (to higher points in the chain) to broaden our potential options, and lower the level of the decision to narrow our potential options. (There are clearly times when we should be focused on choosing a sales manager and not on restructuring the field force one more time.) This ability to move about the chain is almost always an option for the decision maker, but all too often we feel relegated to the level of the decision that we find ourselves facing. (Note that the level is not hierarchical. Frequently, managers at too high a level are making decisions too far down the chain, for example. The appropriate point in the chain varies more with the nature of the issue than it does with one's rank.)

Establishing objectives

There are three components to establishing objectives, which constitute the "destination" for any given decision:

- Establishing the decision statement.
- Identifying resource restraints and expected results.
- Establishing "musts" and "wants."

The decision statement is simply a guide for the ensuing analysis. It consists of the goal to be attained and the means to get to it at whatever level of the chain you choose to act. "To buy a new car" is sufficient. There's nothing wrong with "To buy a new Ford," except that you'll notice the more modifiers you add, the more you limit your options, and the further down the chain you find yourself. For example, "To buy a new, red Ford Expedition SUV from a dealer in downtown Toledo" doesn't leave you with many options. In this case, the decision is already made simply through the constraints imposed by the decision statement!

So, in most cases it's wiser to be pithy. Our example will be:

To choose a new facilities manager.

Decision statements are simple, but they do provide two important focal points:

- They determine what level of the decision chain you choose to enter.
- They enable all members of the groups contributing to the decision to have a common focus, even if geographically remote or infrequently visited.

Identifying resource restraints and expected results

No decision is made in the best of all possible worlds in which time, money, staffing, and latitude for error are all in infinite supply. Consequently, we have to "get our arms around" the decision in terms of understanding what general parameters exist.

Moneysaver
Find out what your restraints are early in the process. Managers tend to go over budget because they promote an alternative that is attractive irrespective of its cost and the resources available to fund it.

Resource restraints are the limitations that we all have to live with. They usually include:

- Investment dollars or budget.
- People, staffing, and head count.
- Time.
- Support and sponsorship.
- Assets, equipment, and facilities.

Results expectations are the general desires that people who own the decision wish to see as outcomes. They usually include:

- Financial return (feturn on investment, assets, equity, sales, etc.).
- Safety.
- Reputation or image.
- Comfort or aesthetics.
- Morale, retention, and people development.
- Consumer perception, market share, and growth.

Resources and results should be gathered in the form of a "laundry list" from all contributing parties, without critique, analysis, or debate. For our prospective new hire, these elements might look like this:

Resource restraints:

- Total compensation package not to exceed $85,000.
- Minimal time in learning phase—needs to "hit the ground running."
- Does not require large staff.
- Can work with current computer system and support.

- Acceptable to three key colleagues who will depend upon him.

Results expectations:

- Will bring heightened level of professionalism to the job.

- Will take initiative to improve productivity and responsiveness.

- Can begin immediately upon selection.

- Can attract, retain, and develop key talent for department.

- Will be a strong contributor to overall management team.

We'll keep this brief for our example, but we now have established the decision we're trying to make, as well as the resources to be conserved and the results to be maximized. Note that the most successful of decisions will always have saved precious resources on the input side, while exploiting the results on the output side. Therefore, every decision is really about some form of return on investment (ROI).

Establishing "musts" and "wants"

From the list of resources to be conserved and results to be maximized we now have to set some priorities. Every decision has objectives that are critical to the success of the decision. If they are not met, the decision fails. These are "musts."

For example, if your resource constraint in buying a home is a maximum mortgage payment of $2,500 per month, but you nevertheless purchase a home with a monthly payment of $4,000, you will fail—go bankrupt—unless you find additional resources. The quality of the outcome is otherwise endangered.

Watch Out!
Beware of arbitrary requirements, especially with people, such as "5 years of experience." That could simply result in 5 poor years. Ask what results you expect, not what tasks have been accomplished. Many people have the exact same year of experience 20 times over, which is not a sterling characteristic.

Other objectives are desirable in varying degrees. For example, air-conditioning might be desired, but isn't critical because the climate seldom gets too hot. A three-car garage might be nice, if it's available, but its absence wouldn't detract very much and its presence would be a minimal advantage, since you only have two cars.

For an objective to be a "must," it has to meet three criteria:

- Mandatory: The objective must be critical to the success of the decision, meaning that if it is not met, the decision fails.

- Measurable: We have to know whether the objective is met or not, so some measure must be attached. It could be quantifiable (for example, a return of 10 percent), binary (access to a labor pool is present or it isn't), or subjective (comfort will be decided by your spouse, who will be the primary driver of the car).

- Realistic: The objective has to be reasonably attainable for it to be considered a must. A criterion of 100 miles per gallon isn't reasonable, nor is "sales of $3 million in the first month" for most new hires.

Objectives that are not "musts," in that they do not meet these three criteria, are "wants." We weigh the wants to indicate relative importance. Since they are not critical, and their presence or absence will not automatically dictate a decision, we need to know which are more desirable than others. Any relative scale will work, and we'll use 10 (high) to 1 (low) for our example.

Note that there should be relatively few "musts" in any decision because, by definition, few objectives will meet all three criteria. If there are too many

Bright Idea
If you have too many "musts," for example, over a dozen or so, you are probably not going to find any alternative that can meet them all. Be very strict on the "musts" and reject any that don't strictly meet the criteria. This will speed the process later on.

"musts," the chances are that utopian conditions are sought which no alternative will meet. However, if there are no "musts," then almost any alternative will have to be considered, which isn't very practical. For the purposes of our example to choose a new facilities manager:

Musts:

- Total compensation not to exceed $85,000
- Successful experience in similar position elsewhere
- Passes screen with colleagues in marketing, sales, and operations
- Can begin within 30 days of our offer

Wants:	Weight
Compensation level below $85,000	10
Potential for advancement within 5 years	8
Has worked with small staffs	6
Familiarity with our computer systems	5
Well respected within business community in general	5
Can begin as soon as possible	3
Has contacts which he can recruit and bolster talent here	2

Timesaver
To arrive at "musts" quickly, examine resource constraints and ask what must not be exceeded at any cost. Then, see if "inverting" them into wants makes sense, for example, if the "must" is "cannot use more than twenty staff members," the want may be to "use minimal number of staff members."

You might have chosen other examples, which is why decisions rely on the judgment and preferences of those who "own" them and have to live with the outcomes. You can see that the "musts" often "invert" into wants—in other words, the "must" of $85,000 maximum compensation becomes a highly desired want of "compensation below $85,000." The "must" of "beginning within 30 days" becomes a much lower desired want of "begin as soon as possible" (since 30 days won't make all that much of a difference).

In our example, the potential for advancement is a relatively high desire, but it is not essential for an otherwise qualified candidate. As the "owner" of this decision, that is my assessment. You, or our boss, may make a different judgment.

We have not yet established the objectives—the criteria or parameters—against which alternatives will be measured.

Generating and evaluating alternatives

Sometimes alternatives are obvious, sometimes not. We seldom bother to investigate thoroughly all the sources available to us. However, one thing we should always try to avoid where possible is a binary (yes/no, do it/don't do it) type of decision.

For example, "Should we go to the mountains or to the beach" is a binary decision statement. There are only two general alternatives permitted. Similarly, "should we hire from outside or promote from within," or "do we use this ad campaign or not" are binary situations. By moving up the decision chain, and asking *why* we are making the decision, we may arrive at a better set of alternatives, guided by a broader decision statement:

- To choose a vacation site
- To find a replacement for the facilities manager position
- To choose a marketing campaign

Generating alternatives

As cited above, we are much too quick to select alternatives merely because we've always selected them in the past. Even when we are selecting three options to choose among, it may not be good enough if there are dozens of other options that ought to be considered. Unlike "must" objectives, the more alternatives considered the better. The objectives will do a good job of weeding them out or putting priorities on them, and subsequent risk considerations will wash out still more. But this is the time to be free-wheeling and creative.

Here is a checklist of sources from which to generate alternatives. It's not a bad idea to use this or something similar tailored to your circumstances at meetings to ensure that you've exhausted all possibilities for alternatives.

- Experience: What have you done before, successfully or unsuccessfully (conditions might have changed).

- Competition and others: What's been done on the "outside" in similar circumstances?

- Customers and employees: Ask those who are closest to the business and the usage.

- Creativity and innovation: Think "outside of the box" and try to raise the bar.

- Research and development: Breakthroughs in thinking or products may provide alternatives.

- Literature and the media: There might be ideas floating around that don't relate to your need until you put them together.

- Recombinations: Combining ideas or existing alternatives often results in a new option.

- Serendipity: Don't rule an option out simply because its "pedigree" isn't solid or it came from an unlikely source.

- Trade and professional associations: Search out what the industry and marketplace are saying.

- Consultants: You often need someone whose nose is not pressed against the same glass that yours is.

Generate a laundry list of alternatives. The unlikely or unsubstantive will no doubt be washed away by the objectives you've set.

Evaluating alternatives

Alternatives are first evaluated against the "must" objectives, because if these aren't satisfied, then the alternative, by definition, fails. This is a "destructive" test, in that we're not trying to support the alternatives, but instead are exposing them to a "go/no go" set of criteria. An alternative either passes or fails.

Suppose we have three candidates from our generating step with these characteristics:

- Must #1: Total compensation not to exceed $85,000

  1. $84,000

  2. $76,000

  3. $74,000

- Must #2: Successful experience in similar position elsewhere

  1. Yes, 4 years

  2. Yes, 1 year

  3. Yes, 2 years

- Must #3: Passes screen with colleagues in marketing, sales, and operations

  1. Approved by all

  2. Approved by all

  3. Approved by all

- Must #4: Can begin within 30 days of our offer

  1. Available in 10 days

  2. Available in 90 days

  3. Available in 30 days

Unofficially...
People will often have "pet" alternatives that they support for personal reasons. By establishing an objective list of "musts" you can quickly "depoliticize" and remove the emotions from the process without having to directly attack or undermine the other party's private agenda.

In the example above, candidate #2 would be eliminated on "must" #4, because the candidate is simply not available in time. No matter how well the other "musts" are met, this one is not, and the decision is endangered. (We could change the time frame if we somehow developed additional leeway to go without a department head, but changing objectives to suit an alternative is backwards and often the result of trying to force-fit a favorite rather than truly meet needs.) While candidate #3 barely meets the final must of 30 days, it is nonetheless met and that candidate stays in contention.

We'll go on with the two remaining candidates. We're going to give each a score, again on a 10 (high) to 1 (low) scale, as to how well the wants are met. We'll then multiply the score times the weight to arrive at a weighted score, indicating approximate desirability in terms of how well our wants are met.

Watch Out!
Don't change musts because you want an alternative to continue in the process without being eliminated. If you change musts without changing the resources or results they are protecting, then you might as well declare bankruptcy and get on with it.

Wants:	Weight
Compensation level below $85,000	10
(1) $84,000	(5x10=50)
(3) $74,000	(10x10=100)
Potential for advancement within 5 years	8
(1) Very high, 4 years of experience	(10x8=80)
(3) Pretty good, 2 years of experience	(7x8=56)
Has worked with small staffs	6
(1) Current staff is same size as ours	(7x6=42)
(3) Current staff is even smaller than ours	(10x6=60)
Familiarity with our computer systems	5
(1) Currently uses same system	(10x5=50)
(3) Currently uses same system	(10x5=50)
Well respected within business community in general	5
(1) Heads trade association committees	(10x5=50)
(3) Unknown outside of present employer	(2x5=10)

Watch Out!
Don't fall in love with the candidate or alternative that seems to best meet your musts and wants. Strong attraction often has strong risks. Always perform a risk assessment prior to making any commitments.

Can begin as soon as possible	3
(1) Can begin in 10 days	(10x3=30)
(3) Can begin in 30 days	(1x10=10)
Has contacts which can be used to recruit and bolster talent here	2
(1) Many contacts through industry activities	(10x2=20)
(3) Contacts solely within present employer	(1x2=2)

The total weighted scores at this point are:

- Candidate #1: 322
- Candidate #3: 288

Candidate #3 has finished about 15 percent lower than candidate #1. But we can't move forward just yet. We still have to see what risks may be present in either option.

Assessing risk

Risk is assessed along two parameters:

- Probability: What is the likelihood of a given event occurring?

- Seriousness: What is the impact or gravity if, indeed, that event occurs?

Probability and seriousness are not equal. For example, if I choose to walk to work on an icy day, the probability of my slipping and falling may be relatively high, but the seriousness of the fall is relatively low—a skinned knee or a wet bottom. But if I choose to drive to work (another alternative), the probability of an accident may be relatively low, but the seriousness is relatively high—personal injury and/or damage to the car. Moreover, I can control my own walking, but I can't control other people's driving. Hence, seriousness always has a greater overall impact than probability.

If something has a very high probability—likely to occur—and a very high seriousness—likely to be very adverse—it's a good idea to give that alternative a wide berth.

Here is an example of risks posed by our two candidates. We'll simply use high, medium, and low to denote risk:

Candidate #1:

- If trade association activities grow, could detract from time on the job. (P=high, S=low)

- If another job is offered before we can provide advancement here, may leave to more attractive position. (P=medium, S=high)

- If requires more compensation in the short term, will exceed our policies and budget. (P=low, S=high)

Candidate #3:

- If not actually available as planned, will exceed our 30-day must requirement, and will not be a part of strategic planning sessions. (P=medium, S=high)

- If has to make inroads in professional community to attract talent, may detract from learning curve here. (P=high, S=medium)

Bright Idea
When subordinates immediately back an alternative and ask for your support, request a risk evaluation immediately. Point out that nothing is perfect, and if they can't come up with the drawbacks, then they've been blinded by the attraction. This takes you out of the role of being the naysayer.

Candidate #1 has three attendant risks that we believe we can manage with an effective employment contract, inclusion in the succession planning system, and effective time management. Candidate #3 presents a risk we can't control (potential unavailability) and another which cannot be ameliorated easily.

On balance, our choice will be candidate #1. Even though more expensive, that candidate is still within our compensation "must" and offers higher desirability with fewer attendant risks.

Note that risks often arise from barely met "musts," in this case the 30-day criterion. The risk step thus enables the decision maker to make adjustments for "must" criteria that may be endangered even though they are met at first glance. The risk evaluation may use any measurement criteria, but we advise against numbers because multiplying seriousness times risk does not provide a useful measure. These two are independent variables, and should be assessed that way.

Best balanced choice

We emerge from this process with the "best balanced choice," which simply means the alternative that meets "musts," satisfies "wants" to an acceptable degree, and provides manageable and acceptable risks. Some of us might choose maximum benefit in the face of strong risk, others may choose minimal risk and sacrifice benefit. The key is to realize that the "balance" is ours, and that the highest score is not automatically the best choice.

The process we have walked through looks like the graphic on the following page.

In this decision-making "funnel," the decision statement sets the boundaries from which we will generate alternatives. The "filters" of "musts," "wants," and risks will eliminate poorly performing alternatives (does not meet a "must," poorly meets "wants," presents too high a risk). The resultant alternative represents the balance of benefit and risk that we (or our company) are willing to accept.

Bright Idea
Ask your team members where you are in the "funnel" process. It's important to ensure that everyone is at the same point, avoiding some people examining risk while others are still generating alternatives.

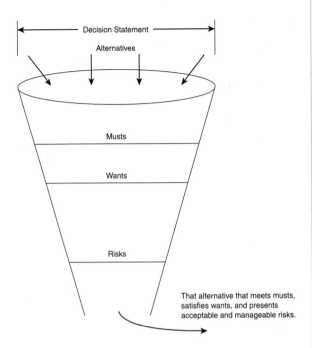

That alternative that meets musts, satisfies wants, and presents acceptable and manageable risks.

This is a process designed to reduce emotionalism and prevent arbitrary leaps onto the "bandwagon." It can be used in shortcuts (making quick assessments against "musts" and/or quickly examine risks) or at length for important decisions. While preserving the manager's judgement and inclinations, it also systematizes the process so that fair hearings and objective determinations can be clearly demonstrated.

Just the facts

- Decisions require both judgment and factual analysis, but what is usually missing is the means to do the latter.
- Every decision of consequence has "musts," the meeting of which represents success.

- Not all desires are equal, so "wants" must be weighted accordingly.

- Risk is the least examined element in decision making, and must be a mandatory part of the process, but cannot be performed until the "surviving" alternatives are known.

- In cases of conflicts about judgment, the owner of the decision—the person with the most at stake, win or lose—must have the final word.

Chapter 10

GET THE SCOOP ON...
Creating a practical implementation plan ▪
Identifying potential problems ▪ Protecting
plans comprehensively ▪ Establishing
contingencies ▪ Setting the "triggers" to
launch further actions

Protecting Any Plan

The fourth and last common management issue is planning, which often gets both a bad name and short shrift. "Let's establish a plan" is a phrase thrown around with the same abandon as "Of course your secret is safe with me," and carries about the same level of credibility. And "planning" is seldom really planning at all, but merely just a set of disjointed and undisciplined actions which eventually evanesce.

Think about how many "5-year plans" or even "annual plans" that not only aren't met, but aren't even monitored. In many organizations, "a number isn't really a number," meaning that plans can always be changed to compensate for the underperformers, rather than focus on why they underperformed! Planning should be about implementing and protecting initiatives, programs, and decisions in a comprehensive, methodical manner. And it is this approach that we will address here.

The plan may be the result of a specific decision that was made: "We've chosen the salary plus profit-sharing option for our incentive system, so let's put a plan together to implement it properly." Or it may arise out of a problem: "We've inadvertently provided inferior product to our European distributors, so get a plan together to restore our credibility with them while we figure out what went wrong." The plan might come about from "raising the bar" as advocated in Chapter 7: "We're going to improve customer response time to within 6 hours of contact, never before done in this industry, so let's create a tight implementation plan and anticipate what might go wrong." Finally, the planning may arise spontaneously, as many things do in work and life: "Let's plan an employee appreciation event, since we're having a good year thanks to everyone working so effectively."

Planning has the following steps, no matter what its duration, content, or gravity:

Bright Idea
When formulating the plan steps, convene a meeting of those responsible for implementation, and have them brainstorm the steps that need to be undertaken. Eliminate duplication, assign substeps, and create priorities, and you'll have a comprehensive set of steps awaiting sequencing and accountabilities.

- Identifying steps in the plan

- Identifying what may go wrong

- Establishing protective actions

- Monitoring the progress of the plan

Identifying steps in the plan

A plan begins with a plan statement. It's a simple, focused explanation of what is to be accomplished. Any of the following could be a plan statement:

- To build a water treatment plant at the Bayonne facility

- To hire a new field force for the revamped cosmetic line

- To establish an educational program for the response center

Once the plan's intent is specified, the plan steps can be established. Plan steps should include three aspects:

- What the step is to be and in what sequence.
- Who is accountable for the step's successful completion.
- What time frame or deadline is to be met.

Example (I've deliberately kept the example brief to merely provide the nature of the process. This isn't intended to be a comprehensive plan, since it's only hypothetical.): Let's assume that the organization has determined that customer service will be enhanced by educating response center personnel in more sophisticated techniques to service and sell over the phone:

Plan Statement: To establish an educational program that will increase sales and service satisfaction for the response center.

Steps:

- Perform needs analysis with clients

   Accountability: human resources manager
   Deadline: 30 days
- Interview response center personnel

   Accountability: each supervisor
   Deadline: 30 days
- Develop learning objectives and methodology

   Accountability: training specialists
   Deadline: 60 days
- Create pilot program with all learning aids

   Accountability: training specialists
   Deadline: 90 days
- Run pilot, get feedback, and revise program

   Accountability: human resources manager
   Deadline: 110 days
- Schedule programs to encompass all personnel

   Accountability: response center manager
   Deadline: 110 days

Timesaver
Most planning is too complex, too long, too oner-ous, and involves too many people. That's why it is done neither well nor in a timely manner. Simplify the planning process as much as possible, which will actually improve its quality considerably.

- Launch first program

    Accountability: human resources manager
    Deadline: 120 days

We now have a plan in place to create and launch a response center development program from scratch within 4 months.

Identifying what may go wrong

The real secret of successful planning is to anticipate what may go wrong. There are three components to this step:

(a) Choose high priority or especially vulnerable steps in the plan, which require protection.

(b) Generate potential problems.

(c) Hypothesize likely causes.

Our time and resources will always be scarce, and as much as we'd like to thoroughly protect our entire plan, we have to focus on those aspects that are most critical to success or most vulnerable to failure. (The airlines are much more concerned about the engines working properly than the quality of the food, although in a perfect world both would be superb.) Thus, we first prioritize our steps.

For the purposes of our example, we're going to select "Develop learning objectives and methodology" as the critical step we're going to address. In an actual plan, with dozens of steps, you might choose ten or twenty to comprehensively try to protect. For our illustration, we'll limit ourselves to this one.

Generate potential problems

We now ask ourselves, "What could go wrong?" We may generate ideas from a variety of sources:

- Experience
- Competition

- Pilots or tests

- Literature and research

- The company critics, cynics, and naysayers

- Creativity and brainstorming

- Focus groups and public samplings

Watch Out!
It's common for people to say, "Here's what went wrong last time," and focus further discussions on these "likely suspects." However, most plans are derailed by the unexpected, not the expected, so spend a great deal of time brainstorming and looking at potential problems that no one has experienced yet.

The idea is to anticipate anything that might undermine or derail us, and then to assign a priority to the potential problem, so that we know where to assign the most resources. We can use the same criteria we used in assessing risk: the probability of the potential problem actually occurring, and its seriousness if it does, indeed, occur. For our critical step of "Developing learning objectives and methodology" we've identified the following potential problems:

- If the customers we interview aren't a sufficient cross section, then we might omit or ignore key problems with certain niches. (P=4 S=9)

- If the methodology isn't accepted or "user-friendly" to the employees, then the intended learning may not be achieved. (P=7 S=10)

- If there is no follow-up or reinforcement back on the job, then the learning, no matter how effective, may atrophy and die. (P=2 S=10)

We have established some very high degrees of seriousness, with enough of a probability of occurrence that we need to establish thorough protection. Before we can do that, we must take one more step.

Identifying likely causes

You'll recall from our problem-solving discussion in Chapter 7 that corrective action can't be taken unless we address cause. Similarly, preventive actions can't be established unless we know *likely* cause.

To determine likely causes, we ask, "If this is a potential problem, what's likely to cause it?" Let's take our highest rated serious potential problem: If the methodology isn't accepted or "user-friendly" to the employees, then the intended learning may not be achieved. (P=7 S=10). What is likely to cause this problem?

- We don't involve the employees in the construction of the program, so they don't feel "ownership" of the process.

- We don't provide a variety of learning methods to accommodate varied learning styles.

- Our instructors are poor presenters or poorly trained.

- The learning environment is distracting or otherwise poor.

We've now selected a critical step in our plan, identified potential problems that may undermine or cause the step to fail, and identified the likely causes of those problems. We're now ready to establish actions.

Establishing protective actions

To this point, we have not spent a penny other than the time invested in putting our plan into a methodical sequence. We're now at a position where we can create actions on paper, again prior to spending money to safeguard our plan. There are two types of protective actions:

1. Preventive actions are those actions that seek to prevent or eliminate likely causes, thereby preventing the problem from occurring at all.

2. Contingent actions are those actions that seek to reduce, ameliorate, or eliminate the effects of the problem if it occurs despite preventive attempts.

If you recall our chart from Chapter 7, you'll realize that we are merely engaged in future problem solving. Only our time frame has changed:

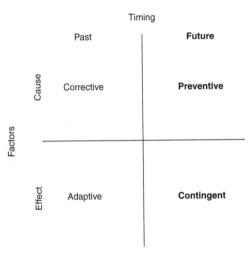

Why take contingent actions if we've spent time and money on effective preventive actions? For the same reasons that you have both a fire marshal and a sprinkler system:

■ Preventive actions can fail. People may smoke in a "no smoking" area, or a rodent may eat through electrical insulation.

■ There may be likely causes that were not anticipated. Combustible materials may come together even though it was thought they were only housed in opposite ends of the building.

■ Preventive action may be too expensive. Every employee can't be monitored every minute of the day.

- Preventive action may be defective. The "no smoking" signs were never posted due to clerical error.

- Preventive action may be impossible. Random lightning strikes can't be entirely prevented.

Preventive actions are intended to remove cause; contingent actions are intended to reduce effects. Note that contingent actions, once called upon, are always more expensive than preventive actions. Once the sprinklers go off (or the "spin control" has to be launched, or the antilock brakes take hold, or insurance claims are filed) there is already damage, money has been lost, time has been lost, injuries may have resulted, and reputation has been lost. So, while contingent actions are critical, nothing can take the place of truly effective preventive actions, even though they may be largely unheralded throughout the plan (fire marshals are seldom singled out, while people breathe sighs of relief for the heroism of the firefighters).

In our example, let's look at the potential problem and likely causes we've isolated: If the methodology isn't accepted or "user-friendly" to the employees, then the intended learning may not be achieved. (P=7 S=10). What is likely to cause this problem, and what preventive actions can be taken to avoid it?

Preventive actions (PA) for each likely cause:

- We don't involve the employees in the construction of the program, so they don't feel "ownership" of the process.

(PA) Create an employee task force to contribute to the objectives and methodology.

(PA) Prior to the pilot, ask the employees to review and comment on the planned approach.

Moneysaver
Preventive actions which are effective will always save money, and those that are ineffective will always cost dearly, because contingent actions are very expensive once triggered. Choose your preventive actions with care.

- We don't provide a variety of learning methods to accommodate varied learning styles.

  (PA) Incorporate discussion, visual aids, role plays, case studies, and small group work.

  (PA) Place the program on CD-ROM as well as in a self-study format.

- Our instructors are poor presenters or poorly trained.

  (PA) Establish a profile for effective instructors and use only people who meet the profile.

  (PA) Establish a comprehensive "train the trainer" program with standards for completion.

- The learning environment is distracting or otherwise poor.

  (PA) Use the amphitheater and its state-of-the-art equipment.

  (PA) Do not allow people to come and go from sessions, and get supervisor commitment to release people for the times required.

We've assigned two preventive actions to each likely cause simply to illustrate that you can assign as few or as many as you wish, within the resource constraints that apply. Generally, the more critical the problem and likely the cause, the more preventive actions you would want to consider.

Bright Idea
Try to determine, using your people's experience and judgment, which probable causes are most likely to create the problem, and assign most preventive measures to those causes most likely to appear.

Contingent actions for the effects should the problem occur

Contingent actions are aimed solely at the problem, since no matter which likely cause is the culprit, the effects will be the same. Sprinklers put out fires before they spread whether the fires were caused by careless smoking, electrical shorts, combustible materials, or arson.

Our current potential problem is this: If the methodology isn't accepted or "user-friendly" to the employees, then the intended learning may not be achieved. (P=7 S=10). The question we then ask is, "If this indeed occurs, what actions can we put in place that will reduce, eliminate, or ameliorate the effects?" In this example, they might be:

- Monitoring by supervisors to coach one-on-one to raise application levels.

- Refresher programs of smaller teams with a facilitator who is flexible about responding to the needs of the team.

- Install an automated menu for customers that directs difficult inquiries to a small team of supervisors while routine queries go to regular employees.

- Bring in external consultants to provide better, more effective, more inclusive education.

Once again, we can assign as many contingent actions as we wish. Sprinklers reduce further damage, first aid stations reduce injury severity, and insurance covers financial loss. In our example, we've assigned a variety of actions to take care of unhappy employees, unhappy customers, and poor training techniques.

Preventive actions are constantly in place—the fire marshal is patrolling, and the employee focus groups are being conducted. Contingent action is placed in "waiting." The hope is that it will never be used, but it's there if needed.

Monitoring the progress of the plan

No plan becomes an "automatic" bet or a "sure thing." The power manager is adept at not only overseeing the creation of the plan, *but also overseeing and monitoring its implementation.* Make no mistake about it: Plans never fail in their conceptualization. They fail in their execution and implementation.

It may seem as if monitoring a plan is simply ensuring that accountabilities and time frames are met. But there are two simple yet vital tools that constitute the difference between luck and planned success.

Triggers and mileposts

Contingent actions do not automatically occur. While preventive actions are always in place (no smoking signs and fire marshals), contingent actions must be "triggered": Someone must call the fire department, and even the "automatic" sprinkler systems must feel heat on their detection units. Insurance won't provide a dime until claims are formed.

Triggers are the actuators of contingent action. Every single contingent action needs at least one trigger, and the more you have, the safer you are in terms of effects being reduced by that contingent action. In other words, a fire alarm might automatically sound when heat is sensed, but the alarm may also be set off by someone pulling a lever on the wall. Not all triggers work every time, some may be incapacitated by the effects themselves, and some may prove ineffective. (Your home alarm system's ability to alert the police may be rendered inoperative if the phone wires are cut.)

Mileposts are those indicators that inform you whether or not your plan is on track and whether or not your actions are in place as planned. They are most important in assuring you that contingent

Unofficially...
If a trigger is a human being (someone supposed to place a call or take some other action), make sure there is a backup trigger—another person. This redundancy can't hurt, and it effectively reduces the difficulty of a person forgetting or panicking about his or her duties in a crisis.

actions will work if needed, because normally preventive actions are already in effect and contingent actions can't readily be tested.

Mileposts inform you as to the progress of your plan by serving as "way stations" or mileage markers. You've seen those little silver keying posts in the hallways of offices, museums, and so forth. The security guard has a key that is inserted, creating a recording that the guard was at that spot at a certain point on the guard's rounds. Security guards can readily fall asleep in the gloom of night, or can read a book with their feet on the desk and simply say they toured the building. The keyed positions, however, if reviewed daily or linked to a computer that automatically monitors the activity, ensure that the preventive action is being undertaken.

The tags on corporate fire extinguishers (or the periodically signed certificates in elevators) are mileposts that the preventive action for the elevator (inspected brakes or whatever) and the contingent action represented by the fire extinguisher (the pressure is adequate or it's been recharged) will be effective if needed. No one wants to turn on the sprinkler system to ensure that it works, or to show up late at night to watch the guards circulate, so mileposts have to be present to ensure compliance with expectations, either in the present or in the future if needed.

Here are our contingent actions from above with examples of triggers and mileposts:

- Monitoring by supervisors to coach one-on-one to raise application levels.

Trigger: Employees are not using the new skills as observed by management or in sample interviews.

Monitor: Supervisors are listening to five calls an hour and interviewing two employees a day.

- Refresher programs of smaller teams with a facilitator who is flexible to the needs of the team.

Trigger: Employees are not using the new skills as observed by management or in sample interviews.

Monitor: Facilitators are identified and prepared, and a tentative schedule is in place.

- Install an automated menu for customers that directs difficult inquiries to a small team of supervisors while routine queries go to regular employees.

Trigger: Employees are not using the new skills as observed by management or in sample interviews.

Monitor: Computer program is tested and working if needed to route calls in this manner.

- Bring in external consultants to provide better, more effective, more inclusive education.

Trigger: Employees are not using the new skills as observed by management or in sample interviews.

Monitor: External consultants identified and their proposals for training received and evaluated.

There is a famous story, which may be apocryphal but which is still instructional, about an engineer who worked at the Atlanta airport. He was at an auction looking for some equipment, and he found an old machine that melted runway ice, which could be purchased for a pittance. His superiors reminded him that Atlanta virtually never experienced icing, but he convinced them that the price was too cheap to ignore it, and they would reap huge savings from keeping the important hub open if and when a freak storm did hit. The

Bright Idea
Any time employees suggest actions, ask them these questions: How will we know the actions are being done? How will we know the actions will be effective when we need them to be? These are triggering and monitoring questions that will help make any suggestions pragmatic.

machine was in working order, and it was placed in the rear of a maintenance hanger.

Many years later, lo and behold, Atlanta's field experiences icing conditions, and the old timers remember the de-icing machine. They move the equipment surrounding it, dust it off, fire it up, and it promptly blew up in a hale of sparks. There were no monitors for this contingent action (preventive maintenance is nothing more than a huge monitoring activity). The best plans go awry when the best actions done receive lowly monitoring.

A few years ago I talked to a client who explained how a fire had shut his operation down for several months, with hundreds of people out of work. I was surprised that the insurance settlement, allowing for temporary quarters and equipment rental, would have taken so long. "It wouldn't have," he revealed, "except no one thought it was their job to send in the claim forms or call the company. We all assumed that someone else had done it—the facilities manager, my secretary, the vice president of finance, our attorney—somebody. But no one did, and our insurance company, in another state, had no idea what had happened."

The best of contingent actions won't work without a trigger.

Permanent and interim actions

People often talk about "interim" actions, but interim really does not relate to a given action, but rather a time frame. The corollary to "interim" is "permanent." The danger is that many interim actions become permanent.

Let's look at air-traffic control, where planning is a life and death issue. If the power fails, then the screens will go blank and controllers cannot direct aircraft already in the air. The probability of that occurring is, unfortunately, higher than it used to be. And the seriousness is quite severe. The preventive action, a highly reliable main power source, can and has failed. The contingent action is to have a backup gas generator that kicks in to supply the power. But let's suppose that the gas generator requires 60 seconds to power up and come fully on-line. In that case, the control center relies on a battery-powered generator that responds instantly when main power is down, but can only last for ten minutes at most. The battery powered generator is an interim contingent action, since it's not preventive and deals with the effects, but is designed to last only a brief time. The gas-powered generator is a permanent contingent action which, though expensive and inefficient, can last as long as is needed.

Preventive actions, also, can be short-lived. If the plan is to move the accounting division to new space across town, one of the preventive actions for payroll being delayed is to process everything on the prior weekend, or to pay people for two pay periods in the prior paycheck. Once the move is completed, the preventive actions simply disappear.

We've all seen people who live with an oil leak in the car by constantly putting more oil in. An interim contingent action to deal with the motor overheating has become a permanent contingent action. At work, the interim contingent action to make up for poor productivity of a couple of performers may be overtime for some of the satisfactory performers. But in many cases, that condition continues ad infinitum: The poor performers are never confronted or improved, and the satisfactory performers are faced with overtime indefinitely. This is both unnecessarily expensive, and horrible for morale. But we all tend to drift toward these "necessary

Moneysaver
Every time you assign or approve a contingent action, place a review date (a monitor) on it. That way you have a built-in method not only to ensure its effectiveness if needed, but to assess whether it has outlived its usefulness if it has been implemented.

evils" because the interim action has at least temporarily removed the pain or avoided an unpleasant
situation.

Knowing when to act and setting priorities: Situation appraisal

How do we know when to choose one of the four
common management issues that Chapters 7
through 10 represent? What tells us that we should
embark on some action or pursue some goal?

These are not idle questions, since a manager's
time can be utterly absorbed merely through the
frantic nature of the workplace and the demands of
others—be they superiors, colleagues, subordinates,
or customers. One of the most common complains
I've heard consistently voiced over the last 2
decades, irrespective of technology, global competition, and mass communications, is "I don't have the
time!"

Management concerns or issues are those
events, ideas, stimuli, and interactions that prompt
you to action. You are prompted to raise the bar,
find cause and fix problems, choose among options
and make decisions, or implement and protect
plans. If you discipline yourself to find the logical
starting point among the true priorities, you'll be
investing time in those areas of most dramatic
return.

A quick way to accomplish this, amidst turmoil
and the heat of battle, is to use the "GVG" method:
gravity, velocity, and growth.

- Gravity is the seriousness or impact of the concern. What is its effect on people, profit,
  resources, image, repute, market share, etc.?

- Velocity is the urgency or acceleration of
  the issue. What is the consequence of doing

nothing? What is the degree to which superiors, the public, the regulators, the shareholders, and other stakeholders may become involved?

- Growth is the stability of the issue. Is it getting worse, staying the same, or improving?

Not all issues are equally grave, urgent, or growing. Despite their nature (remember how everyone runs to problem solving, despite the fact that innovating may be far more valuable) and whether they are problems, plans, decisions, or innovations, this priority-setting device allows you to make objective comparisons.

If you have an idea to improve the customer service response line, someone else tells you that employees are complaining about equipment breakdowns, your boss asks that you make a decision about your potential successor for the succession-planning system, and your colleagues on a task force want your input to build a marketing plan, you can't do all four at once. Which is the most severe, which is the most urgent, and which will get much worse if you don't do anything?

It's always interested me that "growth" is a revealing category. If some issue is declining of its own accord, or is stabilized at a low level of gravity, then it almost automatically becomes a low priority. Conversely, if the trend line is sharply up and the gravity is severe, the issue is hard to ignore for long.

Beware of feeding the wrong concerns

I was working with a human resources vice president who could not get anything done. The entire operation was suffering from his inability to get incentive compensation plans completed, respond to harassment complaints, and make decisions on new hires.

Timesaver
Invest the time to determine how many issues of what type are confronting you. No actions will be effective if they are directed against an undifferentiated and unseparated "mess."

He could never even attempt to raise the bar. He was doing the limbo rather than the pole vault. The CEO asked me to work with him on "time management."

The issue quickly became ironically clear. The human resources vice president was nearly fully consumed responding to requests from none other than the CEO. He showed me reams of memos and e-mail that he received daily, requesting figures on turnover, opinions on office layout, and discussions about assorted company policy.

"How quickly do you respond?" I asked.

"Always within the day," he said, "because I want to show the boss what I can do."

"You're not showing him what you can do, which is precisely the problem," I pointed out. "Most of his requests are mundane and minor. They aren't urgent, they can wait and, frankly, some of them can be ignored, because he's only thinking out loud. And many of them would be answered in the course of your normal job output. But since you respond so quickly, he figures you've got plenty of time for this minutiae, and he continues to pour it on."

"So, the answer is not to respond?" he asked incredulously. "What do I say when he asks why I haven't responded?"

"Tell him you're too busy doing your job."

The vice president, with some struggle, cut down on his immediate responses to the CEO, allowed others to simply wither, and actually began tackling his own issues. The CEO was very pleased that I had improved his "time management" so dramatically.

Don't allow your time to be wasted by these "enablers":

- Don't leave your door open and chat with anyone who wanders in. No one has suggested

Watch Out!
Don't become an enabler of behavior that ruins your own chances for success. Most people who "bug" you, no matter what their rank or position, do so because you allow them to get away with it. Showing displeasure is always better than suffering displeasure.

that a "permanent open-door policy" is synonymous with good management. If you live in a
cubicle, put up a sign when there are no "visit-
ing hours," or go somewhere else to get your
deadline-driven work done.

■ Never allow anyone to leave something on
  your desk, be it a piece of paper, a problem, or
  a grudge, let alone a project, with the exception of the boss. Offer help, but don't become
  a repository.

■ Don't allow whining. Tell people you'll help
  them to think through an issue or provide a
  sounding board, but if they whine, the conversation is over. One of my clients actually has a
  "No Whining" sign on his office wall. He simply points to it occasionally, and people get the
  idea.

■ Don't allow politicking. Tell people that a
  meeting will be the forum for debate and idea
  exchange among competing or conflicting
  interests, but you are not going to engage in
  one-on-one lobbying of any type.

■ Do not suffer fools of any type for any amount
  of time. Tell the troublemakers and instigators
  and rumor mongers that you have better
  things to do with your precious time, which
  happens to be absolutely true.

The separation technique

When you are faced with an ambiguous issue that
you simply can't easily locate in one of the four
areas I've discussed, then revert to a question I've
utilized throughout the book: What's the evidence?

When an employee says "We have a morale problem" (which is an all-too-common catchall for a variety of issues), ask "What's the evidence?"

"Well, our turnover this year is higher than during the last 3 years and industry averages."

"What other evidence do you have?"

"We've had scarcely any volunteers for the United Way campaign or the annual blood drive."

"What other evidence do you have?"

"Human resources is receiving quite a few complaints about working conditions, such as forced overtime, the lack of an incentive bonus last quarter, and poor software."

"What other evidence do you have?"

"We think there is a unionization effort underway."

"Do you know that for a fact?"

"No, I just have a hunch."

So, we've isolated three concerns to work on: High turnover, poor turnout for the volunteer campaigns, and working condition complaints. We can now set priorities (I'd want to find the cause of the high turnover, put together a plan to elicit volunteers, and make a decision about how to test whether working conditions have, in fact, deteriorated) and get on with business.

The separation technique looks like this:

Unofficially...
Psychologically, employees often engage in "transference" when something adverse occurs. They may complain about a supervisor when the real issue is a lack of modern equipment. Don't be lulled by what they claim is the problem, but try to find the stimulus underlying their behavior.

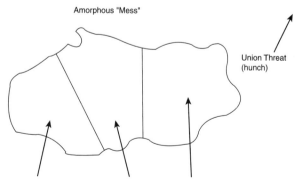

Separation: Blood Drive Off, Working Condition Complaints, Turnover High

It is most useful with these stereotypical concerns and comments, in addition to the "morale problem" shown above:

■ We have a communications problem.

■ We have a "chemistry" issue.

■ There's poor responsiveness.

■ It's an "interface" or "handoff" issue.

■ There's a personality conflict.

■ It's political.

■ It's a cultural thing.

■ There's "history" or "baggage" involved.

The commonality about all of these amorphous concerns is that you can't put your finger on the real crux of the issue. It's like trying to compartmentalize a cloud. The thing just keeps drifting away or slipping between your fingers.

Don't accept amorphous cop-outs. Demand evidence, separate out the real issues (sometimes there are none!), and assign them the proper priority and starting point. Here is the succinct, compressed process:

1. Amorphous concern expressed.

2. Concern separated into component issues using evidence.

   2a. Unimportant or illusory concerns ignored.

3. Remaining concerns assigned priorities using gravity, velocity, and growth criteria.

4. Prioritized concerns assigned starting point: innovation, problem solving, decision making, planning.

5. Proper starting points begun with managerial monitoring and accountabilities.

If you follow this route, you'll make better use of your time, keep your focus (and your head) even in times of chaos, and resolve any and all concerns that are thrown at you in an expeditious manner.

Just the facts

- Planning must be practical, because most plans fail in the implementation, not the conceptualization.

- Preventive actions are always more effective than contingent actions in terms of cost, people, embarrassment, and disruption.

- Since preventive actions are not foolproof and you are not omniscient, contingent actions are always required.

- Consciously decide on whether you are best served with interim actions, and ensure that they don't inadvertently become permanent.

- Rigorously protect your time by clarifying amorphous issues and avoiding being an enabler of time wasters.

The Secrets of Leadership

PART IV

GET THE SCOOP ON...
Why there is no "perfect" leadership style ▪
How to consciously manage time ▪
The true range of leadership styles available to
you ▪ Why you have to sometimes depart from
your "comfort zone" ▪ How to maximize ownership, employee development, and commitment

Choosing Among an Array of Leadership Styles

There is significant debate from time to time as to whether managers are leaders. Some sources maintain that the act of management involves organizing projects and procedures around deadlines and time frames, and that leadership is the act of galvanizing people into action. Others cite the philosophy that leaders need followers, and that people choose their leaders while they are told who their managers are.

While these might be amusing recreational debates, they constitute little more than philosophic fluff. In the actual world of organizations and work, managers are called upon to serve in leadership capacities frequently—sometimes constantly—and must rise to the occasion or fail. No sane manager says to his or her boss, "I'd be happy to lead this initiative, but it's not in my job description, because I'm a manager, not a leader. Perhaps if you provided some leadership training and a nice outdoor group experience, I might be qualified."

Conversely, leaders don't sit around between charismatic engagements biding their time until their followers rally to seek their guidance once again. The last time I looked, they were actively managing some part of the business, large or small, with or without drama.

So let's put the silly debates aside. Managers manage and, in the course of that noble pursuit, often lead others, both actively and by example.

- Active leadership is the formal accountability for reaching some goal, be it mundane (e.g., conducting a meeting) or grand (e.g., implementing a new level of customer responsiveness). In this case, the leader directs and organizes, and is proactive in leading the team.

- Leadership by example occurs when others choose to view the individual as a role model, exemplar, or avatar. In this case, the leader's role is passive in that he or she may be doing what he or she normally does, but others use that behavior as an example (for example, a manager leaves a meeting to take customer calls rather than allow a customer to be frustrated by slow service).

Both of these roles are assumed by managers every day, so they might as well get good at them.

Why the only "perfect" style is for despots

There is no perfect, single leadership style because situations and people vary so widely. A tyrant can afford a single style—belligerently authoritarian—

because he has behind him the brute force to impose these behaviors, no matter how inappropriate or unpopular. However, democratic leaders lead only through the consent of the governed on the political level. In organizational life, the best leaders are effective because followers believe in them.

In every situation, the people, information, results expected, timing, resources, and other important factors are slightly different. If they don't differ at all from one time to the next repeatedly, then we don't need leaders but merely operations manuals. No one has to lead a repetitive action machine on an assembly line.

There are five traditional sources of leadership influence and power:

- Hierarchical—Hierarchical power flows from the height of one's position. It is one of the few remaining throwbacks to the military origins of modern organizational life. When someone is vested with a higher position, more resources, greater responsibility, and the tangible perquisites of rank (office size, parking space, assistants, etc.), then lesser people "salute" the office, irrespective of the person. If I'm your boss, then I'm your leader.

- Power to reward—If I can provide salutary effects, then you will follow me. The power to bestow financial gain, prestige, latitude of action, assignments, and other emoluments constitutes a strong lever over my behavior. People other than direct superiors have the power to provide such benefits, including other managers senior to me, powerful stakeholders

Unofficially...
Hierarchical position alone is the most unreliable source of leadership power. This is because people don't believe in titles, they believe in competence. A title is something they read. Ability is something they can see. Take your title off your card and put your ability on display.

and customers, and peers who can offer inducements that I can't provide myself.

- Power to punish—There are those who can hurt me, either directly through disciplinary action and the removal of benefits, or indirectly, through a stalled career, poor feedback, the anointing of competitors, and so on. While these sources may seem to be the same as the power brokers above, they also include sanctioning groups, such as human resources, legal, accounting, and MIS. There are people who can deny me needed resources and information unless I follow their lead.

- Expertise—There are some I will follow because they are clearly wise in the subject at hand. Despite all other factors, they know more about actuarial tables, molecular structure, publishing a front page article, building a new plant, writing financial software, or selling a car than I or any of my colleagues. I will put up with poor communication skills, interpersonal friction, lack of feedback, and a whole assortment of impediments, because there is comfort, and probably, success, in allowing their expertise to dominate.

- Referent—Referent power means that I follow you because I believe in you. Charismatic leadership relies on referent power, but so does less dramatic leadership in which you simply ask that I trust you because you've never misled me before. Referent leaders seldom have to overtly convince followers. Their honesty, past success, sharing of the load, and clear vision usually persuade people to take their path.

These five sources of leadership power can frequently be found to overlap. Those in hierarchical control, for instance, can wield the power to reward and punish. This, however, is not always guaranteed. It's difficult, for example, to reward and punish union members, volunteers, and those who themselves are referent leaders. Many hierarchical leaders who rely only on reward and punishment are, in effect, weaponless without some other source of power.

Referent leaders may be a part of the workforce, or formally designated managers. Nevertheless, when we look at the five sources comparatively, we can see an interesting relationship:

Bright Idea
Managers have inherent hierarchical power, by dint of their positions. Use that power to deliberately involve others in leadership decisions, not just in the aftermath and implementation. This builds referent power by increasing involvement, ownership, and commitment.

Power Source	Commitment	Compliance	Resistance
Reward	possible	likely	possible
Punishment	unlikely	likely	possible
Positional	unlikely	possible	likely
Referent	likely	likely	unlikely
Expert	likely	likely	possible

Only referent power is likely to gain commitment and compliance, while most reducing potential resistance. In all other modes, resistance is possible or likely, and compliance (begrudging acceptance) is more likely than commitment (enthusiastic support). In most of my clients, managers readily point to their willingness to serve as referent leaders, yet their behaviors reflect the other sources: reliance on position, rewards, punishment, or flaunting of their expertise.

We said earlier that there is no "perfect style," yet it might appear that referent power is such an idea. However, we're merely pointing out that people most willingly follow leaders who operate from a base of referent power. The truth is that there is a variety of styles from which to choose to achieve, support, and perpetuate referent power. (Note that referent power is a key to both the active leader and the exemplary leader we identified earlier.)

The key factors in leadership decision making

There are three key factors in determining what style is appropriate in a leadership situation. (I am indebted to a friend and colleague, Dr. Victor Vroom of Yale University, who has been the leading developer and exponent of what he has termed "situational leadership" models over the past 30 years. His seminal work was *Leadership and Decision Making*, with Phillip Yetton, University of Pittsburgh Press, 1973.)

- Quality of the decision—For the manager as leader, quality in decision making with others has this connotation: Does one outcome have a qualitatively different impact than others? If I'm to decide how to allocate parking spaces, and my options are by seniority, by first arrivals, by employee performance, and so on, yet I have a covered parking space beneath the building which isn't affected, then the quality of the situation is low. Any outcome is as good as any other to me. On the other hand, if I'm to decide who to appoint as the new sales manager in our largest region, that outcome (the differing candidates) might have a huge impact on me and, hence, has high quality.

- Commitment to the decision—Commitment is the enthusiastic support of those who have to implement a decision. In the case of the parking lot, while it may not matter to me what option is chosen, the people who have to implement it (the drivers) had better enthusiastically support the alternative chosen or the plan will fail. If I've chosen seniority, but those who arrive earliest simply take the best spots, then the decision is unsuccessful. (Yes, I could place guards out there to enforce my selection by brute force, but then we're back to tyranny, aren't we?) Commitment in this example is high. However, in the case of my new hire, it would be nice if the field force in the region staunchly supported and was committed to my choice, but it's not essential. They may prefer one of their own while I know that an outsider is required to introduce new methods that no insider can provide. Here, commitment is desirable but not essential.

■ Timing—Timing is always a factor in leadership decision making, because it is a rare, nonrenewable resource. Yet it's often viewed incorrectly. Simply because it's nonrenewable does not imply that it must be conserved at any price. Some leadership situations require that more time be invested. Sometimes acting rapidly is not advantageous, even if rapid action is possible. My parking lot decision can probably wait until I can assure myself of the necessary commitment. After all, people are parking somewhere, somehow currently, and getting to work on time. In my new hire example, I may never be able to acquire the commitment of the field force to anyone other than the choice of an insider, and the longer I

Timesaver
In leadership situations, ask two questions immediately: Does it really matter what course we take? Do we need enthusiastic support if this is to work well? If the answers are "yes," then you should probably invest more time; if "no," then you can act more quickly if you choose to.

wait the longer a key leadership post is unfilled and resultant sales growth suffers. I can't afford to wait for commitment.

The dynamic of these three factors looks like this:

$$\frac{\text{Quality} + \text{Commitment}}{\text{Time}} = \frac{\text{Situational}}{\text{Success}}$$

The quality of the issue (degree of difference in the options being considered) plus the commitment required (enthusiastic support of the implementers) underlain by time availability and management, will equal situational success. If all three are taken into account and managed properly, success is likely; if any one or more of the three are ignored or mismanaged, success is unlikely.

The range of leadership styles

There is a range of styles available to the manager. There are no magic descriptions, words, or labels to apply. No value judgments are implied by any of the terms of descriptions, but we have to call them something, so here is my offering:

Autocratic Inquiring One-on-One Group Consensus

Autocratic

In autocratic leadership, the manager acts alone. He or she consults no one, and simply makes the decision or takes the action required. We all make autocratic decisions every day, usually in the course of the routine aspects of our jobs. The more empowered one is, the more likely one is to make autocratic decisions, provided the requisite information is available.

This style could be called "acting alone" or "solitary." On a small scale, the manager may see the

Unofficially...
We have no "perfect" style, and informing subordinates that "this is my style" can lead to trouble. Allow yourself the flexibility to adjust and amend your style as the situation dictates so that you don't become a dogmatic tyrant.

need to schedule overtime and does so, posting the
list to inform employees that overtime is necessary
and who will be required to provide it. On a grand
scale, a manager may decide to suspend a customer's credit until payments in arrears are
received, and may do so without consulting the
client, the sales representative, customer service, or
anyone else. Similarly, hiring and firing decisions
may be made in such solitary conditions.

Inquiring

In an "inquiring" mode, the manager seeks out others to provide information, but does not reveal the
reasons for the request or disclose the issues at
hand. The manager may make a phone call to
inquire about payment status, or go to human
resources to ask about turnover in underwriting, or
might encounter someone in the hall and raise a
question about staffing requirements. In all of these
cases, the manager doesn't reveal anything else, or
responds briefly if the other party requires more
information before replying.

This mode is reminiscent of Detective Sergeant
Friday in the old *Dragnet* series who constantly
reminded witnesses, "Just the facts, ma'am." These
managers come across as "all business" and highly
time efficient. If asked what's going on (what's generating their questions), they tend to reply "Oh,
nothing" or provide the briefest possible explanation. This style is barely interactive and highly time
conscious.

One-on-one

This is a consultative style in which the manager
talks to people singly and, unlike the inquiring
mode, shares the nature of the issue, provides

Bright Idea
Tell people at
the outset who
will make the
final decision on
any issue. Input
will vary consid-
erably if people
believe the
leader is ulti-
mately making
the decision
(let's take some
risk and be bold)
or they are mak-
ing the decision
and are account-
able (let's go
slowly on this
one).

details, and actively solicits the other party's ideas, facts, opinions, and feedback. The manager may do this with a trusted protégé, a few people, or scores of people, until satisfied that he or she has obtained a good cross section of opinion, all of the available information, and a variety of insights.

This interviewing style is common to managers who enjoy personal conversations and minimum confrontation and debate (which often arise in group settings). In this case, the manager may see people formally in the manager's office, at the other person's work area, over lunch, in the halls, or wherever a one-on-one conversation is comfortable and private. Some managers use the same select, trusted group to interview each time, while others prefer to vary their sources.

Group

This is one of the most common and one of the most abused of the styles. In this case, the manager convenes a meeting, which may be regularly scheduled or called specifically for this issue, and actively elicits input, debate, information, and opinions from the group. The manager makes it clear that he or she will make the final decision, but only subject to what is heard in the meeting(s). This is the "one-on-one" approach with the extra dimension of debate, confrontation, interchange of ideas, compromise, and so on.

The advantage of this technique is that everyone receives and responds to the exact same set of information from the manager (unlike "one-on-one," where selective hearing can take place or the manager might not disclose the exact same information to each person, advertently or inadvertently). The disadvantage is that the group is often disappointed if a consensus is reached but not acted on by the manager (who retains the decision-making prerogative). Also, meetings are often endless, circular debates if not run well. In these settings, the manager may choose to take a role, or may sit back and simply absorb.

Consensus

This style is the same as the prior one, with one large exception: In consensus mode, the manager tells the group that he or she will accept and act on the group's decision, whether by unanimity or consensus, as agreed. The manager clearly surrenders the decision-making prerogative, and proceeds upon the group's recommendation (hence the need to identify whether that recommendation is the result of total support or consensus support).

If the manager chooses to take an active role in the debate (and sometimes that may mean merely remaining in the room as a highly intimidating presence), then the style is actually "group" despite the superficial attempt at consensus, because the manager is nonetheless influencing the outcome. However, if the group is confident enough to ignore the manger's presence, or the manager is confident enough to not be present, then this is a true consensus style.

Before we go on, read through these two examples, and select a style from above which you think you would use in each of the situations presented. We'll return to these later in the chapter:

Example #1:

Suppose that you are the manager of a group underwriting division in a large insurance company.

Moneysaver
Employees who can participate in and make decisions about their own jobs tend to conserve company money, protect resources, and utilize time well. Conversely, they tend to ignore these economies when simply "following orders."

You have 30 underwriters, working for four supervisors. In the past, the supervisors have decided amongst themselves about issues such as staffing, sharing resources, performance evaluations, and overtime. There is low turnover and high morale. However, the company has recently acquired a huge new contract with a major automobile company. There will be weekend work required to process everything by the effective date, and this weekend is predicted to be beautiful with ideal beach weather. You know that virtually everyone in the unit will want to be heading for the ocean, which is only an hour's drive away.

What style would you use to schedule the overtime?

Example #2:

You are newly appointed to manage a team of outside salespeople who have managed to consistently hit their quotas, but with questionable ethics and a large amount of ensuing customer complaints about promises not kept. You've been told to shape the unit up while not losing market share. You're immediately faced with the decision to reorganize the unit, since new technology has made much of the support staff obsolete. You have never sold in this area yourself, you're seen as an outsider, and the salespeople feel that management is trying to arbitrarily limit their earnings. You must make a decision about the reorganization immediately, so as not to lose focus on sales goals.

What style would you use to determine how to reorganize?

The dynamics of style

A variety of dynamics change across these leadership styles.

Autocratic Inquiring One-on-One Group Consensus
For example, as we move from left to right, the following factors are affected:

- Time investment increases.

- Commitment will tend to increase.

- Validity of information will tend to increase.

- Ownership of the solution or course of action tends to increase.

- Amount of people involved increases.

- Managerial skills needed increase.

- Knowledge about the issue increases.

- Subordinate development tends to increase.

These and other factors all need to be assessed and actively managed. In other words, no subordinate development will ever take place when an autocratic style is used, despite how much time is saved. Conversely, more time is required when employee ownership is sought.

The factors are important, because managers otherwise have a tendency to stay within their comfort zones. If I despise running meetings and can't tolerate confrontation, I'm going to tend toward one-on-one interactions at best, and autocratic decisions when I can, whether or not I have enough information or require employee commitment. If I am most comfortable surrounded by people at meetings and don't like taking a clear stand, I'm going to eschew anything except the group and consensus styles, despite the fact that time may be of the essence, or that the employees have vastly different agendas than does the organization.

Power managers are those who can best do the following:

Watch Out!
When some of
your decisions
are startlingly
successful and
others are hope-
lessly disastrous,
you are probably
stuck in one
style of leader-
ship despite the
circumstances.
Diversify your
style by reaching
out at least to
adjoining ones.
A leader who is
50 percent suc-
cessful is 100
percent in
danger.

- Recognize the appropriate range of styles for any situation.

- Develop the skills to utilize the entire range of styles.

- Inform others directly or indirectly of the style chosen.

The last point may seem odd, but it's important for two reasons. First, any search through the literature about leadership—and it's voluminous—reveals that the most successful single attribute of leaders isn't style but consistency. People like to know what to expect. Many managers try to meet that need by always leading in the same fashion, despite the situation. A better approach is to inform people as to the style chosen in any particular situation, and remain consistent to it.

Secondly, informing people about leadership styles is vital to preventing misunderstandings and hostility. How many times have you been in a meeting in which people apparently reach consensus only to learn later that the leader has chosen a course of action that they did not recommend? The result is a cry of "foul!" and people muttering in the hall that their opinions are not respected, their time is wasted, and they have no input.

What happened in actuality is that the employees thought they were in a consensus meeting, but the leader had really convened a group meeting. The leader always intended to retain the decision-making prerogative, but the employees' perceptions were different. Hence, the nature of the meeting and the type of decision making needs to be apparent. This can even apply to the extent of rapidly seeking data:

"Sue, I'm in an 'inquiring' mode here, so can you tell me quickly what the delivery times have been to the Southwest this month?"

You might not say it that way, but you do want to get the point across that all you want is information, and you don't have time to go into details about why you're asking. That's better than an abrupt question, a refusal to share background, and the responder left wondering and suspicious about your motives and intent.

We don't all possess the skill sets to employ the full range of leadership behaviors equally well, so we should focus on developing our abilities in areas where we're least adept. Comfort zones should not be the decisive parameters in choosing leadership style. Decision variables should be.

The seven leadership decision variables

There are conditions that are either present or absent in most leadership situations. You might want to add some to our list, but the list is concise, practical, and easily applied. Note that they are "binary," in that a simple "yes or no" response is possible.

Quality variable

Does it make a difference which course of action is chosen?

This means that some options have demonstrably differing payoffs versus all options being about equal, as in our parking lot example.

Information variable

Does the manager have adequate information to make a decision alone?

Prior to acting alone, the manager first needs to determine whether existing information even allows such an approach.

Bright Idea
Share the variables with trusted aides and assistants. Have them participate in the determination of which variables are present. This will ensure your accuracy as well as quickly enlist them into the appropriate leadership style.

Structure variable

> Does the manager know exactly what information is missing and how to retrieve it?

The colloquial question here is, "Do we know what we don't know?" or "Is it true that we don't know what we don't know?"

Commitment variable

> Is implementation or resolution critically dependent on the commitment of others?

Commitment is "enthusiastic support," not merely compliance, by those responsible for providing information and implementing the actions.

Participation variable

> Will the implementers commit to a decision made by the manager without their active participation in the analysis?

Experience will be crucial in determining the extent and circumstances that govern whether employees will simply accept a decision as valid or whether they will require ownership to produce validation.

Goals variable

> Are the implementers aligned behind organizational objectives?

Called "goal congruence" by psychologists, this measures whether employees share organizational objectives or have separate, and perhaps conflicting, goals.

Alternatives variable

> Will alternative options probably produce conflict among the implementers?

This is the converse of the goals variable, in that goals may be shared, but the routes to achieve them are not agreed upon.

When these variables are combined, behaviors from our original range may be eliminated in terms of being feasible for the current situation.

For example, if the answer to the quality variable is "yes," and differing options provide differing values, and the answer to the information variable is "no," the manager does not have adequate information at the moment to make a decision, then what leadership behavior should be eliminated?

In this case, the autocratic style simply won't work, because it is predicated on independent action. If the issue is important, and the information does not reside with the manager, he or she can't make an independent analysis, no matter how much a factor, such as time, may be pressing. So "autocratic" behavior is eliminated, not through a value judgment but through sheer practicality to protect the integrity of the leadership.

In another example, suppose that the quality variable applies (quality is important) and the goals variable shows us that implementers are not aligned behind organizational goals (for example, there is a union that is militantly antimanagement). What behavioral style should be eliminated?

Here, the consensus approach would be fatal, because the decision making would be left to people whose agenda is not the same as the organization's (instead of reaching a business goal, they want to undermine management). Despite the strength of the leader in meetings, despite the urge for "participation" from the motivational gurus, and despite calls from union leadership to share the decision, consensus leadership cannot be applied here without the probability of disastrous results.

Through the application of the variables in a variety of ways, inappropriate leadership styles can

Watch Out!
Human resources people and consultants will frequently urge participation for a variety of "feel good" reasons that may fly in the face of prudence and pragmatism. Use the variables as an objective test as to whether participation in decisions can be successfully applied.

be eliminated, leaving a selection among those most likely to be situationally successful. These are far superior reasons for supporting a particular leadership style than just relying on one's comfort zone, the latest fads, or trying to participate for participation's sake.

Here is a quick way to check your appropriate and inappropriate leadership behaviors. It may look like a map of the New York subway system, but it is merely a graphic representation of the leadership decision variables placed in a "binary fork" format. For our purposes, we've assigned the following identifiers to the behavioral range:

Timesaver
When in doubt about whether or not a group's objectives are aligned with the organization's, opt for a group style at best, not a consensus style. Uncertainty in this area can be fatal if you surrender a decision to the employees whose interests may be opposed to those of the organization.

- Autocratic: A

- Acquiring: B

- One-on-One: C

- Group: D

- Consensus: E

As you can see in the figure on the following page, if the first question is answered "no," quality isn't an issue, then we skip the questions about adequacy of information and how to we know what's missing, because they are irrelevant. Similarly, if commitment of others isn't critical (variable #4), then we skip the question about whether they will commit to a leader-alone decision (variable #5).

Example #1:

Let's take our example through the process. Here it is again: Suppose that you are the manager of a group underwriting division in a large insurance company. You have 30 underwriters working for 4 supervisors. In the past, the supervisors have decided amongst themselves about issues such as

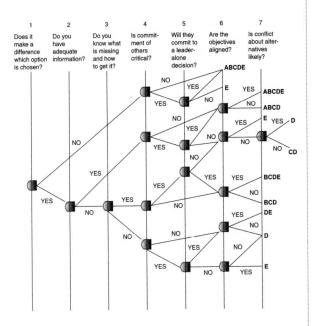

staffing, sharing resources, performance evaluations, and overtime. There is low turnover and high morale. However, the company has recently acquired a huge new contract with a major automobile company. There will be weekend work required to process everything by the effective date, and this weekend is predicted to be beautiful with ideal beach weather. You know that virtually everyone in the unit will want to be heading for the ocean, which is only an hour's drive away.

What style would you use to schedule the overtime?

Let's examine the variables in sequence:

1. It does make a difference which course of action is adopted, because if people are

unhappy they will not do a high-quality job processing the new account information.

2. You do not have adequate information to make a quality analysis, because you're not sure of what actual plans people have. Nor do you know who worked overtime the last time this happened.

3. You do know what information is missing and how to get it (talk to people and to the supervisors).

4. Commitment of others is critical to effective implementation. If they don't show up, it's fatal.

5. They will probably not commit to a leader-alone decision, because of the burden on their family time.

6. The objectives are aligned—there is low turnover, good feelings toward supervision, and a history of support.

Unofficially...
One of the best reasons to establish high levels of trust is that subordinates will increasingly accept leader-alone decisions. While that option should never be abused, it is of tremendous benefit when deadlines and time pressures become severe.

The suggestion, then, according to the model, is to turn this over to consensus decision making. Note that if you felt that they would have accepted a leader-alone decision (variable #5), then all but an autocratic style would have been acceptable (you would still have had to ask about personal plans and availability).

On our graph it looks like this:

How does the choice of styles compare with what you chose originally?

Now let's run our second example.

Example #2:

You are newly appointed to manage a team of outside salespeople who have managed to consistently

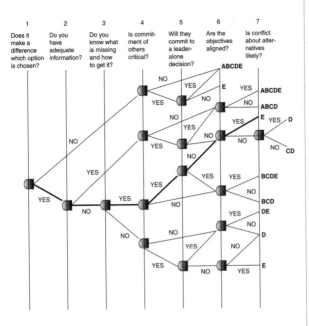

hit their quotas, but with questionable ethics and a large amount of ensuing customer complaints about promises not kept. You've been told to shape the unit up while not losing market share. You're immediately faced with the decision to reorganize the unit, since new technology has made much of the support staff obsolete. You have never sold in this area yourself, you're seen as an outsider, and the salespeople feel that management is trying to arbitrarily limit their earnings. You must make a decision about the reorganization immediately, so as not to lose focus on sales goals.

1. It certainly makes a difference which options you choose.

2. You do not have adequate information.

3. You do not know what is missing or how to get it quickly.

4. Commitment of others is critical.

5. The group will never commit to a leader-alone decision.

6. Objectives are not aligned.

On the chart:

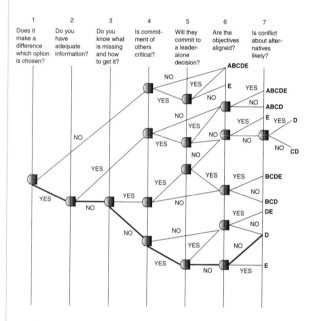

Here the choice is for the group option. You can't afford to make this decision alone, nor can you simply turn it over to the group. The model suggests that only by convening the group can you establish the debate, surface the concerns, and share the needed information uniformly and quickly, but that you must retain the decision-making prerogative. The idea is to safeguard quality while maximizing group participation within safe bounds.

How does this result compare with the style you chose earlier in the chapter? Was your reasoning similar or did you fail to consider some of the variables?

There is nothing magical about the process or the "map." What we're suggesting is that your *likelihood* of success is far greater when you stay within the appropriate range of behaviors allowed within the variables that exist for that situation. You can certainly "violate" this advice—for example, you could have chosen "autocratic" in example #2 if you so desired—but the chances of your success are diminished significantly when the variables are ignored.

Some basic guidelines or "rules of the road":

- Time-efficiency is always to be found on the "left" of the feasible range, but it may sometimes be limited.

- Ownership and development will always be greatest on the "right" of the feasible range.

- The "middle road" is an attempt to work time-efficiently while still creating ownership.

- Your comfort zone is an appropriate choice provided that it is within the feasible range.

As you are offered professional development opportunities or pursue individual education on your own, ask yourself what skills and behaviors are needed to assist you in embracing the entire range of leadership styles. As a rule:

- Autocratic style demands comprehensive knowledge of the area of your accountability, high self-confidence, and the ability to frame issues quickly.

- Acquiring style demands precise questioning, the ability to quickly separate the germane

Timesaver
Whenever the model suggests a range of behaviors applicable in a particular situation, use the one on the extreme "left" if you are seeking to be most time-efficient.

from the mundane, and firmness (in resisting return questions).

- One-on-One requires an approachable, coaching-type of attitude, with high persuasiveness to encourage people to talk.

- Group skills include conflict resolution, priority setting, presentation skills, acute listening, and summarization.

- Consensus requires the group skills listed above plus patience, ego subordination, and prudent risk taking.

All managers are leaders at one time or another, sometimes daily, often in times of great consequence. The only question is what kind of leader you intend to be: effective or ineffective.

Just the facts

- Managers are leaders passively, by example, and actively, in accountability for initiatives and action.

- Situation variables, not style preferences, should dictate management behaviors in leadership positions.

- Trust is a key factor in supporting leader-alone decisions.

- Time efficiency is important, but has to be weighed with the quality of the outcomes and the commitment necessary for success.

- Sharing the leadership style being used is a fundamental factor in helping followers see consistency.

GET THE SCOOP ON...

What is really negotiable and nonnegotiable ▪
Ensuring that agreements stick ▪
Decisions in tough times: downsizing, mergers,
and so on ▪ Handling contemporary problems:
drugs, harassment, abuse ▪ When to hold and
when to fold

How to Negotiate Successfully Without Resorting to Weapons

Chapter 12

Negotiation is not armed combat, at least not at first, although one of my undergraduate political science professors was fond of defining warfare as "the least subtle form of communication." We negotiate on a daily basis, often unknowingly and, therefore, unaware of our processes, skills, and weaknesses in the area.

Negotiation is the art of conferring with others to reach a settlement, when necessary through compromise and bargaining.

This means that:

- At least one and sometimes numerous others are involved. All parties who have an ability to influence the outcome and affect our objectives must be included.

- Communication must be open, frequent, and is most effective if done in person, adequate when at least oral discussions are possible, and weakest when limited to the written word.

■ A settlement is not automatically a compromise, though that is the conventional view. Quite practically, one party's position may be entirely satisfied in a settlement, meaning that compromise is possible but not mandatory.

The last point is especially salient because negotiating is not always done on a real-time reciprocal basis. That is, I may gain complete satisfaction in my short-term needs in return for a longer-term complete satisfaction in your needs; for example, we may see the science fiction film I badly want to see tonight in return for my promising to see the period drama you favor next week. On the job, I might agree to help you out with some staffing needs for a special project in return for your future consideration, if and when I may need it. (In the latter case, the exchange is simply for "goodwill," which may or may not actually be required.)

With some exception, the best negotiating is done in person, when you can watch the other parties' body language, provide immediate feedback in both verbal and nonverbal ways, and use the dynamics that are endemic to physical proximity. However, the role of emotions, temper, loss of control, and other visceral factors is not reliant on personal meetings. Just read some of the vitriolic e-mail messages we all see every week and you can appreciate the fact that people can become belligerent and aggressive without necessarily seeing their negotiating "adversary"!

Determining the negotiable and the nonnegotiable

The most important step in negotiating, bar none, occurs prior to ever initiating or engaging in

Bright Idea
Only negotiate with peers. No matter how effective you are, you are undermined when the other party says, "Now I'll run our agreement past my boss" (who can disavow it while knowing what your position has become). Conversely, attempt to have your subordinates negotiate all preliminary phases before "final approval."

conversation with others. It is rather the prepara-
tory step of determining what you can give away,
what you can amend or alter, and what you cannot
give away under any circumstances.

Since all negotiation concerns either present
or future actions, we can steal a page out of our
decision-making chapter and use this key question:
What are my "musts" and what are my "wants"? You
have to establish, clearly, unequivocally, and conclusively, what you can modify or concede while
remaining successful, and what can't be altered or
given away if you are to remain successful.

Example: If you are attempting to merge two
departments into one operation with the objective
of a productivity improvement that your own boss
has demanded, you may have this set of objectives:

- Reduce staffing to at least 75 percent of cur-
  rent level
- Completion within 30 days, prior to year-end
  work
- No disruption in customer responsiveness
- No expenditures outside of existing budget
- Reduce staffing as much as possible
- Complete as soon as possible to minimize
  disruptions
- Create conference room out of saved space
- Transfer out poorest-performing employees
- Use opportunity to purge all client files 5 years
  and older

You realize that to accomplish the task you need
the enthusiastic support of your six supervisors,
three in each current department. Their lead will
be important in the speed and accuracy that

Watch Out!
If you allow one of your "musts" to be compromised or sacrificed, you will have a poorly negotiated resolution, no matter what else you may have gained. If you lose a true "must," you have lost a key ingredient to your success.

employees use to get the job done over the next month, including long hours and weekends.

The supervisors have come to you with their concerns. They include:

- No lost supervisory positions
- People handled humanely and helped to find other company jobs
- No weekend work
- Temps hired to assist throughout the process
- Creation of kitchenette and lounge area from saved space

What we have here is a typical conflicting set of objectives, with the potential for acrimony and adversarial positions. Yet the manager prefers not to simply "order" the moves required, because a lack of supervisory support will undermine the effort, especially with timing and productivity such urgent needs.

The answer is to take the manager's list of objectives and apply our musts and wants separation, which we will say for the sake of our example, is this:

Musts

- Reduce staffing to at least 75 percent of current level
- Complete within 30 days, prior to year-end work
- No disruption in customer responsiveness
- No expenditures outside of existing budget

Wants

- Reduce staffing as much as possible
- Complete as soon as possible to minimize disruptions

- Create conference room out of saved space
- Transfer out poorest performing employees
- Use opportunity to purge all client files 5 years and older

Now we have a very different template, just with that simple separation. The manager knows that jobs cannot be guaranteed, particularly all of the supervisory positions. People can be helped ethically, and supervisors can be assigned to use performance as a standard for retaining employees, and to gather the profiles of the others for attempted transfers to jobs appropriate for their skill levels. Weekend work will be a necessity and temps are out of the question, due to budget restrictions. However, the conference room can be sacrificed (you can continue to borrow the boardroom when not in use) for the kitchenette and lounge (or perhaps there would be room for both).

This doesn't make the manager's decisions any easier—after all, some of the supervisors will have to find other work—but it does make the right decisions clearer and provide a focused priority. Too many managers get bloody negotiating for conference rooms and wind up retaining full staffing.

As a case in point, we all see mergers and acquisitions in which a clear and unarguable objective— reduced expenses through synergies and staff reductions—is never met, because the new entity can't bring itself politically to reduce head count among employees, take on a union, or, most commonly, terminate highly paid executives (or at least do so without expensive termination packages).

In our example, the manager knows that he or she absolutely cannot guarantee staff reductions or temporary hires, but can make concessions on space and how excess personnel are handled. And that's a very solid start. So, the first, key, and most critical step in negotiating is prior to talking to anyone: Establish your personal musts and wants.

How to conduct effective negotiations

Here are the 10 secrets to effective negotiating, based on the conditions that you have already established for yourself, the musts to be preserved, and the wants that are desirable but somewhat expendable.

1. Use your turf. The worst case should be a neutral setting. But, if possible, try to use your environment, which has a psychological effect. Create this dynamic by offering something if you must—you have a bigger conference room, more support resources, more privacy, or you have a meeting immediately after that you can't miss and meeting in your office will permit you more time. (This is why it's tough to negotiate with the boss, since you're usually on the boss's turf at the time!)

2. Use your subordinates, if possible. Have your people enter into preliminary negotiations, so that you can test the other party's musts and wants, you don't have to abide by any tentative agreements (do not surrender the final approval authority), and you remain above the initial fray.

3. Listen more than you talk. Try to keep the ratio to 3-to-1 or more. The more the other party speaks, the more you learn about objectives, fears, timing, pressures, and so on. Volunteer very little, and when you do, be factual. There's a big difference between saying

"I would like to complete this within 2 weeks"
and "If I don't get this done in 2 weeks our
entire plan could be jeopardized." Listen particularly for needs expressed by the other side
that you can meet fairly cheaply from your
perspective.

4. Keep a mental or written private list of your
musts and wants, and track progress.
Summarize often. Many discussions backslide
as the other party begins to realize that you've
taken an edge or they may think that everything is continually up for discussion until
there is some final, written agreement. Make it
clear that "We've already decided on the location of the response unit, and I can't continue
like this if we constantly revisit every decision."

5. Try to be collaborative and not adversarial.
Talk about "decisions we're making" and
"prices we have to pay," and not "you'll get this
if I get that."

6. Never make it personal. Do not attach your
counterpart's self-esteem, ego, self-worth, or
abilities. As they say in the movies, "this is only
business." If you allow it to become personal—
in either direction—emotions will hold sway
over objectives. You may well "one-up" someone at the price of an important objective
being missed. British Prime Minister
Chamberlain received "peace in our time"
(which lasted barely a year) while Hitler
received Czechoslovakia uncontested just prior
to World War II. Congratulate the other party
on how well they've negotiated, no matter
what the actual outcome in your eyes.

7. Remember that the other party may well have a dominant "client." In other words, it's not just what another manager needs, but it's his or her boss who's really the issue. The union representative may be concerned with the rank and file reaction, or with the way in which the regional representative views the result. The media may be an issue, or government regulators, or lobbyists, or other interested parties. Try to think through to your "counterpart's customer" so that you can really gauge what to offer.

8. Negotiate privately and confidentially. Don't allow ego or other interests to compromise that sanctity. You're liable to get much more leeway and flex from your counterpart if the proceedings aren't public and concessions can be made in private.

9. Never renege. Unless you've inadvertently agreed to something that will kill you or the organization, stand by your word. Even if you've made a major error—but a nonfatal one—live with it and make the best of it. Trust is everything in negotiating, and if you're deemed not to be trustworthy, your position will be intolerably weakened in the future. If someone got the best of you, admit it and learn from it, but don't retaliate through a failure to hold up your end of the bargain.

10. Always summarize in writing. You need a document of record. You don't have to record embarrassing concessions or painful truths, only the outcome, consisting of who does what to whom in what time frames. Without this, the "beer truck scenario" (a famous "what if" used

by all salespeople: What if the buyer is run over by a beer truck tomorrow? Will the deal stand up?) can undo you.

There is a world of other advice you'll receive on negotiating, but if you separate your musts from your wants at the outset, then live by these 10 rules, you'll "win" a lot more than you'll "lose."

Handling the tough issues of our times

Managers are called upon today to deal with some issues that were rare or unheard of 20 years ago (and not dealt with in MBA and other educational programs). These issues include:

- Substance abuse and alcoholism

- Sexual harassment

- Discrimination of all types

- Sabotage and theft of real or intellectual property

- Cheating, embezzlement, and fraud

- Technological invasion, include e-mail abuse and hacking

- Workplace ills, real and imagined (for example, ventilation, ergonomics)

How do you negotiate when faced with the hot topic, the sensitive issue, or incendiary opinions?

First, ensure that you are dealing with a negotiable issue. Organizational policies—whether or not frequently used and whether or not you completely agree with them—often dictate response. Indica-tions of a hostile workplace, for example, may be subject to immediate referral to legal or human resources. Any kind of theft may warrant immediate dismissal, regardless of circumstances. Responses in these areas also have to be highly

Unofficially...
Sensitive issues are better dealt with through open and candid negotiation rather than being "swept under the rug." However, it's often more useful to go slowly and hold several sessions, rather than attempting to reach agreement on sensitive issues quickly.

consistent, otherwise an elitism and prejudicial environment is formed in which one's rank, tenure, or connections, rather than the facts, actually dictate response.

Here is a case example taken from a client. How would you negotiate the response?

Example: A district manager in the field force has reported to the vice president of human resources the following story, which has been validated with the other parties concerned. A sales representative purchased a fax machine for his home (from which he works) so that he can deal with customers more efficiently. He paid for the machine himself. When he told his own district manager that he had done this, the manager told him to submit a series of lunch bills with clients over the next several months until the $450 price of the machine had been recouped. The salesman did so, mentioned the "system" to another salesman, who requested the same treatment from his district manager, who filed the complaint with human resources.

Your sales director says that it's a minor matter, that the two people involved have spotless records, are both top people, and the issue should be minimalized, with the money repaid by the salesman. The human resources vice president wants both people fired and a clear policy statement (which already exists) reissued and emphasized.

The matter has landed in your lap. What would you do? Which side would you support?

Here is an example of what the musts and wants might be:

Musts

■ No unethical activity is permitted

■ The organization has a clear, unambiguous message and example

- Rapid resolution
- Top management presents a uniform front

Wants

- No top talent is lost
- Policy is examined for reasonableness, and changed if required
- Organization enthusiastically supports decision
- Minimal distraction to operations and morale

Using these parameters, an arbitrary firing was rejected unless a pattern of deceit and personal gain was found. However, clear accountability and a firm policy had to be manifest. The manager in charge decided on the following:

Since neither the sales rep nor the sales manager had any kind of infraction on his record, there were no terminations. Further, the action was clearly not for personal gain on the part of the manager, and salesman did not have that original intent. However, a policy was clearly violated (truthfulness in expense reporting and fax machines were not a reimbursable item for the field), so the district manager was placed on probation for a year and his bonus was set at 50 percent of what it would normally have been at year-end. The salesman reimbursed the company immediately and was also put on probation for 6 months. The manager reporting the incident received a phone call of thanks for his initiative and honesty.

Both the sales director and human resources vice president arrived at this outcome, although the manager could have simply invoked it. However, this created true ownership, even though the resolution was not as strict as the latter wanted and not as lenient as the former recommended.

Watch Out!
Make sure that negotiations revolve around the organization's best interests. At times, rival parties will joust over purely personal parochial matters. If the organization won't benefit from the outcome of the negotiation, no matter what the outcome, walk away from it and deny both parties.

Negotiating tough responses

Some of the issues above are not always true negotiating situations. Often the manager has to take
strong, unilateral action, based on judgement or
organizational policy. But there are times when
either the resolution has to be negotiated with
peers, as in the example above, or when the most
desirable outcome is remediation, counseling, and
rehabilitation that is agreed to by the individual
involved. That accommodation often also involves
negotiation. (If you doubt that negotiation is
important in issues involving discrimination,
harassment, substance abuse, and the like, think
about the situations that have developed in recent
years at Astra Pharmaceuticals [sexual har-
assment], Texaco [blatant racial epithets], the
Navy's "Tailhook" fiasco [sexual harassment], and
Denny's restaurants [racial discrimination of cus-
tomers].)

Too often managers have been afraid to confront colleagues, or have accepted "necessary evils"
or been drawn into inappropriate environments
because they have not negotiated resolutions with
peers and superiors.

The same dynamic applies with downsizing and
layoffs. If you want to protect staff and save jobs, for
instance, simply digging in your heels and trying to
shield people will not work (especially since it's
often external consultants doing the arbitrary cutting). You're far better off trying to negotiate by
demonstrating the following:

- Outsourced work or transferred work will
  result in more expense and lower quality than
  the present configuration.

■ The current unit can accept additional work from other areas that are being reduced or eliminated.

■ Customers will be inordinately affected by the loss of this unit.

■ Problems for the overall reorganization (or merger or whatever) will be severe because this unit represents unique union, discrimination, or legal potential problems.

Negotiating with customers

Logic makes people think. Emotion makes them act. When negotiating with customers (or prospects), keep emotionalism in the picture.

There is a reason that auto dealers encourage test drives. It's because no matter what the gas mileage, the soundness of the construction, and the safety features of the car, the purchase of an automobile has become a basic lifestyle decision. The buyer wants to feel good and look good. I asked one of my friends why he had purchased a rather impractical sports car when he had been shopping for a sedan. He told me, sheepishly, "The car looked good, and the sales guy told me to take it for a spin. I told him I wasn't interested in that type of car, but he said it was a slow day and I might have a good time. It was a great experience. I saw some people looking at me. When I got back, the sales staff commented that I looked really cool in the car."

"So you simply purchased that model?" I asked, stunned.

"No," he muttered, "I purchased an upgraded one with a spoiler, because that one looked even cooler."

Unofficially...
When tough decisions are being made about staffing behind closed doors, there is a feeling of hopelessness. But those meetings are using some criteria to make choices, and the criteria might as well be yours. Present a solid negotiating case early, before your counterparts, and you can influence the outcome.

Negotiating with customers demands that you listen carefully and offer options so that the emotional quotient can be met. Does every customer have an emotional need to be filled? No, there are some who are simply matter-of-fact and objective, or for whom the issue is mechanical. Buying paper clips is not an emotional decision. However, buying a desk is.

Here are the steps necessary to negotiate with a customer successfully every time (and this holds true for internal customers, as well).

Do not focus on features and benefits, but on results and outcomes

Features and benefits are simply things that vary in attractiveness depending on the customer, and which you can arbitrarily focus on too early, forcing the customer to decide, "Nice, but I don't need that." It's far better to focus on results and outcomes.

Example: You want to sell a piece of property.

Wrong way: Focus on the short distance to schools, or the three-car garage. The buyers might prefer a private school despite the distance, and have only two cars, viewing the rest of the garage as wasted space.

Right way: Ask what the family situation is, listen for the couple's objectives, and provide support for the buyer's preferences. If they are athletic, point out the country club only a mile away. If they love to entertain, point out the circulation patterns in the house.

At work, if you want to provide a training program to a line customer, don't focus on the brevity of the course or the interactive technology, no matter how fabulous you think it is. Instead, demonstrate the customer service skills that can be immediately

Timesaver
When negotiating with an internal or external customer, ask fairly early what their ideal outcome would be. That will tell you quickly what their musts probably are, and what emotional factors are important. You now have information about them that they don't have about you.

transferred and used to improve the department's progress toward improving response time.

Take easy-to-accommodate issues "off the table"

Negotiations often get stuck on the mundane and easily resolved. Don't allow minor points to become stumbling blocks because of your own ego or emotions. The more you concede minor points, the more chips you build up as deserving some quid pro quo.

Example: The client has asked, if the purchase is made, that shipments be sent to three locations instead of a central one. This is not the usual policy, but you know the cost is minimal and that your shipping area can do it easily. Instead of saying, "Well, we can look at that, depending on other issues," say, "Done. What else do you need?" If the client says that a single contact is required, don't say, "All of our people are well trained to help you," but "I can give you a single name if you realize that the person may not be immediately available and may have to call you back, but always within 2 hours."

Having "taken off the table" all of the relatively minor points, you can then say, "I'm happy to have accommodated these five important issues that were stumbling blocks. Now, I only need one thing: We'll need payment in advance in return for these services and options that are exceptions to our policy." You've traded a raft of minor issues for one major one.

Always provide a "choice of yeses"

One of the most successful negotiating gambits of all is to provide options instead of a "take it or leave it" fork in the road. I call this the "choice of yeses." This is a powerful psychological tool that subtly changes the dynamic from "should I do this?" to "how best should I do this?"

Example: You're attempting to get the boss to provide a pool of incentive money for the inside support team, which feels left out of the sales incentive system even though they are key to its success. The boss has steadily refused such requests in the past, pointing out that measurement is difficult, the precedent is worrisome, and there is no budget for it. Most people have argued about fair play, morale, and teamwork.

Your tack is different. You tell the boss that there are three options to do this successfully:

■ Insiders are teamed with their outside counterparts, and only share in incentive money generated by profits from that team above and beyond their plan.

■ The entire inside operation gets a common percentage from a pool formed if the entire division exceeds its plan, thereby generating bonus monies.

■ The inside people are rated as always, on individual performance, and the top 25 percent receives a strong bonus if the division exceeds plan, the next 25 percent receives a more modest bonus, and the other 50 percent receives no bonus, regardless of profit.

The boss cannot debate the merits of each and decide which is safer, more equitable, and so on. Moreover, the key must of not spending money that isn't there has been dealt with by basing all of the options on excess profits.

Don't allow any negotiating opportunity to pass without at least examining if there's the possibility to present a "choice of yeses."

Bright Idea
If you want to defuse a negotiating situation quickly, begin with, "Why don't we examine our options?" Assuming that there are alternatives, this gives both sides the opportunity to change an "us versus them" mentality into a common exploration of resolution options. (This also works very well with kids!)

Never discuss costs—always discuss value

Every single person negotiating an issue will be understandably concerned about costs, especially clients and customers. But no one wants to sacrifice value. Hence, the discussion you create should always be about value, and never about cost. (Once salespeople focus on cost, their products and services have become nothing more than commodities, and the cheapest price will prevail. But this is not a normal condition, as sales of Mercedes-Benz, Bulgari, and Armani will attest.)

Example: You are negotiating a consulting contract with a prospective buyer. The buyer says that $225,000 is expensive, there is no budget for it, and the buyer is sure that the job can be done less expensively by internal people or by other external sources. You point out that the buyer is deriving productivity improvements—identified by the buyer in putting the proposal together—which are worth a minimum of $4 million on an annualized basis. If this could have been done internally it would probably already have been done, and if it's to be done right, then the best qualified resources, not the least expensive, are needed. Moreover, the investment (not the "price") is about 5 percent of the first-year savings alone—only a nickel of every dollar that will be saved. On the longer-term basis, the investment virtually disappears, and every investment the buyer makes should be this good.

Whether internal or external, talk to customers about the value they are receiving, and the investment and return on investment that it entails, not the "fee" or "cost" or "price." And remember that a significant part of value is emotional, so in addition

Watch Out!
Set a minimally profitable and acceptable fee level as your "must." During negotiations, should you choose to reduce your fee in return for reducing deliverables and value, you'll know clearly what line you can't cross. Without such a minimal must, you can easily close on a non-profitable deal.

to actual financial return, conditions that are important include: safety, comfort, security, quality, reputation, image, aesthetics, and tranquility. The more value placed on these emotionally important issues, the more the investment is minimized.

These negotiating dynamics are largely controlled by you, and are not a function of the other party, the situation, or the issues. These are process points that are constantly available if you choose to employ them.

Never lower a price or reduce a fee without a commensurate decrease in value

Sometimes you'll have to reduce a customer's investment if you are to get the business. There may be an inflexible budget, competitive pressure, or other business conditions that warrant such a move. However, do not lower price without a tangible reduction in value. Otherwise, the client's negotiating strategy will always be, "How low can they go?"

If you're offering a consulting contract, then remove the international work, or the follow-up audits, or the one-on-one interviews. If you're selling computers, remove the free servicing, or the software updates, or some peripherals. If the customer is internal and you're offering MIS support, remove the 24-hour availability, or the usage summary reports, or the new programs written expressly for that client.

Never take part in a unilateral reduction of your fee, value-received, or well-being. That is not negotiation. It is surrender.

The negotiation flow

Negotiating is all too often a circular path, leading from nowhere to nothing. It should be a linear flow, which shouldn't be entered into unless the preceding steps have been successfully concluded and, thereby, never revisited.

The chart below shows the sequence:

START

Establish non-violable musts

Establish a constructive tone, but on your turf or neutral turf

If possible, have subordinates begin discussions

When you are involved, listen much more than you talk

Concede "wants" when necessary, but never "musts"

Always focus on the other side's value, not the price or cost

Do not concede price without a tangible reduction in value

Summarize and reiterate to ensure both parties understand the same thing

Put it in writing

FINISH

You can embellish on this as much as you please, but the point is that there is a starting point and an ending point. We've all been involved in negotiations that went on endlessly because of these basic weaknesses:

■ Agreement on concessions and compromise are never concluded, but are left open as possibilities.

Suggested remedy: Place the contested issues on an easel sheet (not a blackboard or whiteboard that can be erased). Post the sheet at each meeting, and mark those items that have been settled by indicating the appropriate action, for example, Staffing: Three staff members to move from actuarial to underwriting on a permanent basis.

■ You (or the other party) realize a must has been violated and attempt to return to undo the damage.

Unofficially...
The more people
that are present,
the more that
negotiators are
subject to ego
needs and inter-
personal dynam-
ics, to the extent
that logic and
pragmatics won't
necessarily carry
the day. Try to
limit the number
of people present
severely, and try
to avoid subordi-
nates who are
just present
watching their
bosses
"perform."

Suggested remedy: On your part, keep your musts clearly in front of you (privately, of course), so that you are constantly aware of them and don't lose track in the heat of the discussions. If your counter-part is clearly trying to regain a critical point, allow it to happen but only in return for several of your objectives, since the value of regaining a lost must is so enormous.

- New people join the discussions and claim that they never agreed to prior concessions.

Suggested remedy: At the outset, get absolute agree-ment on who the participants will be, and who among them has the ability to make final decisions. Demand that the decision makers be at every meet-ing or the sessions will be cancelled. Further, do not allow any new people to enter at any time except as observers and information resources. The more people present, the more that "face" and ego enter the picture.

- The other party becomes intransigent because they perceive that there is too high a cost to be paid (whether in money, repute, resources, and so on).

Suggested remedy: Focus on the value and help the other side realize that the investment being made is wise and will be appreciated in terms of the return. *Example:* Although you are losing six staff members, you will no longer have the financial reporting obligations that have caused unexpected and unwel-come weekend work on occasion. (This technique is especially useful when dealing with union represen-tatives or customers.)

- The agreements are later denied, rejected, or reneged on.

Suggested remedy: The decision maker—the "owner" of the outcome—must be involved, preferably early, but certainly well before the conclusion. We talked earlier about trying to have subordinates conduct preliminary discussions, but substantive discussions must be between responsible decision makers. Never negotiate, yourself, with someone else's subordinates who are not the decision makers for their team. Also, it's helpful to summarize each meeting and commit to writing the progress (for example, the issues on the easel sheets that have been settled in one direction or another) and to commit the final resolutions to paper, which both parties sign. (These written agreements should go to mutual superiors.)

What if you make a mistake? What if you conclude a negotiation that turns out not to be in your best interest, or has violated your own musts, or that colleagues and subordinates have critiqued as poor results? Don't panic. Few negotiating mistakes are fatal. You may have to live with a poorer result than you would have preferred. You may be temporarily inconvenienced.

Don't panic and don't be too hard on yourself. Learn from your mistakes and become a better negotiator the next time. Negotiating is art and science, and no one is perfect. Practice on lesser matters, so that you've honed your skills (and made your mistakes) by the time you arrive at the major matters.

Just the facts

- A constructive settlement results in both parties being satisfied, not one exulting in victory over the other.

- The absolute key to your success is to be clear on the few musts that cannot be sacrificed.
- Never concede on price or investment, unless value is reduced.
- Document agreements along the way, and as a final step.
- Don't allow ego—yours or theirs—to overly influence practical outcomes.

GET THE SCOOP ON...
The difference between strategy and tactics ▪
What vision, mission, and values really mean ▪
Aligning objectives behind strategy ▪
Demystifying culture ▪ Why tactics can succeed
but strategies fail

Setting Strategy That People Can Actually Use

Chapter 13

Strategy is not just for the executive boardroom, the most senior managers, or external, pricey consultants. Every manager has both a strategic role and a tactical one. Ideally, managers at every level should be actively embraced in and supportive of the corporate strategy. However, at the very least, managers create their own strategies on a regular basis, so they might as well get good at it.

Power managers recognize the difference between strategy and tactics, and don't allow themselves to believe that success in one equals success in the other.

Most simplistically, strategy is "what" and tactics are "how." Your strategy determines the goals, outcomes, and ending points that make sense, even though the target may intelligently shift as conditions change and strategies are redefined. However, most managerial strategies are surprisingly short-term, so that they are actually met (or missed) within a brief time frame.

If strategy is the destination, then tactics constitute the execution and implementation. Peter Drucker would call strategy "doing the right things," and tactics "doing things right." It does no good to do wrong things well, it does no good to do right things poorly, and it's a disaster to do wrong things poorly.

Yet most managers only work along one dimension, either strategy or tactics, rather than managing the synergy between the two. That's why most strategies are vibrant and exciting in the planning, and dismal failures in the execution. No one is managing the transition from ideation to implementation.

The surprising difference between strategy and tactics

Timesaver
As you might suspect, most people are more inclined to jump into tactics ("action"). Before they do, demand to know what strategy is being implemented and how those actions will lead to the goal. You'll at least learn quickly if they are capable of strategic thought or are merely implementers.

If you're playing chess, your strategy might be to gain control over the middle of the board, and the tactics you employ might be to sacrifice a pawn early in order to gain that territorial advantage. However, if you were guided only by tactics, you might be impelled to never endanger a piece, thereby foregoing that particular strategic advantage (which is probably the most powerful strategy in the early part of a chess game).

In the war in Kosovo, NATO's tactic of absolutely minimizing allied casualties greatly affected strategy, probably prolonging the hostilities until they could be brought to a conclusion with the "safest" tactics that would still be effective—massive air power, but no ground combatants.

If you are hiring people for operational supervisory positions, do you hire simply the "best" candidates with the strongest résumés and the best interviewing skills, or do you pursue those with better strategic talents because supervisors have to anticipate, plan, and organize around future customer needs? Some "brilliant" hires have turned into duds not because anyone mistook their abilities but because they had the inappropriate abilities—tacticians were required but strategists were hired, or vice versa.

In the graphic, you can see the simple but crucial relationship between strategy and tactics:

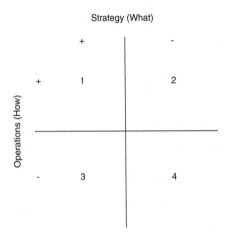

Strategy (What)

In quadrant #1 we have organizations (be they companies, divisions, departments, agencies, nonprofits, schools, and so on) that have a clear strategy and effective tactics. Examples from a wide array of organizational entities might include:

- Microsoft
- Pfizer
- Continental Airlines
- Dell Computer
- Girl Scouts of America
- U.S. Federal Reserve
- Yale University
- City of Baltimore

These are organizations that plan their future well and execute their plans well. They may change. For example, Sears and Boeing would have been in quadrant #1 at one point (and may be again, some day).

In quadrant #2 are those organizations that employ effective tactics but do not have cogent strategies. Consequently, they may be making money quarter-to-quarter, and may be attracting and retaining customers and employees, but they are vulnerable to sudden shifts and twists. This is where most organizations, particularly in the United States, have resided, and where most managers have traditionally placed their emphasis and focus. It has resulted in a short-term view of the organization, and has doomed many of them to peaks and valleys, sudden downsizing, and inaccurate forecasting.

Such organizations are often resting on their laurels or entirely consumed with meeting short-term earnings forecasts or nonfinancial goals (customer acquisition, publicity, and so on). Examples of these companies at this writing might include:

- General Motors
- Eastman Kodak
- Boeing
- United Way
- Internal Revenue Service
- Harvard Law School
- City of Philadelphia

These organizations may be doing well, but their success is erratic and not predicated on a clearly defined future. Harvard Law School has commissioned consultants to determine why student morale is so low, and the City of Philadelphia has managed

Bright Idea
When unsure of the merits of a proposed course of action, ask, "What strategic goal is this meant to achieve or support?" If no one can answer that—or a strategic goal is created on the spot—then your instincts were probably right and the proposal is a random one.

to greatly reduce its debt and improve its services, yet still struggles with its long-term finan ing strategies, swinging from reinvestment in the aging shipyard to trying to attract other enterprises.

Quadrant #3 is the converse of #2. These organizations have clear strategies (for example, "to be the leaders in microchip technology"), but don't have the operational savvy, expertise, or talent to be making money and creating an efficient operation. Quadrant #3 organizations, which are frequently start-up or high-tech companies, either move up to quadrant #1 as they become more competitive and efficient (Microsoft) or drop off the board as inefficiencies do them in (Osborne Computer).

Examples of current quadrant #3 organizations might be:

- Amazon.com
- America Online
- Most cellular phone companies
- City of Washington, D.C.
- U.S. Immigration and Naturalization Agency
- U.S. Postal Service
- Amtrak

You'll note that, in government, "dropping off the board" is usually not an option, so that more money is thrown at the problem even though efficiencies might not improve. Amtrak, for example, continues to spend hundreds of millions to modernize its operation while never having shown the ability to make a penny's profit.

Finally, quadrant #4 is the area for those who don't know where they're going and don't know how to get there. (The philosopher Santayana's definition of a fanatic was "someone who loses sight of

Bright Idea
Have all key decision makers participate in your strategy formulation because it's vital that they agree on current status and desired future status. When you present a strategy as a fait accompli, it will not be embraced by the very people you need to support it the most.

his goals and consequently redoubles his efforts.") Many of these organizations simply disappear, but some descend and recover. Chrysler was a good example of an organization in quadrant #4 that re-emerged under the leadership of Lee Iaccoca. Sears has also visited this area periodically as it lost sight of its customers and its rivals (at times it has tried to compete with both Wal-Mart and Bergdorf's). Apple Computer has also gone from quadrant #1 to #4 and back again.

Current quadrant #4 candidates might include:

- TWA
- U.S. Bureau of Indian Affairs
- Greyhound Bus
- City of Camden (has requested that New Jersey take it over)
- Howard Johnson's

In the private sector, quadrant #4 organizations go bankrupt or are acquired. In the public sector, they have more money thrown at them or are left to languish with minimal funding. In the nonprofit arena, they generally fail to help their customers and abuse their volunteers.

While these are global and organization-wide examples to make the point, the fact is that managers face similar dynamics on a daily basis. So, before we go on, let's establish a simple set of definitions:

Strategy is a framework, within which tactics that affect the nature and direction of the organization are established.

Tactics are decisions that are made within a strategic framework, which affect the nature and direction of the organization.

The manager's role in strategy

The graphic below illustrates the manager's role in strategy implementation:

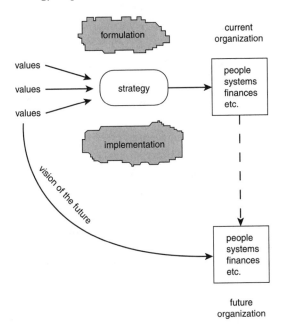

Values

Values are simply those beliefs that determine what strategy will be. On an organizational level, Merck & Co. believes that it exists in order to take the greatest ability in scientific research and apply it against the greatest areas of human health suffering. Virtually any Merck employee, whether in finance, sales, research, or any other area, will tell you that in so many words.

On a departmental level, the values may be to respond to customers with speed, accuracy, and honesty, no matter what the problem, the complexity, or the cause.

Watch Out!
Strategies, whether organizational or personal, never fail in their formulation, which is usually a pristine paper exercise. They generally fail in their implementation, which is a real-world, practical exercise. Strategy implementation is the talent in short supply.

Values precede strategy because they represent what the enterprise believes in, what its purpose is, and why it exists. We hear a lot about "culture" these days, and how difficult "cultural change" is. Culture is nothing more than that set of values which governs behavior. Values can, indeed, change. But behavioral change without a fundamental change in values is merely movement. I once consulted for a high-risk auto insurer that made it clear to employees that, although the customers tended to be high-risk and financially insecure, the customers were to be treated with the respect and courtesy due any customer of any business. Yet the employees really didn't believe this, and, when management wasn't looking or listening, treated the customers quite poorly. The result was an inefficient operation that had trouble sorting out valid claims from illegitimate ones, and constant threats of regulatory oversight.

Vision

This is the glimpse of the future that the strategy is intended to realize. It constitutes what the organization (or department or agency) is supposed to look like, feel like, sound like, react like, and be like in the future. The vision flows from the values, from the raison d'être of the organization. Strategy is the means to achieve that desired future state.

Strategy formulation

Strategies, whether grand or simple, have to be constructed. This usually includes an examination of the goals to be achieved, the environment, the competition, potential threats, potential opportunities, timing, and so forth. Strategies on the organizational level are often for extended periods, for example, five years, but, in reality, they are seldom effective for more than a year or two, and ought to be at least revisited and revised annually.

Strategy implementation

This is the "translation" that managers must make to adjust the conceptualization of the strategy to operational realities. The current organization contains people, systems, finances, procedures, customer relationships, and so forth. The future organization will contain these factors as well. However, how must they be changed, altered, nurtured, protected, and supported in order to make the transition from the current organization to the future organization? That is the manager's great challenge.

Most strategies fail in the implementation because management does not do an adequate job of managing the current organization in the direction of the future vision.

The manager's role in strategy is not to take the hefty three-ring binder with the corporate strategy and place it neatly in the bottom desk drawer, although that is precisely where most probably rest at this moment. The manager's job should include the following:

- Understand the strategy in its entirety, and how it relates to the manager's specific accountabilities.

One should be able to articulate the strategy briefly for the sake of subordinates and colleagues (the former to guide their work, the latter to reach effective compromises). If the strategy is "To become the premier provider of financial security to middle-income Americans," and the manager is in the underwriting department, then what are the implications for underwriting? Should the strategy

Unofficially...
Any vision of the future is, by definition, uncertain. In the best case, as conditions change, it's a "moving target." The idea isn't to hit a certain spot, but rather to move in the right direction. Strategy implementation is really about direction, not destination.

become more risk-averse for security, or more prudently risk-taking in a boom market economy? If one is managing sales, does this mean that potential customers should now include early retirees, or does it preclude people who no longer have college tuition and house payments in their futures?

- Review the human resources and talents required to meet the strategic goals.

Do not start with what you have now. Rather, create the picture of the future, otherwise you will be constrained by growing what you have rather than creating what you need.

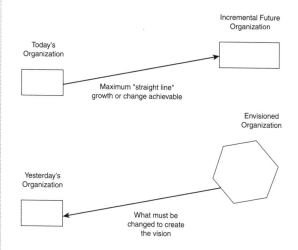

If you begin with today and try to turn it into tomorrow, you will be constrained by maximum growth and change permitted by today's organization and resources. But if you begin with the picture of the future, you can then "work backwards" to determine what has to be changed today in order to reach tomorrow.

This is a crucial management consideration in effectively implementing strategy: You cannot begin with the assumption that the current people and talents will be able to grow and change at the rate needed to gain the future vision. You must begin with the vision, and then ask, "What people and talents must be in place today in order to make progress toward our vision of the future?"

■ Review the procedures, systems, policies, environment, and resources that must be changed in order to support people in achieving that future state.

The current organization's mode of operating will not allow you to support the talent required to help you reach the desired future state. By definition, it has been designed and reinforced to help maintain and solidify the status quo. Although there might be some flexibility, the new organization is not within its paradigm.

Here's an example of the above elements: Hewlett-Packard recently decided that one of its major customer response centers needed to be changed in order to support a strategy of rapid, customer-controlled problem solving. The current center directed 90 percent of all calls to individual technicians for response, while 10 percent were deemed appropriate for an automated menu and response system because those issues were generic. Managers in the unit decided that the exact reverse was required to meet corporate strategy: About 90 percent of calls would have to be automatically answered with customers controlling the menu to find their own resolutions, and 10 percent, representing the most difficult and complex problems, would be directed toward a human response. (Believe it or not, most questions still revolved around things like plugging in machines and how to plug in peripherals.)

Some coasts are set aside for shipwreck.
—Loren Eisley

This meant that the current human resource talent was used incorrectly. There was a wide array of people, most of whom were qualified to handle the mundane and simple questions, while directing the tougher ones to a small team of specialists. What would be needed in the future was a small cadre of experts to whom the automatic system would direct those calls that didn't fit into automated response categories.

The technology had to change in order to handle many more choices and types of problems, but had to offer rapid menus so that a customer who actually did need to speak to one of the expert technicians could do so fairly rapidly. Finally, the system had to be established without compromising the current one and losing existing customers through poor service during the transition.

The organization and the manager of the response center created the following sequence:

1. Understand the strategy (rapid, customer-controlled response) and determine how the current unit could meet and support that vision. It did not begin with the current operation, but asked what the "ideal" solution would be for the customer.

2. Determine what kinds of people and talents were necessary to implement the desired state. In this case it meant far fewer people but with much higher skill levels.

3. Determine what technology and procedures were required to support the people and talents in the desired organization. Here it meant higher pay levels, less hectic surroundings, access to the most sophisticated diagnostic equipment at the response center, evaluation

not by number of calls answered (for the humans) but on problems solved the first time, and much more sophisticated technology and options to handle the "standard" calls.

4. Develop an implementation plan with accountabilities and time frames to create the new organization. Among other things, this means a dual system for a number of months so that the new structure can be created without disruption to the current service levels. At a given point, calls are simply switched from the old unit to the new. The plan also calls for the redeployment and placement of the excess people who remained after the original unit shuts down.

This is how managers at all levels participate in and support the corporate strategy. However, there is nothing stopping the response unit from embarking on a strategy of its own, so long as it supported the corporate vision. That's why step #1, understanding one's role in the corporate strategy, is so vital.

Aligning corporate objectives with individual objectives

Corporate objectives, goals, and outcomes are useless if the talent of the organization is not working in active support of them. That may sound obvious, but in the majority of cases people are working—with the best of intentions—isolated from corporate goals or in opposition to them.

Most individual goals are misaligned because:

■ The organization's strategy isn't clear.

Some organizations don't have a cogent strategy, but only a vanilla mishmash of goals and values

Watch Out!
Many times, organizational strategy is not known, due to the absence of one, or poor communication, or unreasonable secrecy. Don't assume that you know what it is. It's your superior's job to provide connections to your job, and if you don't know it, you can't provide connections for your people.

("We will be the highest quality food flavoring company in the world."). We've all seen the banners in the cafeteria that proclaim "Simply the best," as if that's a sufficient rallying cry for people to mold their jobs and behaviors after. Many nonprofits confuse the strategy and governance with fund-raising and revenue generation. Consequently, the only strategy they have seems to be to raise as much money as possible as often as possible.

- The organization doesn't communicate the strategy.

This is due to the mistaken belief that strategy is an executive and sophisticated notion that the general organizational population can't understand, much less utilize. In some cases, strategy does become lofty and abstruse, and we see reference to EVA (economic value added), shareholder value, and discounted future earnings. Those indicate a grave management error, since strategy is the framework within which tactics are decided, and people can't make tactical decisions if the framework is unintelligible or confusing.

- The strategy isn't interpreted at the individual performance level.

The performance evaluation system should have objectives built in that are in direct support of organizational strategy. In the vast majority of cases, however, individual goals have no relationship to organizational goals, and sometimes only fuzzy connections to more local, departmental goals. Managers often don't have the skills, volition, opportunity, or interest in making the proper connections because they, themselves, aren't being evaluated in that manner.

- The strategy changes but the individual goals do not.

Individual goals seem to be cast in cement for the year, and are seldom reviewed or altered (see Chapter 4) despite organizational upheaval and turbulence. Strategies are often changed because of new technology, new competition, changes in senior management, perception change, demographic shifts, global business developments, and the like. Yet people continue to labor under a reward system that is providing incentives for a strategy long since abandoned.

■ There is no reinforcement and monitoring.

Moneysaver
Monthly, review your goals as they support corporate strategy with your boss. Then do the same with your key reports, and have them do the same with theirs. Any change from your boss probably requires a change below you. You are accountable, whether your boss instigates these discussions or not.

Even when strategic goals are translated into individual performance objectives, if there is no oversight, performance easily slips. And while the performer can be "punished" at the annual salary and incentive evaluation, that's much too late to compensate for the misguided performance. It's far better to monitor monthly to ensure that performance is in line with organizational needs. But this is rarely done since everyone is rushing to resolve that day's fires and priorities. If organizational goals aren't the fires and priorities, then what are?

Hence, one of the fundamental jobs of the manager is to align individual goals with clear and understood corporate goals, to ensure that the performer is actually meeting those performance objectives, and that any shifts in strategy are reflected in altered performance goals. Too many managers are efficiently guiding subordinates to the wrong objectives. (There is an old Bob Newhart comedy routine where the pilot announces to the passengers that he has good news and bad news. The good news is that the plane will land about an hour ahead of schedule. The bad news is that he's uncertain whether that will be in New York or Buenos Aires.)

The process of goal alignment is critical for the manager because it involves both the business side and the cultural side of the business, as illustrated in the graphic below.

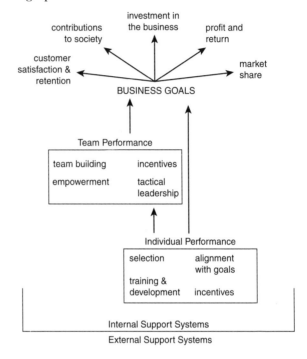

Organizational strategy (business goals) may be defined in any number of ways: on a customer basis, a societal basis, financial basis, competitive basis, some combination of these, and so on. There are two primary, potential supporters of the goals: individuals and teams, though the latter is composed of the former, as well. Individual performers are necessary in that they comprise legal, technical, research, and similar individual contributors. Teams are essential because functions such as marketing, sales, service, and manufacturing can't be successful without them.

Both individuals and teams require connections to organizational strategy if they are to function effectively in support of organizational goals. The manager's key interface is shown in the next illustration.

Bright Idea
Evaluate any developmental, educational, or training recommendation from this vantage point: Does this improve the performance that will accelerate our ability to support corporate strategy? If the answer is negative, then the development is suspect, at least.

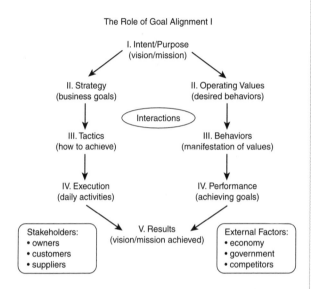

The Role of Goal Alignment I

I. Intent/Purpose
(vision/mission)

II. Strategy
(business goals)

II. Operating Values
(desired behaviors)

Interactions

III. Tactics
(how to achieve)

III. Behaviors
(manifestation of values)

IV. Execution
(daily activities)

IV. Performance
(achieving goals)

Stakeholders:
• owners
• customers
• suppliers

V. Results
(vision/mission achieved)

External Factors:
• economy
• government
• competitors

In the graphic, the vision of the organization is to guide both sides of the equation toward the desired results: the business side and the cultural side. Managers are vital to the role of facilitators, overseers, and guides that create the best interactions between business and cultural needs. One cannot succeed without the other.

Many of the attractive consulting interventions have viewed only the business side as important: reengineering, downsizing, and right sizing, to name a few. Many of the behavioralists have opted strictly for the people side: empowerment, participative management, and open book management. However, it's actually a blend between the two that will drive the organization toward strategic goals.

Unofficially...
Every organization has a strategy, so don't accept the rebuff that "we don't have one formulated yet." The problem is that it's often unconscious or created by default by competition or regulators, but it's a strategy nonetheless.

Strategy should generate tactics which, if executed well, derive the results expected and create the future state desired. However, the values of the organization also drive the operating values, which create behaviors and actually determine performance. If both sides of the equation aren't managed and aligned, then progress is minimal (or aggressive but wrong, as in the flying to New York or Buenos Aires story) and the results are endangered.

Since we've established that culture is nothing more than that set of beliefs that governs behavior, and we need those behaviors that will generate the performance levels required for the tactics specified, you can see that the manager's goal is more critical than ever in the success of the strategic process.

Historically, managers have derived power from control of information and control of people (the infamous "headcount"). In days of leaner organizations and computers on everyone's desk, the traditional power bases have disappeared. However, the new power base is that of achieving results through others, of leveraging talents, and of creating synergies. Ironically, that role has become more strategic than ever.

Managers who can understand corporate strategy and translate it for "local" guidelines, interpret it for individual and team objectives, and coordinate the business and cultural aspects of the enterprise, are in possession of more power than ever before. That interface cannot be managed by executives far removed from the work, and it can't be spontaneously managed by employees, who lack the perspective and frame of reference.

Power managers take the time to understand
and translate corporate strategy and use it as the
parameter within which to marshal resources, lead
others, and achieve results.

Just the facts

- Strategy is based on organizational values, not
  vice versa.
- Tactics are the "how," and must support strategic goals.
- Alignment of individual and team goals is the
  critical factor.
- "Culture" comprises a set of beliefs, and can be
  changed.
- People must be considered separately from
  support and technology.

Speaking, Presenting, Facilitating

PART V

GET THE SCOOP ON...
Why what you say and how you say it are
equally important ▪ Handling questions
effectively ▪ Making your points with the
media ▪ Taking command of a room ▪
Captivating the crowds

Presenting Like a Pro

Chapter 14

Virtually all managers are called upon at one time or another to address a group, conduct a meeting, present a report, make a formal recommendation, or facilitate a session. All of these events help you to stand out in a crowd, and it's important to look good while you're standing there.

Many people become nervous and tense when addressing others, even when just responding to a question in a meeting. While I've never believed the "greatest fear in surveys is public speaking" line, I have observed that managers with excellent points have been "underwhelming" in their presentations and lost the day, while others with moderately good ideas were embraced as heroes after giving captivating presentations.

Whether a small, internal meeting, or a large, external conference, there are three clear and simple keys to presenting like a pro:

1. Prepare thoroughly and well in advance.

2. Maintain a poised, enthusiastic, and controlled demeanor.

3. Expect the unexpected. Nothing ever goes completely as planned.

These three keys will help you avoid panic and attacks of nerves, which are anathema to standing up in public because tension paralyzes one's movements, compromises judgment, and saps energy. (Other than that, tension is great.) However, don't expect to be completely stress-free, because you need a certain amount of adrenaline coursing through your body to create an urgency and a keen focus on the present. (Walter Winchell, in his heyday, commanded the attention of the great preponderance of radio listeners. It was said you could walk down any block and not miss the show, since every radio was tuned to his program. He deliberately drank a quart or so of water just prior to his broadcast, and didn't allow himself to visit the rest room, thereby ensuring an urgent, high-powered, energetic delivery!)

The opposite of distress is eustress, and the idea is not to eliminate all stress—which makes one complacent—but to achieve enough tension to motivate and energize, while avoiding the higher extreme that paralyzes behavior. The chart on the following page illustrates the relationships.

Prepare thoroughly and well in advance

Every time you stand up, whether informally or formally, to deliver a message or talk, people will learn two things, not necessarily in this order: The first is the content of what you want to convey, and the second is your own competency. While there are all kinds of claims about the power of nonverbal communication (and most of them are bogus or exaggerated), "how" you present something is almost as important as "what" you present. (Albert Mehrabbian made a famous psychological study of

Bright Idea
Open every presentation, except those that contain dire news, with a smile. A smile will loosen your own facial muscles and alleviate excess tension, as well as reassure your audience. Watch any outstanding speaker and you'll find them smiling frequently.

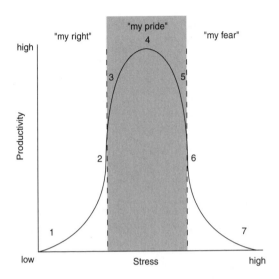

people standing in line who were interrupted. When the person attempting to "cut" the line was pleasant and smiled, rather than abrupt and aloof, the chances were far greater that they would be allowed the favor they requested. Some people have extrapolated that phenomenon to speeches, though certainly without Mehrabbian's blessing.)

Listeners tend to judge sincerity, support, enthusiasm, and commitment of the speaker by nonverbal means. In other words, no matter what you're saying, your behaviors are louder. "What you are speaks so loudly I can't hear what you say," said Ralph Waldo Emerson.

I once observed a senior vice president in a manufacturing company announce to the assembled home office staff that, due to the excellent year just concluded, there would be maximum bonus participation. Yet he said so in such a dry, unenthusiastic, halting manner, that many people present walked out thinking something bad had occurred. One woman actually commented to me, "It's too bad we couldn't have done better."

Treat any "public" appearance, even in a small, internal meeting, as a chance to demonstrate your willingness to help, confidence in your abilities, and command of the topic. Even when you may only be introducing someone else, or "warming up" the audience with introductory remarks, never take the assignment lightly. In earlier chapters we discussed "referent" power, and how some people are followed because they instill confidence and others choose to follow them. There is an opportunity to create referent power—or to forever lose it—every time you stand before a group of subordinates, peers, superiors, media, or customers.

Here are the keys to careful preparation: Understand the audience and organize your remarks.

Understanding the audience

Orient your remarks to the nature of the group. If they are subordinates, they will accept a great deal from you on faith, but if they are superiors, they may have to be convinced with facts and numbers. The educational levels will dictate what kind of language is appropriate. If you're speaking before an international group, whether on their turf or yours, don't use cliches and American idioms. People from the field might not understand home-office technical language ("The comparatios were TQC for the PAR"), and relatively new people might not relate to company lore and war stories.

Carefully delineate whom you'll be addressing and, if the same message is to be delivered to highly diverse groups in differing settings, adjust the delivery to be most relevant for each group and environment.

Organizing your remarks

Presentations of any type have three components: a beginning, a middle, and an end. This should come as no surprise, yet many speakers begin in the middle and conclude without an ending!

The beginning should be brief, containing a "hook" or attention-getter that draws the listeners into what follows. Presentations are usually successful or unsuccessful in their first 2 or 3 minutes, because it's during that period that the listeners decide whether the content is going to be of benefit or not. Yet what they are really being affected by is the *delivery* far more than the message. Use your first couple of minutes to "grab" the listener so that he or she wants to hear what else you're going to say.

In an informal setting, this may be nothing more than: "The weekly staff meeting is going to focus on turnover today, because we've found that our rate is the highest in the industry and the people in this room can do a lot to erase that dubious honor." In a more formal speech: "Thanks for inviting me to address the industry leaders. My passion for this business demands that I be honest with you—the factors that have accounted for our success over the past decade are disappearing, and we must embrace a new set of factors for tomorrow's success that, frankly, we may not be ready for."

Some examples of "hooks" or "grabbers" to use to open your presentation:

- Facts and statistics: "Ten years ago we were the forty-seventh largest firm in this business, and today we are the seventh. We didn't get there by accident, and I've identified five areas that have been our core strengths."

Watch Out!
Humor is fabulous in presentations, but it's deadly if it doesn't work. Don't tell a joke, tell a story. Don't go for a big laugh, but for heads nodding in agreement. And if there's pain or embarrassment involved, make sure you tell it on yourself, not someone else.

- Rhetorical questions: "We've grown dramatically and profitably over the past decade. Why have we prospered while others have failed? Will we be able to continue our growth without making major changes in our product line? Will we need different talents? I'm going to address those issues."

- Analogies: "If our growth over the past decade were applied to the high-tech industry, Microsoft would be twice as big as it is and Dell Computer would be 50 percent larger."

- Clever phrases: "We've been the overachievers in our market. And, as with all overachievers, things have come pretty easily to us. Now it's time to raise the bar, and to see if we can reach a goal that no one else has managed to reach."

Unofficially...
Audience members will make a tacit decision about whether and how intently to pay attention to your remarks in the first 2 minutes or so of your presentation. Spend an hour of preparation on these 2 minutes if you have to, but make them very strong!

- Humor: "We've been called a 'best kept secret.' Well, I don't know about you, but I'd just as soon not be such a secret when bonus and incentive time rolls around. In fact, I'd like to be standing out in front with everyone pointing!"

- Brief story (with emphasis on "brief"): "Hank and Marie actually began this company in a garage. My mentor told me that he found a dark spot on several of the early blueprints, which we still use. When he asked what caused it, he was told it was oil from a leak in Marie's car that they were never able to fix."

- Recognition: "I don't want to begin my remarks without formally recognizing the home office support team that enabled us to beat our service goals for a record tenth month in a row. Let's have them stand and give them the recognition they deserve."

- Demonstration: "What you see here is an example of our latest portable generating unit. You'll note that you can't even hear it in the rear of this room because it's so quiet."

- Illustration: "If you'll turn your attention to the screen (or the handouts), you'll see that despite higher sales our profits are slightly lower this year, and we need to make sure that we don't keep working harder, but instead, start working smarter."

The middle, or body, of your talk should contain the basic information that you'd like the listeners to think about, act on, or take away to others. A good way to diversify and vary your presentation or talk is to use this formula:

- Select the key points that constitute your overall message. For example, if your message is "Work smarter not harder," your key points might be:

    1. Don't continue to fix problems, but find out what caused them so we can eliminate them altogether.

    2. Track customer complaints to see if there is a pattern that can isolate chronically weak areas of service.

    3. Work with colleagues, not in isolation, so that we're not all reinventing the same wheel every day.

    4. Use our online research capability to find out if similar situations to the one you're facing have already been identified and resolved.

    5. Ensure that the customer is happy before you engage in time-consuming investigations.

- Once you have the points that support your theme, build an example and suggested actions around each. For example, if we chose the last points above: "Ensure that the customer is happy before you engage in time-consuming investigations," then we might build around it:

  1. "We had a case just last week where a customer was asked to wait for a week while we determined why the refund check hadn't been sent. We knew within 2 hours that auditing has questioned the refund, which we knew was due. We should have immediately issued a manual check, then worked out our differences with auditing. Instead, we argued internally while the customer waited . . . and waited . . . and waited . . ."

  2. So, here are the actions I recommend in this situation:

- If the issue can be resolved quickly externally, even though we have internal problems, do so.

- If the issue can't be resolved externally until internal problems are resolved, then give the customer a precise time at which you will call back with a progress report.

- Prior to that progress report time, if you cannot resolve the internal matter, then raise it to my level. If you do not come to me, it is your fault.

To summarize about the body of your talk: Break your overall topic or theme into separate points, then back up each point with an example or story, and provide a set of actions, guidelines, or responses.

Timesaver
When you have to create an oral or written presentation, work "backwards" from your overall theme, to your points which support the theme, to the examples and actions that illustrate and support each point. You can then create methodical presentations in a very brief time.

Build your visual aids and handouts around those points and actions. In other words, for each point have a slide, or a page in the handouts, or an easel sheet. This is a systematic way to compose the body of your talk. Note that you don't start with a joke, six points, or handouts, but you begin with your theme, work "backwards" to develop the points which support it, then work "backwards" again to develop a story or example and action steps around each point, supported by your visual aids. (This process works for written or oral material, and is the answer for those people who say they "just can't get started" or have "writer's block.")

The third part of the presentation is the ending, and it's almost always ignored or downplayed, which ruins much of the work that preceded it. If the opening of the speech is the key to whether people will want to listen to what follows, the ending is the key to whether people will do anything differently when they leave. Yet, most of the time, the speaker drones to a close with the hackneyed, "Are there any questions?" (No, there aren't, because we're all dying to get out of here.)

The close should be relatively brief (there's nothing wrong with saying, "In summary," to let your listeners know that you're concluding and they had better pay close attention). It should contain the following:

■ Reference back to the theme or topic of the presentation.

"We've been discussing the need to work smarter, not harder, beginning immediately, and helping your people to move in that direction."

▪ Review of the key points.

"The five points that are essential for us in this division are:

1. Don't continue to fix problems, but find out what caused them so we can eliminate them altogether.

2. Track customer complaints to see if there is a pattern that can isolate chronically weak areas of service.

3. Work with colleagues, not in isolation, so that we're not all reinventing the same wheel every day.

4. Use our online research capability to find out if similar situations to the one you're facing have already been identified and resolved.

5. Ensure that the customer is happy before you engage in time-consuming investigations."

▪ A call to action.

"When we leave here this morning, let's all do the following:

1. Hold a brief meeting with our staffs to review these five points.

2. Ask our people what else we should be doing to work smarter.

3. Talk informally over the next day to share what we've learned.

4. Agree on an incentive to help people focus on these goals."

You can use humor at the end of your presentation, so long as you tie it to your summary points. You don't want people leaving saying, "That was a great story!" but forgetting what it is you wanted them to do. Your ending should be crisp and clear,

Unofficially...
Numbers and lists tend to help people to focus their attention and remember issues. For some reason that psychologists aren't sure about, sets of three are particularly easy to remember. In critical presentations, for maximum retention, try to use three key points.

and never conclude with questions (take questions during the talk and save a summary for the end).

A quick guideline:

1. Opening: Brief, has a "hook," grabs attention. Requires only 5 to 10 percent of the time allotted for the entire presentation.

2. Middle or body: Has a theme, specific points in support of the theme or topic, uses examples and action steps to illustrate each point. Visual aids can be organized around the points. Requires 85 to 90 percent of allotted time.

3. Ending: Brief, contains a restatement of the theme, summary of the points raised, and a specific call to action afterwards. Requires no more than 5 percent of allotted time.

If you prepare around these parameters, you'll create an engrossing, sequential, and well-organized presentation.

Maintain a poised, enthusiastic, and controlled demeanor

When you're making your presentation, whether to a roomful of known colleagues or an auditorium full of strangers, there is an understandable "panic zone." But the way to overcome it and to shine is not by trying to visualize your audience naked (a cliched technique) or anything else that silly.

If the presentation is a major one before an audience, have a "dress rehearsal" the day prior or in the morning. Get comfortable with the environment and your ability to move around. Use the mike and run your visual aids. Wear the clothing that you'll wear for the presentation to make sure there are no problems. (This sounds overzealous, but a tie or scarf can get caught in a projector, and jewelry can clank against equipment. Sometimes, a certain choice of clothing doesn't offer a good location for a lavaliere mike. You don't want to discover this as you're about to walk on stage.)

You may find that the lighting is wrong for your visuals and needs to be adjusted. Make sure the visuals are large enough to be seen. (Informal rule: Don't put pages of text on a screen from a report. Use major points only, and use graphics with them.) If you're not the only speaker, find out how and when you'll be introduced and take the stage.

Whether the presentation is to a large audience, the media, customers, or a small group of colleagues, here are the keys to a poised, enthusiastic demeanor:

Smile

We've covered this above. Don't grin and gape as if you've lost your mind, but smile pleasantly as if you've just been introduced to people you've always wanted to meet. Your tension will lessen, your facial muscles will relax, and you'll tell the audience that you're confident and prepared. As one wag put it, "If you're really happy, don't forget to tell your face!"

Use eye contact continually

In a small room, eye contact should be established with everyone present. It should typically last from 2 to 5 seconds. Shorter than that is distracting, and longer than that tends to be uncomfortable. If someone looks away when you look at them, move on. Begin with known friends and supportive people. They will smile back at you and will provide positive nonverbal behavior (nods, supportive gestures). This will give you the "momentum" that you need. (If you're facing customers or the media, have some of your own people there to serve this purpose.) Eventually work your way to all those in the room. This typically works in a room with up to 25 or 30 people.

In larger settings, look to points in the audience. (Don't look at the far walls as some people advise. This technique makes you look spaced-out and unfocused.) Make sure you look to six areas: right front, right rear, center front, center rear, left front, and left rear. If you're comfortable as you look to these six areas, you can pause midway between each, thereby increasing the eye contact.

If you're in a spotlight and cannot see the audience at all—which is common in that situation—during your dress rehearsal study the hall with the lights on and simply memorize where you'll look. From the audience, it will appear as if you're looking at people around the hall, even though you actually can't see them.

Eye contact is one of the most important of all the nonverbal indicators in presentations because, effectively done, it conveys caring, interest, and confidence.

Move around the front of the room

Try not to be bound to a lectern or audiovisual device. Ask someone else to change your overheads, have a remote control for the slides, use a lavaliere or handheld mike instead of a fixed mike. The ability to move around even moderately projects great command and informality, which are powerful messages. Moving around, combined with effective eye contact, provides a strong impression. (One woman told me at an awards ceremony that I was the most impressive speaker the event had ever hired. "What did you enjoy the most about my remarks" I asked. "Oh, your remarks were okay, I guess," she said, "but we've never seen anyone talk and move at the same time!")

Moving around means that you are not reading your presentation or confined to prepared remarks. Here are some ways to avoid those restraints:

- Use your visual aids as your "notes." Simply speak to the points that each slide, overhead, or PowerPoint frame reveals to you and the audience.

- Keep written notes in one place, and walk over to glance at them as needed. Make sure your type is large and easy to read. You should be familiar enough with your topic so that you can speak conversationally from bullet points, and not read the script. Politicians often sound pompous and artificial because they are forced to read scripts verbatim that someone on their staff wrote and that they're seeing for the first time.

- At large, formal meetings, request a tele-prompter with your remarks on that system. These are increasingly common as technology improves.

- At smaller meetings, simply keep your notes on the table or somewhere else that's convenient. (Many people write notes on the overhead slide frames, or on an easel in front of the room.)

Try to never read prepared remarks. This is the most boring of all presentation styles. Keep your tone conversational, as if you were speaking to three or four people, no matter how many are in the room.

Use gestures

In a smaller room with fewer people, use normal gesturing. In a larger room with more people, exaggerate your gestures so that they will be seen by everyone. (It's actually hard to gesture too much!)

Bright Idea
When you're presenting to a small group, distribute a copy of your key points to everyone, and simply work from that. If you find yourself uncertain about what's next, simply ask the group, "Where are we?" They'll put you back on track.

Gestures include use of your hands and arms to accentuate and dramatize your points. Obviously, you can't do that as well if you have notes in your hand or are rooted behind a lectern. Nonverbal gestures both emphasize your points and vary your delivery, providing greater interest among the audience.

Watch speakers within your own organization. You'll find that the ones who are most interesting to listen to are those who use gestures. If you are able to move around, establish eye contact, and use gestures as you speak, you'll find that your ideas, recommendations, and calls to action will be much more readily accepted despite the logic or illogic of your reasoning. That's why the medium is as important as the message. I've seen dry financial reporting come to life because the speaker knew how to deliver in this fashion, and I've seen exciting sales results lose all impact because the speaker failed to use these tactics. Whether or not they seem "fair," they are the keys to influencing an audience, large or small.

Use the power of your voice

Except in small rooms, always use a microphone to amplify your voice. Most conference rooms are not engineered well acoustically, and your points will be lost on the rear third of the audience if you don't provide for amplification.

Try to vary your voice and projection to produce these results:

■ Volume should vary. If you are constantly loud or constantly soft, your voice will be either annoying or tedious. Change the volume of your projection to dramatize—and drama can be created by softness as well as by loudness—certain points. Audiences need changes in volume periodically.

Timesaver
For an important presentation, practice your remarks using a tape recorder. When you play it back, time it. Then assume that you'll actually deliver it in only 75 percent of the time on the tape. We speak more slowly in practice, and have much more adrenaline flowing during the actual event.

■ Use inflection. This is the stress that you want to provide for certain words or phrases. It can change the entire meaning of a phrase. For example, the italicized word in the following sentences will receive special stress:

1. We're happy to report that some of you have *exceeded* the old performance standards.

2. We're happy to report that *some* of you have exceeded the old performance standards.

3. We're happy to report that some of you have exceeded the *old* performance standards.

In the first sentence, it sounds like a very happy condition. In the second, it sounds disappointing that only some have exceeded. In the third, it sounds rather depressing that they were the old standards.

Plan to provide the proper stress and emphasis so that the interpretation of your remarks is the same as your meaning.

■ Change your tempo. This is pacing or speed. An overall too rapid delivery will frustrate and exhaust people, and an overall too torpid delivery will make them comatose. Use a fast tempo to show excitement and to jolt the audience, and a slow one to show reflection and to provide a rest. In between, keep the tempo upbeat, and faster rather than slower.

■ Use "power language." There is a nuance that outstanding speakers use that most audience members don't immediately realize. Here's the difference:

1. What we would like to do is try to have our customers tell us regularly that we've met their service and support needs.

2. We will ensure that our customers tell us
   daily that we exceed their expectations.

Sentence one is passive and mildly hopeful. Sentence two is assertive and ambitious. "Power language" is never passive or tentative. It is assertive and strong. For example:

Non-Power Phrase	Power Phrase
We would like to . . .	We will . . .
When we are able . . .	In August . . .
We will try to be ready . . .	We will begin on . . .
There is reason to believe . . .	We believe that . . .
It's possible to exceed . . .	We will exceed . . .
Our hopes are that . . .	Our expectations are . . .

You can see the difference in a half hour or hour of phrases on the left versus those on the right. After repeatedly hearing the former, the listeners are wondering if they'll be successful. After repeatedly hearing the latter, listeners have no doubt of what's to be accomplished. This is the secret of "power language," and you should use it as much as possible.

Audience involvement

You can get any audience involved, no matter what its size.

For small groups, you simply engage them in conversation as you talk with them. You might pause and ask, "What do you think about this idea?" or simply say, "Before I move on, the floor is open. What are your questions, concerns, or uncertainties?"

For larger groups, you can ask that people turn to a neighbor and discuss a given point, or develop a response to a challenge. You can request that they turn to a page in the handouts and solve a problem, or respond to an issue, or make a note of something.

Bright Idea
Most questions are a sign of interest, not a challenge. Treat the question as an opportunity to enlarge upon that interest, not as a threat needing to be beaten back. The former attitude will produce a much more appealing and acceptable response.

Audience involvement is a fine technique because it takes the focus off of the presenter, varies the tempo, forces people from a passive into an active role, and gives the presenter a brief respite. Case studies, role plays, and similar exercises are often effective, if they're relevant to the topic. A good guideline: Any audience involvement in a large room shouldn't exceed about 5 minutes, and in a smaller room about 10 minutes. Longer than that and the presentation is disrupted and continuity is lost.

Handling questions

In larger groups this is sometimes not done, although it's not uncommon for microphones to be located in the aisles or passed around for questions even when hundreds of people are present. In smaller groups, it's virtually mandatory.

There's nothing wrong with encouraging people to ask questions as you proceed (although this is usually logistically impossible in large groups). This enables people to stop you and clarify points before you move on. Similarly, it's a very effective technique to tell people that there will be time allocated for questions later in the presentation, and you'll be happy to respond at that time. This enables listeners to get more of a perspective before formulating their questions.

There are two essential rules for handling questions:

1. Never end your presentation with a question-and-answer period. As noted above, this destroys your ending and your call for action. If you say to people, "This concludes my remarks, are there any questions?" you will have people mentally (and often physically)

departing your presentation. What you should say is, "Prior to my summary remarks, I'm happy to answer any questions at this point, and then I'll make my final comments." This sets the proper level of expectation, and allows you to finish properly.

2. There are three components to effectively dealing with questions.

■ First, you repeat the question. This is obviously because some might not have heard it (particularly if the questioner has no microphone), but not so obviously so that you have additional time to consider it.

■ Second, respond to the question. If you don't know the answer, admit it, and offer to find out and get back to the questioner. If you can't provide the answer, tell them. Always be honest, and respond to questions as succinctly as possible, so that others have a chance to ask their questions. Remember that the question may only be of interest to a few in the room, so answer it and move on.

■ Third, review the response with the questioner. Ask, "Did I answer your question?" or "Does that provide you with the information you need?" This is the way to gain closure, but also to find out if your answer might have been insufficient or unclear.

If you get a hostile question, repeat it and respond, but *do not* review it with the questioner, who might want to seek a debate with you. After responding, move your eye contact to another person and say, "I see we have another question over here. . . ." If there are no other questions, then

Watch Out!
You have the respect and support of the audience at the outset, since most people want an effective speaker and interesting presentation. Don't lose that respect by trying to humiliate a heckler. Deal with the interference professionally, and the audience will help to silence the heckler for you.

move your eye contact away and say, "I'm now going to provide that summary I promised."

To review: Never end your talk with a question-and-answer session. When you take questions, use three steps—repeat, respond, and review. (With hostile questions, don't review.)

Finally, if you're in a small group, use my "volleyball" technique. Bounce some of the questions back to the group. Say, "Before I answer that, what do some of you think about that question?" or "Does anyone want to comment on that before I respond?" This technique gains group involvement, gives you time to think, gets ownership from the participants, and may just provide you with a better idea than you had! It's not your job to field every question and hit it out of the park. Bounce some back across the net and you'll find that the ball might stay in the air for a considerable time.

Using visual aids

A few comments about visual aids. Always try to prepare them in advance, even if they are nothing more than easel sheets. Always test for readability and clarity from the most remote point (what works in your office or living room doesn't always work in a conference room or auditorium). Use appropriate visuals for the audience size and composition.

Generally:

- Easel sheets can be seen well by no more than about 30 people, even when on a stage or elevated.

- Overhead slides are effective for groups up to about 100, but require mild lighting adjustments, especially near the screen. However, they are flexible (you can use one over and over again or draw on them).

- 35-millimeter slides can be seen by almost any size group with proper equipment, but they require that lights be changed significantly and are not flexible.

- Computer-generated slides are very sophisticated and can be changed easily to reflect recent events, but they are unwieldy, require significant equipment, and are subject to endless technical problems. They can also overwhelm the message.

Rule of thumb: Never use visuals for their own sake (everyone is using computer-generated graphics) and use the appropriate visuals to make your point given the size of the room, the nature of the audience, and with the least disruption to your presentation. Visual aids can enhance a presentation or absolutely destroy it. They have to be used intelligently, not merely because they're available.

End on time

The final part of a poised, enthusiastic, and controlled demeanor is to get off the stage on time. An audience's interest drops incredibly once it realizes that you're not finishing as planned. Very little you say after that—which includes your ending and call to action, unfortunately—will be heard or heeded. (Just one very real example from my platform experience: A professor with a 20-minute time slot went on and on for 90 minutes before he was reluctantly pulled from the stage, throwing an entire conference agenda out of whack right from the outset.)

It has never been recorded that any audience filed a complaint when a speaker ended a few minutes prior to the scheduled time. But when that time is exceeded, the outrage is tangible. Keep track of your time (contrary to some advice, there's nothing

Watch Out!
Hope for the
best and expect
the worst. Have
an extra bulb for
the projector and
know how to
insert it. Bring
an extension
cord. Be pre-
pared, ultimately,
to present with-
out the visuals
at all if they col-
lapse. Don't let
the presentation
depend on the
visual aids.
Murphy is
watching.

wrong with looking at your watch, and most smaller meeting rooms have clocks on the wall), or ask someone to do it for you and cue you when you have 10 minutes remaining, 5 minutes, and so on.

End on time and people will say you were a terrific speaker.

Expect the unexpected

Nothing ever goes completely as planned. Here are some common problems and responses or reactions:

- The visual aids fail. Acknowledge the problem, state that you knew it would happen to you, and you're prepared to go on with the presentation using the handouts and your notes. On a projector, quickly check the plug and move to the spare bulb. If that doesn't work, get back to your presentation.

- A phone rings. If it's a cell phone, ask that the conversation be taken outside, and other phones and pagers be turned off. If it's a phone in the room, ask someone to answer it, transfer the call, and then unplug the phone. (All of these things should have been done in advance.)

- Someone enters late. Don't acknowledge them other than with a smile, and never, ever embarrass them.

- Someone enters seeking one of the participants. Stop what you're doing, ask if you can help them locate someone, then move on. Do not become upset—it could be a legitimate emergency.

- A staff member is disruptive (for example, someone is noisily clearing tables). Pause and ask if they could stop the activity and do it after you've concluded.

■ An audience member seeks to dominate the meeting with questions or challenges. After handling the first two or three, suggest that the two of you meet after the presentation to deal with the issues that are obviously very important to this person but which you don't have the time to do justice to at the moment.

■ People in the room are disruptive by talking or using personal computers, for example. Don't forget that many people take notes on their computers, so this could be a form of rapt attention. Two people might be trying to clarify something you said. If you are distracted by it, simply inquire, "Is there something I can help with, or something I've confused you about?"

■ Your time is cut because someone else took too much of it themselves. Admit to the audience that you have X minutes less than you expected, so you'll try to cover the main points, and do just that. It's a good idea to ask yourself in advance, "If I had to shorten this by 15 minutes, what would I remove?" and then do just that if you have to.

If you prepare carefully, comport yourself confidently, and expect the unexpected, you will be seen as an outstanding presenter and, fairly or unfairly, your message will receive a much higher degree of acceptability despite its content.

Most managers do not present well because such skills were never a part of their former jobs or professional development. Power managers learn to do this well as an essential element in their ability to persuade and influence others.

Just the facts

- Presentations are key power points, whether large and formal or small and informal.

- Preparation constitutes most of your later effectiveness.

- Confidence in front of an audience is the compilation of a set of learnable delivery skills.

- Questions are vital for acceptance, but must be handled in a certain manner and never after your summary.

- Something always goes wrong, and excellent presenters take it in stride.

GET THE SCOOP ON...
Organizing for results ■ Reducing the number
and frequency of meetings ■ Running the show ■
Sticking to the clock ■ Dodging meeting bullets

Running Meetings (Instead of Meetings Running You)

Chapter 15

The good news is that we know meetings are
time-consuming black holes of management
life. The bad news is that meetings are time-
consuming black holes of management life.

So why do we put up with so many of them?

There is an entire industry devoted to effective
meetings, including seminars, books, cassettes, and
videos. In this last genre, the semi-legendary John
Clease effort, "Meetings, Bloody Meetings," from
Video Arts, has been much more successful at generating a fortune for its creators than it has at
improving meetings.

Making sure the meeting makes sense

Let's start at the beginning: What is it that meetings
ought to accomplish (what are the desired outcomes)?

■ Decisions made around a common management issue.

Timesaver
Unless you need input, debate, and commentary from the group, consider not calling a meeting. They are notoriously poor forums solely for information exchange, which can be accomplished far better with modern electronic media.

The issues examined in Chapters 7 through 10 often require that disparate points of view and frames of reference be accessed with "live" debate that e-mail, phone conferencing, and memos simply don't support well. A meeting is a good place to thrash through the data, gather information, and formulate some knowledge. Agreed-upon actions ought to emerge.

■ Generating consensus and ownership.

There are times when a group (a "family" group of people who normally work together, or a "stranger" group of people who do not normally work together) has to support a given initiative or goal. In many of those situations, the only way to effectively do so is to gather all of the players together. (Meetings are the given alternative in two of the leadership styles in Chapter 11, for example.)

■ Conflict resolution and negotiating.

When there is disagreement over either alternatives or objectives and there are several people (or the representatives of larger groups of people) on each side of the issue, a facilitated meeting is generally the best resolution vehicle (see Chapters 3 and 12).

■ Ensuring a uniform message.

Messages about issues such as potential mergers, compensation systems, new policies, the results of legal action, and so forth are often best delivered to large groups of people simultaneously, so that everyone receives the same initial message without distortion.

■ Providing recognition.

When public recognition of performance is merited, assembling people to honor the recipient is a traditionally appropriate role for a meeting.

- Creating a knowledge transfer.

Many organizations have a policy that shift supervisors will meet briefly at the change of shifts to convey knowledge needed by their successors. Department heads who support each other often do this on a regular basis. However, note that this is "knowledge" exchange, and not "information" exchange. Information is best provided in written form and usually doesn't require conversation or explanation.

- Providing for image, public relations, and symbolic opportunities.

Although not the best means for doing so, the CEO addressing the troops and offering to take questions from the floor is a powerful symbolic device in many organizations once a quarter (or once a year). Similarly, inviting a customer, government regulator, or former competitor to speak to employees can serve several objectives in terms of morale and access to information.

Unfortunately, meetings are too often used for these illegitimate reasons:

- Because they are scheduled and have always been there.

- To exchange information.

- As an excuse to discuss and not take action.

- Because an executive ordered it ("create an inventory task force").

- When people are lost and feel that getting together will help somehow.

- They are status symbols attendant to a certain rank or accomplishment.

Bright Idea
When someone suggests a meeting, the immediate response is usually, "Where can we find a conference room?" Instead, ask this question: "Why?" If it is for a reason other than those listed here, or can be served better by an alternative other than a meeting, don't look for the conference room.

The first thing to do is to ensure that a meeting, as an alternative, makes sense for the issues at hand. If the meeting is not a regularly scheduled one and has been suggested, then examine two things:

1. Does it meet one of the objectives cited above?
2. Is it the best way to meet that objective?

Relative to the second point, you may choose to recognize someone through a feature article in the organization's magazine or newsletter, rather than a meeting. Or you may decide that a conflict is so emotional and so explosive, that one-on-one interviews are superior to a group meeting. If conditions are appropriate, you may choose a leadership style that will be highly effective without any meetings being held at all (see Chapter 11).

If the meeting is regularly scheduled and you find yourself enmeshed in it (or your people constantly among the missing because they are enmeshed in them), ask these questions:

1. What is the origin of this meeting, and is it still applicable?
2. Does it meet one of the objectives above?
3. Is it the best way to meet that objective?
4. What would be the adverse consequence of terminating this meeting?

We're asking a few more questions of long-term, regular meetings because we might have lost sight of the reasons for their existence, or there could be a political or cultural problem in canceling these meetings (for example, employees feel that the meetings are one of their few opportunities to voice feedback, or they are deemed to be one of the few perks of certain supervisory positions).

Here is the first and most critical key for doing away with unnecessary meetings: At least once a quarter, and more often if you prefer, review every regularly scheduled meeting affecting you and your subordinates, and pass them through the test above.

Here is the second key, for preventing proposed meetings: Immediately pass them through the test above prior to agreeing to schedule, lead, or participate in them.

If you apply these two keys with vigor, I guarantee that you will both reduce existing, standing meetings, and avoid new ones from sprouting. Before examining how to run meetings better and exploit them for best results, it's important to be ruthless in reducing their number, otherwise you'll find yourself running poor meetings very well. That is, you'll be efficiently running a meeting that has no reason to exist.

Meeting efficiency is based on your skills and competency to either run them well or participate in them well. But the effectiveness of meetings is dependent on whether the beast is at all needed at that time for that purpose. You must answer that question before attempting to improve them.

The relationship looks like this:

Timesaver
Any attention paid to improving meetings is wasted if the determination isn't made first as to whether the meeting is necessary. The last thing in the world you want to do is run useless meetings well.

Meeting's Worth and Purpose (Effectiveness)

	Low	High
High	Wasted time: Eliminate when possible	Most Productive: Don't touch
Low	Useless: Eliminate immediately	Wasted time: Improve structure

Meeting's Efficiency

Ideally, meetings should serve a valuable purpose best accomplished through the meeting; those that serve such a purpose and are already run well don't require any further scrutiny (although any meeting can probably be improved somewhat), and those that aren't run well require improvement in efficiency because the purpose is important.

Those without a valid purpose (low effectiveness) need to be eliminated either immediately (they are poorly run, poorly attended, and so on) or more gradually (they are longstanding and may cause some hurt feelings, some small aspects need to be attended to in other ways, and so on).

Once you've been rigorous in deciding whether a meeting makes sense, you can then look to improve the ones that are left.

Results-oriented agendas

The greatest single improvement that can be made in almost any meeting is to move it from a task focus to a results focus. Fortunately, there is a perfect device for accomplishing that: The meeting agenda.

Many meetings don't have agendas, and that's fatal, because there is no guarantee or even probability that anything of merit will be accomplished within any particular time frame. However, just as seriously, many more meetings have an agenda that is nothing more than a sequential time list of activities. Let's create a hypothetical meeting on the formulation of a new sales compensation system. Here's what the typical agenda might look like on a time and task basis:

SUBJECT: NEW FIELD COMPENSATION SYSTEM

9:00	Opening remarks	Joan Shelton
9:20	Report on work to date	Jim Sawyer Jan Smithens Jess Sloan
10:15	Break	
10:30	Discussion of priority issues	All
11:30	New assignments and next meeting	Joan Shelton
12:00	Adjourn	

Watch Out!
If a meeting does not have an agenda with start and stop times, that's an immediate indication that things are out of control. For everyone's planning purposes and especially your own, demand that beginning and ending times be set, and that people abide by them.

Now, that looks like a nice, concise, agenda, but it's actually a pernicious time-killer that guarantees only a single action: To hold another meeting! In fact, that's what most meetings routinely agree to do—hold another one.

(I once consulted for a hospital client who had a Friday morning executive council meeting every week, without fail. There was about $3 million of salary among the two dozen regular members present. Invariably, they spent the morning moving priorities from one easel sheet to another, but none was ever resolved or removed in all the weeks that I observed them.)

Troubles of the agenda

In the example above, the time frames are arbitrarily made to fit into a morning. Opening remarks don't require 20 minutes, but an update from last time might take 2 minutes. Work to date could have been distributed in writing or electronically prior to the meeting (remember that information exchange alone is never a good reason for a meeting), and there are no results objectives that lend themselves to resolving this issue. Work will always expand to fill

Unofficially...
If there's a meeting you can't avoid (for example, called by the boss) and there's no agenda, ask what time it's scheduled to end. If it's a bore, tell the boss you have other commitments based on the ending time, and ask whether you should cancel them, or leave the meeting. It's worth a shot.

the available time (this was Parkinson's Law), so you can be sure that Jim, Jan, Jess, and even Joan will take at least all of the time provided. However, they don't need it.

Here's a far better example of an agenda for the same meeting:

Goal: Selection of a new field compensation system

Pre-session work required: Read, evaluate, and note any questions about work submitted by Jim, Jan, and Jess, and be prepared to discuss their recommendations.

Starting time: 9:00

Ending time: 10:30

Results/ Objectives:	Accountability:	Timing:
Select sales manager to lead field focus groups	Jim	10–15 min.
Review and select from outside consultant benchmarks	Jan	30–45 min.
Perform risk analysis of sales reps concerns	Joan	15–20 min.
Identify priorities, accountabilities, and next meeting date, if required	All	5–10 min.

Post-session work: Sales manager chosen to be informed, consultant chosen to be contacted, random interviews conducted with sales reps, all information gathered to be sent in common format electronically to Joan's secretary for dissemination by May 9.

What we now have is a meeting that will take 90 minutes at the outside and as little as 60 minutes if the discussions proceed well. Everyone will enter with the same work accomplished and information digested. Joan can coordinate the meeting using approximate time frames, and there's the flexibility to end it early. Distinct results and decisions emerge from this meeting.

In half the time of the prior agenda, we've accomplished a great deal more because we used a results-oriented agenda to do the following:

- State a goal to be accomplished
- Specify the work to be done prior to the meeting
- Organize around a few, specific results
- Provide timing flexibility
- Specify what is to happen between this meeting and the next one

The simple use of this kind of agenda, and not a task and time list, will immediately enhance meeting efficiency, and is one of the best doses of medicine for the meetings in the lower-right quadrant of the figure earlier in this chapter.

Running the meeting with firmness

You can tell which meetings are immediately doomed because, at the appointed starting time, you and the bagels are the only ones there. At many organizations, this has become so much of a joke that people say, "Are you talking about real time, or meeting time?"

But it's no joke. The more people realize that everyone won't assemble for at least 15 minutes after the starting time, the more likely they will take another phone call or check additional e-mail, and the cycle is perpetuated. The meeting host or facilitator simply makes it worse by saying, "Let's wait a

Bright Idea
If you have an assistant, provide a list to be checked prior to every meeting, and let that person do your legwork. An often overlooked basic: Verifying that the meeting room is still yours for the times required. Clerical errors—and bribes—have often "lost" a meeting room at the last minute.

few more minutes, because we don't want to have to repeat everything for the latecomers." Most meetings start late and end late. Could there be some causal connection there?

If you are running the meeting, tell people it starts on time, and begin it that way. Whenever a person enters late, at the first appropriate break in the discussion, ask publicly why they were late and, unless a truly important cause or brilliant piece of lying is supplied, tell them that this won't be tolerated in the future and they'll be expected to find out what they missed. It's not a bad idea to assign extra accountabilities to the latecomers—while crude, it does break the habit in a remarkably short time.

(If you are a participant in a chronically late meeting, show up on time, but bring work with you, and keep at it until the meeting is brought to order.)

Similarly, don't allow people to come and go randomly, or to be interrupted by phone calls and assistants. A trip to the rest rooms takes 5 minutes, not 50. If people feel that they can wander in and out, they will, and this not only deprives you of their contribution but it also casts a degrading pall on the importance of the matters being discussed. You owe it to people to run a brief, meaty, interesting meeting. They owe it to you to give it their undivided attention for that period of time.

So, here is the recipe for running a firm, organized meeting:

1. Distribute the agenda and any pre-session work well in advance.

2. Call (or have an assistant call) every participant a day or two prior and remind them of the times, venue, and pre-session work needs.

3. Call the meeting to order on time.

4. Keep introductory remarks to a minimum (this is not a speech or presentation, it's a meeting), although some humor never hurts if you're good at it.

5. Review the agenda quickly, ask if there are any questions or concerns, and move to the first item.

If it's your meeting, don't sweep in at the last minute like some ancient potentate. Make sure that all audio/visual needs have been taken care of, and that refreshments are present. Disconnect the phone, it's only there for you in emergencies. Talk to people casually as they arrive and break the ice.

Power meeting techniques

Aside from the mechanical aspects of logistics, timing, and discipline, there are meeting techniques that power managers use subtly to keep things moving. You may not always have noticed their use, but you probably have been able to clearly distinguish between those of your managers who ran dynamic, interesting meetings, and those who appeared to be directing a glacier.

Stopping road hogs

Some people tend to dominate a meeting, because they're loud, or opinionated, or confident, or just plain insensitive. They have to comment on every single position and issue—including the refreshment break—and can cause a tremendous delay because no one can move past them. After the first two or three such interruptions or lengthy diatribes, step in and say, "Ralph, I appreciate your inputs, but I've got to hear from others. Your position is clear,

Timesaver
There's nothing wrong with having "ground rules" on the easel or walls that set the parameters for participation and involvement. I've seen the same rules work well for grammar school students and senior executives (e.g., respect your colleagues)!

and you're free to see me after the meeting, but let's give everyone a chance while we're together."

Meetings are not about civility at all costs. They are about reaching objectives. If someone is hogging the road, politely tell that person to change lanes.

Ending circular discussions

Just when you think a point has been thoroughly debated or a tentative decision reached, someone goes back to square one and begins to debate well-trod ground. You can both avoid this (preventive action) and stop it quickly if it occurs (contingent action).

The preventive action is to have someone keep track on an easel or whiteboard of the progress in the discussion. Periodically, you should paraphrase or summarize with, "Let's pause and review: We've determined that the new compensation system will be internally designed, and not contracted to outside consultants. The debate now is whether the human resources function should take the lead, or line management should lead and use human resources simply as a resource. Does everyone agree?"

In that way, with the easel reading, "Design Internally," for all to see, people will not be prone to return to that decision. They'll have a clear idea of progress and of direction.

The contingent action occurs when someone says, "I have an idea. There's a firm in Westwood that worked at my wife's company, and she says they did a far better job than the internal people would have. Shouldn't we ask them to at least come in and give us a proposal?" You then reply, "We've already agreed that external firms are not sensitive to our culture, would cause suspicion, and we don't have a budget for them in any case. Given those facts, we're not going to go back and reopen that level of the decision chain."

Resolving conflict quickly

We've talked earlier (Chapter 3) about resolving conflict, and those skills can certainly be employed in a meeting. In addition, however, you can prepare the ground in this manner, "We know there are going to be strong opinions on various sides of this issue, and I want to encourage you all to air them while we're together here. We'll track them on the board. All I ask is that you be candid, factual, and respectful of every other person's point of view. Other than that, let's hear the strongest debate we can muster."

Too many meetings proceed with a "pretend" consensus, because the real issues aren't thrashed out during the meeting but rather await the "hallway" and "closed door" conversations that follow.

I worked with a division of a Fortune 500 company in which meetings were fictitious. No matter what was discussed or agreed upon, everyone present knew that several of the participants would gain the vice president's ear at the earliest juncture and lobby for what they actually wanted to happen. The vice president would then modify the meeting results accordingly.

What you decide at the meeting should be with all conflicts openly aired and final, unless you subsequently receive brand-new information. And, if that information could have been raised during the meeting, the provider should be confronted with the inappropriate use of that information outside of the meeting.

Timesaver
Appoint a scribe to record key points on an easel sheet, and post them around the room. People can focus much better and move faster if the points are visible for everyone to see, because otherwise my notes might differ from your notes in style and substance.

Overcoming cultural barriers

At times you may have participants who are from different parts of the organization, different backgrounds, or have different behaviors, which means that they might not be as vocal or participative as you would ordinarily prefer. Silence does not necessarily indicate agreement, and passivity does not necessarily indicate consensus.

One way to overcome this is to place people in smaller teams—even of twos and threes (known as dyads and triads in the facilitating world)—and have them examine issues during the meeting. This not only provides a break in the meeting routine, but it allows a team to report back without any one individual in the spotlight. The person reporting is merely the spokesperson, and may or may not be influential in the smaller team's conclusions. Teams can also report back in writing.

It's important to have the teams report back while the entire group is still together, so that overall consensus can be reached and accountabilities determined. But this is a fine device to encourage all parties to participate more actively, without having to speak up individually or take on a known strong proponent on a given position.

Maintaining high energy

Some of your meetings may have to be fairly lengthy, because the circumstances (for example, flying people in from widely dispersed locations) or the issues (for example, a time urgency to make decisions) demand that the group meet until certain goals are met. In addition, some people will unavoidably be coming from or going to still more meetings.

To maintain high energy in longer meetings, consider one or more of the following techniques:

- Take a short break every hour. Traditionally, breaks are 15 to 20 minutes (and they are generally stretched still longer by weary participants) every 90 minutes or 2 hours. But if you take a 5- to 10-minute break every hour, people are re-energized faster, and don't leave the meeting as often.

- Use a brief, creative exercise. These can't be too long or they soak up precious meeting time, but a 2- or 3-minute challenge (for example, a word puzzle, company history test, or logic challenge) will get vital mental juices flowing and provide some competitive fun.

- Utilize small teams. This is a great device for two reasons, in addition to the cultural one presented above. First, people are focused in a smaller group, so that they are forced to participate, can easily be heard, and move around their seats for variety. Second, you can move an issue along much more rapidly by breaking it up among the teams: Team one takes customer feedback, team two takes employee feedback, team three takes competitive feedback, and so on. All meeting issues do not have to be processed in a linear fashion, and small teams provide a concurrent means of resolving several issues contemporaneously.

- Use effective visuals. Don't dim the lights and show a hundred boring slides. But a comedic videotape, some slides of the last company picnic, or some overheads with pithy quotes and insights might be ideal for breaking up the tedium and creating interest.

- Invite guests. You don't want a droning "talking head," but meetings can be substantially

Bright Idea
Getting people back to meetings after breaks is the worst job in the world, so don't do it. Assign two people to herd everyone back on your signal. This frees up your time and avoids an onerous chore. (Using one male and one female employee for this task is a good idea, so that rest rooms can be emptied.)

enlivened with a short discussion with a customer, a brief update from the head of a department the group supports, or a question-and-answer session with an executive. The key is to control them so that they are informational and lively.

How to avoid meetings that are weighing you down

We've focused during much of this Chapter on meetings that you control, run, facilitate, or influence. But what about those meetings that you merely participate in and that seem to eat up your entire day? I have, quite literally, coached executives who are concerned about not being able to get to their chief accountabilities without working a killing 60-hour week, only to find that they are spending 6 to 8 hours a day, 4 to 5 days a week, in captive meetings.

Here is a template of 10 questions to determine whether you should be in a meeting or not, at least by objective comparison. If less than half the questions are answered "yes," you simply don't belong there. If more than seven are answered "yes," you probably need to attend. Between five and seven is a gray area, but I'd recommend a tough stand and interpret that as your presence being needed on occasion, but certainly not at every meeting.

1. Is my competency, talent, or viewpoint critical to the successful running of these meetings?

2. Are decisions made at the meeting that directly influence me, my people, or my accountabilities in terms of getting our jobs done?

3. Do I need to be present to set an example to subordinates or colleagues who are critical to the success of the meeting?

4. Am I attending for some reason other than the fact that my position, title, or predecessor in this job created a precedent for attendance?

5. Is there an issue that I want to personally discuss, protest, or support that will be decided at this meeting?

6. Will there be internal or external customers at the meeting whom I must support through my attendance?

7. Are the issues discussed or other attendees such that I cannot send a representative in my place?

8. Is there something occurring at the meeting, in terms of either the nature of the issues or the timing or the participants, which can't be resolved or decided in any other venue at any other time?

9. Is this a meeting that I enjoy, learn from, and look forward to?

10. Have I been directly ordered by a superior to attend this meeting?

Remember, if you can only answer affirmatively to four or less of these template questions, you don't belong at the meeting. (Some of you are saying that if your superior ordered you to go, #10, that's reason enough! But it's not. If the other questions are answered "no," then you have reason to question your superior's decision.) If you answer eight or more affirmatively, you need to be there. If you answer five to seven affirmatively, then you can probably either attend only on occasion or send a delegate.

Inappropriate meetings will eat you alive, especially when they become regular items on your

Unofficially...
Many meetings include a raft of people for safety's sake. That is, if they are present, no one can say later that decisions made were inappropriate or secretive. If you're one of those "safety" people, stop going or send a representative. Others' paranoia is not a good reason for meeting attendance.

calendar each month. They sap not only time, but energy and focus, as well.

How to get the most out of participation

All right. We've established that this is a meeting you ought to attend, because all 10 of the answers in our template are "yes," and it's not a meeting you run. You are strictly a participant, surrounded by colleagues, in a meeting run by your boss or another division head.

Your choice now is to simply grin and bear it, right?

Actually, you can get the most out of meetings if you care to invest a few moments of time and preparation. So on the assumption that the meeting makes sense, here's how to exploit it for your own best interests.

Arrive a bit early, and bring some work

If you arrive at the last second or are late, and the meeting begins on time, you'll stick out like a severed thumb and create ill will. On the other hand, by arriving about 10 minutes early, you'll not only avoid that fate but you can also:

- Secure the seating that you prefer. You might be most comfortable next to the door, or with a view, or away from a noisy projector, or close to the boss. Choose the seat that makes you most comfortable. (I always choose one at a corner, where I can stretch my legs during the meeting.)

- Chat with some colleagues you don't normally get to see, who might also show up early. You can do some networking or exert some influence if some of them can help your area.

- Get some work done. If no one shows up, read the reports or make the phone calls you brought along until the meeting time approaches. In the worst case, read *The Wall Street Journal.*

Read through and highlight any pre-session work of importance

Don't allow yourself to be surprised. Read any advance work and mark those parts that pertain to you and can help or hurt you. Be prepared to make your case or ask for specific, additional information.

Bring equipment you'll need

Bring your own pad, pens, highlighter, and calculator. Bring whatever reports or statistics you'll need to support or refute others' claims. (I once saw the CEO of Burlington Industries crudely throw his chief financial officer out of a meeting when the latter admitted he had not brought last year's comparison figures. "What do you think we keep you here for?!" the CEO bellowed.)

Be prepared to present

If you're on the agenda, come early and practice with your overheads or slides. Know what lighting you'll require. Distribute handouts at the seats if appropriate. Make sure you'll have a dark marker for the easels or whiteboard (light colors do not show up well in the lighting of a typical conference room). Pour yourself a glass of water. You can stand out as a presenter, or fall on your face. Don't begin by shuffling papers and mumbling about not being prepared. Begin by saying, "I've been looking forward to this, and I want to thank you in advance for your attention and consideration."

Watch Out!
If you're not on the agenda, don't waltz in and relax. Determine if you might be called upon for input, given the agenda and the people present. If so, prepare something informally—notes, or a diagram—that can be used if needed. You'll look brilliant by being able to respond "extemporaneously."

Determine what you'll "volunteer" for

If the meeting is run well at all (and even if it's not), there's a high probability that accountabilities will be parceled out to further progress toward the next meeting. If you have some ideas about what these may be, volunteer early for the ones that are least distasteful (or most advantageous) to you, so that you don't get stuck at the end with the ones no one in their right minds wants. "Well, let's see, we need someone to lead the fund-raising drive, and we can't use Smith, who's already volunteered for the cafeteria improvement project . . ."

Make an early excuse to leave

Tell the person running the meeting that, based on the agenda or the advance information, you've scheduled a client conference call for 15 minutes after the stated meeting completion time. That means that once the meeting starts to run over, you can simply signal to the responsible person that you're taking off as planned on other important business. (This is also a good reason to get there early and sit near the door.) You can't very well interrupt something at the last minute, but by "planning" your departure in advance, you can almost always get away with it, because the meeting facilitator will always say, "Oh, we'll be finished on time."

Plan to be involved

A lot of people (and I plead guilt, here) bring things to meetings to occupy them. They surreptitiously (or, if they're rude, obviously) do their own work during the meeting, or they'll do a puzzle, or name all the states, or doodle through a ream of paper. Actually, that kind of "forced diversion" creates tedium and sleepiness. You're much better off planning to be actively involved, by questioning others, raising new issues, using some prudent humor, or taking notes to share with your own team and subordinates. As long as you're there, you should try to contribute and learn.

Meetings are what you make of them. There are clearly many that you can avoid as a participant, or as a manager who decides to use other styles in decision making and leadership. There are those you run that can be run better and be turned into instruments of productivity and camaraderie. And there are those in which you participate where your participation is really your choice of interest or disinterest.

But here are two final rules of thumb:

1. No normal business meeting should last longer than 90 minutes, whether regularly scheduled or specially arranged. The exceptions would be crisis meetings, where some dire event needs to be resolved, and wide-scale meetings where people are brought in at great expense from far afield, and the opportunity to be together outweighs the disadvantages of long meetings. But the vast preponderance of meetings should be 90 minutes at the most, and preferably shorter. This is easily accomplished with pre-session work, the right attendees, a results-oriented agenda, and a strong facilitator running the show.

2. No one day should have more than two formal meetings, preferably one in the morning and one in the afternoon. Otherwise, you're not available for your people or your customers. When meetings "overlap" to early morning or after hours, you're in the equivalent of an uncontrolled dive. There is simply no valid organizational reason to take key managers and

Unofficially...
Just as two meetings per day and 90 minutes per meeting are clear parameters, if you and your people can't get your jobs done in a 40-hour week in most circumstances, there is something wrong with either the job demands or the people. In either case, this is a management responsibility to correct, not something to "live with."

hold them captive so frequently. You are not called a "meeter," after all, but a "manager."

Just the facts

- Meetings aren't ends in themselves, but rather instruments to meet business goals.

- Every meeting should have a results-oriented agenda circulated in advance.

- Just because you're invited to a meeting, it doesn't mean you should attend.

- Just because you are told by your superior to go to a meeting, it doesn't mean you should attend.

- You have as much responsibility for meeting success as a participant as you do when you are the facilitator.

How to Be a Memorable Manager and Role Model

GET THE SCOOP ON...
Responsibilities of an exemplar ▪ The four key
interpersonal traits ▪ Controlling ego ▪
Developing people for your own benefit ▪
Why you should lead a diverse life ▪
Crisis management

The "Complete" Manager for the Routine and the Crises

Chapter 16

I n our last two chapters we're going to discuss what Hegel might have called the "über manager." This is the manager who is above and beyond the crowd, who can be relied on in tough times, and who has mastered the routine of management so that, while it is never taken for granted, it is second nature. This is the manager as role model.

Any of us who worked in organizations of any kind early in our career can remember two kinds of managers:

- those we urgently wanted some great evil catastrophe to befall, so that they'd disappear from our lives, and

- those who we would follow into hell and back, such was their charisma.

All the others were lost in an indistinguishable stew of mediocrity. But if we were lucky enough, there were a very select few who actually had a profound effect on our lives, not just our work.

Here are the 10 traits of memorable managers (that's the famous, not the notorious):

1. Serves as positive role models for others.
2. Integrates ethics and values into business goals.
3. Subordinates ego to organizational needs.
4. Shares credit but accepts personal accountability and blame.
5. Innovates and attempts to raise standards.
6. Sees people as assets, not expenses, and develops subordinates.
7. Takes prudent risks; looks at return, not just investment.
8. Possesses strong communication and interpersonal abilities.
9. Views the customer as the primary focus.
10. Lives a complete life, with work as simply one component.

To what degree do those traits describe you or guide your own developmental goals?

Serves as a positive role model for others

People watch the manager closely for "cues" about acceptable behavior. Note that I didn't say "effective behavior," which denotes goal fulfillment, but "acceptable" behavior, which denotes cultural inclusion. Others are constantly seeking clues to tell them which behaviors will guarantee continued acceptance by the local culture, and which might threaten to exclude them.

When you take action—be it as minor as a "good morning" on the way to your office, or as major as a decision to terminate an employee—you must consider the standard you are setting for those who look to you for their cultural guidance. This may seem like an inordinate burden to place on a manager who merely wants to get the work done and finish the day, but unfortunately, it comes with the turf.

I was consulting for a division president who had a direct report notorious for his brutal conduct at meetings and with subordinates. He was profane and loud, viciously attacking those around him whom he perceived were against him or not supporting him well enough. When I finally had gathered enough factual evidence, I went to the president and advised that the man be terminated (several attempts at counseling had failed).

"It's just his way," said the president. "He gets the results, and although I would never act that way, everyone understands it's just Rick's approach."

"No," I said, "everyone thinks this is your approach and your philosophy because you tolerate it and reward Rick for his efforts. In fact, if you look into Rick's unit, you'll see a lot of "junior Ricks" developing who are harsh and abrasive with their own people. The ambitious managers think this is the behavior you most admire."

Rick was gone within 2 weeks. If you are cold and aloof and work only behind closed doors, some people will assume that such detached behavior is the key to success. What examples do you want to provide, what examples do you want your subordinates to provide, and what examples are you looking toward for your own guidance?

Watch Out!
Who have you chosen to look to for your cues about successful behavior? Are you following someone who is tolerated as a "necessary evil" and generally not respected, or someone who is touted as a "bold" decision maker who stands up for others?

Integrates ethics and values into business goals

We discussed in our strategy material (Chapter 13) that values preceded strategy. That is, what the organization stands for and why it exists direct its strategy for the future. Similarly, personal values and ethics should guide a manager's business judgment and decisions, not simply financial goals, project objectives, and quotas.

Bright Idea
Find what resources exist if a "whistle blower" is required. Some organizations have ombudsmen, some Employee Assistance Programs (EAPs), some strong human resources or legal departments, and some have formal links to external help. There is often help available, but it pays to know where it is ahead of time.

One of the reasons that we've seen egregious behavior in organizations go unstopped until the media were alerted is that business and cultural acceptance often takes precedence over values and ethics. The widespread use of racial epithets among high-level managers at Texaco, and the sexual harassment and discrimination that occurred at Astra Pharmaceuticals, were longstanding and widespread. How could they have gone on for so long?

The answer is that many otherwise decent people stood around and did nothing, justifying their passivity with "this is the way it is in this company," or "what difference can I make," or "I need my job." Consequently, bizarre and illegal activities can take on lives of their own and become part of the organization's culture.

These are the most dramatic examples. But every day there are "minor" ones threatening to grow into similar horror stories: The salespeople who ship materials before a client needs them in order to boost commissions; the managers who look the other way when company materials are appropriated by employees; the individuals who cheat on their expenses because "everyone does it" and "the company owes me this because our pay isn't up to the competition."

Organizations can do well by doing right, and so can individual managers. It's up to you to meet your goals within the ethical parameters that you know are correct, and to set that example for others. It's also your duty to provide an example by confronting and challenging those—at every level—who are clearly violating those standards. When asked why you tolerated thievery, cheating, racial stereotyping, sexual harassment, or bribery, it's rather weak to reply, "It was my boss. What could I do?"

Subordinates ego to organizational needs

Ego, itself, is not a shameful facet of our beings. It is an understandable and quite natural need. It's fine to exult when we've "won," because we are often so hard on ourselves when we "lose." But ego has to be controlled, and its "turf" usually ends where someone else's ego begins.

Managers should be proud of their accomplishments but place them in proper perspective. None of us is irreplaceable. There is always someone who can do something better than we can.

I once met a manager who constantly barged into her subordinates' work because "it could be done a little better." Since she had come up through the ranks and had been, in fact, a superb performer, she actually could do most things better than most subordinates. "Here, let me take that call and show you how to respond to a demanding customer." "Don't call the warehouse, go over and see them because they'll respond faster if you're there in person." Her advice was usually accurate, but dysfunctional.

Unless a fatal mistake or irretrievable error is about to be made, subordinates need to "win and lose" on their own. Setbacks can teach great lessons, learned far better than with someone else always showing you the "right way." Most excellent managers probably can do something faster, more accurately, or more efficiently than most subordinates, but that's not the point. The point is to allow people to develop through management coaching, not management ego.

Another ego component is competition. It can be healthy to compete with another unit for the best service or the most sales because the results improve the organization in any case. But it's never appropriate to win at someone else's expense. If the objective is to "show up" another unit or beat them irrespective of the impact on the organization, then ego has outweighed organizational goals.

I worked with a utility where I found two adjacent divisions "dueling" with perquisites. The respective general managers were in a private contest to prove each was more popular than the other. When one provided for a half day of work on Friday during the summer, the other provided a half day to be taken at any time during the weak. When one allowed people to dress casually, the other allowed pets to be brought to work. This went on and on as productivity dropped and dropped.

Their boss told me that he couldn't understand how two such popular managers could run such unproductive divisions. I told him that the popularity was at the expense of productivity, and he had better take out a big stick to knock some egos back down to size.

Shares credit but accepts personal accountability and blame

"Share credit and take blame" has never proved to be bad advice. Those managers who can graciously share credit when goals are achieved actually bring much more credit to themselves than they would have by trying to stand alone. And those who singularly accept responsibility for setbacks and loss and do not attempt to pass the buck are deeply respected by subordinates and colleagues.

There is the apocryphal story about the manager who had recently made a $16 million error, and promptly walks into his boss's office to resign. The boss, of course, tells him to get back to work since the company cannot afford to let him go, having just invested $16 million in his education. Management is both art and science, as this book has tried to illustrate, and mistakes will occur, some of them, unfortunately, significant ones, despite all precautions and planning.

Own up to the setbacks, even when the mistake was not yours personally or the problem could have been averted by someone else who was asleep at the switch. I observed one manager, whose subordinate had just lost a key client through neglect, take the blame with her own manager. "Look," said her boss, "this was Kelly's error, so just fire him, and then see what you can do to regain the client."

"No," said the manager, "I should have caught this. Kelly was wrong, but I'm supposed to be the backstop, and this was ultimately my responsibility."

Her boss said that it was her unit, so she'd let it stand there. The manager determined that Kelly wasn't ever going to fulfill the job well, and moved him to another position. Both the boss and the other subordinates, without a word being said, had immense respect for the manager's actions, and both superior and subordinates worked hard to support her in the future and avoid similar client problems.

Bright Idea
If there is public (organization-wide) recognition for an achievement, allow your subordinates to determine who among them should accept it on behalf of the department, and don't take center stage yourself. This will create more focus on your character and standards than any personal appearance could have done.

Lowell Anderson, when he was CEO of Allianz Insurance in Minneapolis, announced over the public address system one morning that a $100 check was awaiting every home office employee in the human resources department, and was a symbol of the company's gratitude for their help in achieving goals that year. The amount of money was minor, but the gesture and sharing of credit was enormous.

Innovates and attempts to raise standards

We've discussed the need to continually innovate in Chapter 7. Outstanding managers don't simply coax along the present, they establish new futures. Power managers are constantly monitoring these areas for possible innovation:

- Unexpected successes: What has worked beyond expectations that can serve as a springboard for other advances?

- Unexpected failures: What has failed so dramatically that we might learn of an entirely new need or market that we've obviously missed?

- Unexpected event: What new internal or external occurrence lends itself to new approaches?

- Process weakness: What "weak link" of our own or of our competitors might provide for improved products or services?

- Market/industry change: What is changing about our structure or the industry that will allow for new standards?

- Combined technology: How can we reconfigure and recombine technology to give us a competitive edge?

- High growth: What growth have we experienced beyond projections and forecasts that can lead us to leverage other things we do?

- Demographic change: What is changing about our customers and their income, education, or dispersal that may lead to new products or services?

- Perception changes: What differing societal perceptions can be built on or managed for new ideas and approaches?

- New knowledge: What have we learned, created, or developed that lends itself to new products and services?

Managers who maintain the status quo will always be appreciated and "safe." Managers who challenge the status quo and attempt to improve performance regularly will be needed and given resources and attract the support and attention of others.

Sees people as assets, not expenses, and develops subordinates

This is a pragmatic need, not just a smart managerial technique. One of the greatest causes of managers *not* being promoted is the absence of anyone to take their place. I can't tell you how many times I've sat in succession planning meetings or promotion review meetings and heard "He's a good one, but there's no way I can afford to let him go; he'll just have to wait for another opportunity," and "She's certainly the best candidate, but would it do us more harm to lose her in her current job than the benefit we'd be gaining in her new job? There are others who can do the new job, even if not quite as well."

Timesaver
Create an "innovation team" with rotating membership, and allow them the time to meet as they desire to produce new ideas and suggestions to "raise the bar" within your area or department. Innovation requires focus, and it's a fine project for your people on a regular basis.

The old managerial mentality saw equipment as assets and people as expenses. Hence, preventive maintenance and investment were provided for the former, and little was done for the latter. That equation, of course, has changed (although not in all places and not always very rapidly).

The signs of resistance to this tenet are often subtle. But they can be seen in the manager who says, "Times are tough, so let's cut the training budget." Or: "You're going to have to put off that 2 week trip with the family, because with the new acquisition pending there's no way we can afford to lose you here for 2 weeks." Or: "There's nothing in the rotational assignment that you can't learn right here, and this way you won't be gone for 3 months."

Managers have to be prepared to make sacrifices for these assets, which include investing in development, providing time off for personal fulfillment (call it "preventive maintenance"), and allowing top performers to proceed at their own rates.

However, there are two keys above all here:

1. Scrupulously develop your own successor(s) since the lack of one will undoubtedly hinder your own chances for advancement.

2. Spend more time developing the top performers than trying to save the poor performers or boost the mediocre performers.

One of the greatest of all management errors with people is to ignore the high-flyers ("They can take care of themselves") and to lavish precious time on mediocrity. Developing people means weeding out poor performance as well as developing top performance.

Takes prudent risks; looks at return, not just investment

There are a raft of managers in organizational life who are very good at asking a single question: What does it cost? They are asking the wrong question. They should be asking: What is the return?

Opportunities arrive regularly, and the key question is what will they do for you, not how much they cost! There will be educational opportunities, customer invitations, competitive breakdowns, technological discoveries, societal changes, and other unforeseen happenings that can constitute great advantage. Are you prepared to evaluate them for return on investment? Are you prepared to separate out wild gambles from prudent risk?

Prudent risk has these characteristics:

- There is a demonstrable and measurable gain to be achieved if the initiative works as planned.

- There is expertise, experience, and precedent to suggest that the opportunity can be successful if managed well.

- The "downside" is not fatal. That is, damage control is possible and the loss can be sustained and eventually made up.

- There is no danger to safety, image, product quality, or other unassailable factors.

- You control the variables. There is no major outside factor that is outside of your control (or at least with strong influence).

- You have the support of your superiors; that is, the initiative is not a secret and there will be no unpleasant surprises even in failure.

Unofficially...
Budgets virtually never allow for the unexpected and serendipity, so don't be swayed an iota by the fact that there's no budget for a given opportunity. Ask instead: What return will this provide that will not only pay for itself but accelerate us past our goals?

- You feel passionate about the likelihood of success and can enlist exactly the support that you deem necessary.

If this template applies, you have the makings of prudent risk, not wild-eyed-bet-the-farm gambling. In other words, you already are holding three-of-a-kind, and you're not trying to fill an inside straight.

Strong communication and interpersonal abilities

Chapters 6 and 14 dealt with a variety of communications issues. Power managers are "socially initiating," in that they don't sit back and wait to be contacted, because, inevitably, such contact occurs only after something negative has already happened.

Excellence in communication and interpersonal abilities rests on four central qualities:

1. Reading with comprehension. You should be able to read a memo, a customer's letter, a procedure, or an e-mail and understand more than simply the words. You should be capable of interpreting the intent and the "between the lines" issues.

Example: A customer writes in great consternation and fury about a check that wasn't received. You're missing the details, and you have to contact the customer to get more information, but the letter is far out of proportion to the $84 check that's missing. You realize that the writer is overwrought about something else, which is probably unrelated to this matter. Rather than delegate this to a subordinate, call on the phone, or put it in a file for a week, you write back with just the facts, unemotionally, and

Timesaver
"Triage" for mail: One pile of what should be read immediately (for example, customer letters), another of what needs to be read in the next day (for example, field reports), and a third of background and information which you will get to when you can (for example, magazines). Throw everything else out.

ignore the harsh words the customer has written. You know that this will give the customer a chance to reflect and provide the information you need, whereas a phone call might generate more over-reaction and might cause you to respond in turn. But a letter from the person in charge, asking for a few specific details and offering immediate help on receiving them, should do the job.

Suggested action: Read widely, and compare what you've read with someone else who has read the same material. Recognize the differing perceptions, and develop the ability to interpret material in more than your traditional manner.

2. Writing with expression. You should be able to write succinct, pithy, and interesting memos and letters, so that your meaning is conveyed clearly and the reader finds the material to be of interest.

Example: You have to write a memo on customer response time to remind your staff that there has been a pattern of complaints about a lack of empathy extended to callers who have been on hold for several minutes. You want them to remember this simple need, which helps to make customers feel better and requires only a few seconds of commiseration. You start your memo with "Please read before disregarding . . ." which you know will both cause a smile and get their attention. You keep it to four sentences, and remind them that the phrase, "Hey, there are people who have waited for 2 days!" is not considered to be especially empathetic.

(There is a famous story of two German hotels, each with a sign in the guest rooms. The first hotel sign says: "Breakfast is included in your room rate, but failure to eat breakfast will not result in any decrease in that rate." The second hotel sign says: "We are pleased to offer you a complimentary breakfast." Both signs accomplish the same end, but the second with much more grace and goodwill.)

Suggested action: Try to reduce what you write by as much as 50 percent, then give it to someone to test for what they understand from it. Keep customer letters and memos to a single page. Keep e-mail to two paragraphs at most.

3. Speak with influence. When you address a group, a meeting, or a few people in the hall, you should have a command of vocabulary, analogy, metaphor, and usage.

Example: Managers who consistently violate correct speech are often disregarded by superiors and mocked by subordinates. I know several managers, stuck at given places in their careers, who consistently use terms such as "irregardless," "between you and I," and "should I imply that you want me to work on this?" (Correct: regardless or irrespective, between you and me, and should I infer—speakers imply, listeners infer.) When this happens at formal meetings and presentations, whatever follows the incorrect speech is lost for a minute or so on the audience. I once heard a speaker refer to "anecdotes" as "antidotes," which distracted everyone's attention.

Suggested action: Whenever you read a word you don't know, write it down and look it up later. Add the word and its definition to a formal list you keep on your computer or in a small file. At the end of a few months your vocabulary and usage will have improved tremendously.

4. Listen with discernment. Most managers can't
   listen because they are too busy talking. Don't
   just allow others to speak, but actively interpret
   what they're saying. Take notes, but don't barge
   in. Show that you are an empathic listener.

Example: Many people are satisfied to merely be
heard. Taking the extra 5 minutes to allow someone
to complete their thoughts and explain them fully is
worth the investment in terms of their confidence
that you've listened to them carefully. You may know
exactly where they're going after the first sentence,
but then again you may not. Prosecutors love to
allow witnesses free reign because they tend to
incriminate themselves. Similarly, allow people the
freedom to speak and you may just learn something.

Suggested action: Wait until there is a demonstrable 2-second silence before responding to someone,
whether in person or on the phone. Count "one
thousand one, one thousand two," and then
respond. If they say, "Are you still there?" or "Are
you with me?" simply respond that you were thinking over what they had said.

Views the customer as the primary focus

Whether you manage in a small auto repair shop, a
midsized supermarket, or a global insurance group,
you have customers who pay the bills and keep the
lights on and the phones working. It might make
sense to take them rather seriously. I find myself constantly reminding those who are ostensibly being
paid to provide me with service, "Wouldn't your job
be terrific if customers just didn't get in the way?"
Several have agreed with me quite strenuously!

Bright Idea
Many people
don't say what
they mean.
Reply: "This is
what I think I
just heard . . ."
and give them a
chance to clarify
or elaborate.
When they hear
the "echo" of
their words they
often realize
they haven't
communicated
well. This puts
the onus on
them, and not
on you.

The old system of priorities in the business world used to be:

descending
priorities

Senior Management

Shareholders

Employees

Customers

In this sequence, senior management took care of itself, then made sure that shareholders were happy, then looked after employees, and finally may have had something left over for the customer. This was the day of great executive perks and aloof fortresses, quarter-to-quarter returns that pleased investors, and keeping employees at bay and unions mollified. Especially in the old regulated worlds of banking, airlines, and utilities, the customer be damned.

Today, however, superb management has to have this sequence in mind:

descending
priorities

Customers

Employees

Shareholders

Senior Management

Customers are the lifeblood. Employees come next, because they are the ones dealing with the customer (and there is no such thing as unhappy employees and happy customers). Then please the shareholders and, as a result, management will be rewarded nicely. This is the new business reality for world-class businesses and world-class managers alike.

The customer may not always be right, but the customer deserves a few things consistently under your management guidance:

- Polite interaction, whether by phone, mail, or in person.
- Rapid responsiveness.
- Accuracy and quality.
- Truthfulness and consistency.
- Judgment applied to legitimate exceptions and unique situations.
- The opportunity to speak to management and be heard.

In any and all of these "customer rights," bear in mind at all times that you are the exemplar for those around you. If you exemplify these values, they will be employed by others. If you give them only lip service or reject them, they will atrophy and disappear. That choice is yours, alone.

Lives a complete life, with work as simply one component

The finest managers are well-rounded managers. They are best able to appreciate the perspectives of customers and employees, understand that they are not (generally) dealing with the fate of the world, and don't take themselves overly seriously.

Managers who are able to enjoy family, friends, hobbies, travel, entertainment, recreation, and other diversions are able to communicate better with a diverse array of people. It's hard not to get along with someone who enjoys waterskiing as much

Watch Out!
Some customers will attempt to carry the day through sheer volume and bravado, often in public, to embarrass you into capitulating. Immediately tell such people that you'll be happy to hear their issues in private, but that if they don't change their current behavior you will refuse to deal with them.

as you do, or has just visited London as you have, or who also has children in school. Note that these issues transcend culture, ethnicity, origins, and upbringings.

Investment people and financial experts will tell you that your entire financial future should not rest on your employment. In other words, since your salary and bonus already derive from your employer, and your benefits package is a part of your remuneration, and you may also have a stock purchase plan or 401(k) dependent on company performance, you should deliberately ensure that other investments are not in the company, to avoid complete catastrophe if you lose your job or the company suffers hard times. They say you should diversify.

The same holds true for your life and interests. As much as one-third or more of your life is invested in your work, and that's not counting issues that you take home, conversations about work, seeing friends developed at work, and so on. (For those of you who travel as part of your job, this investment is heightened significantly.)

Consequently, you should "invest" outside of work. Find friends, interests, and passions divorced from your occupation. This isn't a mutually exclusive undertaking. One doesn't replace the other, but merely supplements it. But if you work a 40- to 60-hour week, take work home, play softball for the company team, see friends only from the workplace, possess only company stock, and can only speak the company "language," you're not much different from the company person of the 1950s, except that this is a much more volatile world with changes in employment and status sudden and common.

For your well-being as much as your safety, you should diversify your interests and lead a complete life. The office will still be there on Monday.

Taming the crises

Crises will occur. The best planners and most methodical managers can't avoid the occasional crisis.

Someone said once that there are no great people, but only ordinary people who rise up to meet great challenges. "History is only the biography of great men," said Thomas Carlyle.

You never have quite the chance to excel as when a crisis occurs. Let's define "crisis" as the following: An unstable state of affairs requiring decisions and resolution prior to a return to normalcy. Certainly, after some crises, nothing is "normal" ever again. But most business crises involve some aspect of the following:

- Key talent leaves or defects.

- Important customers depart or are lost.

- Financial matters decline precipitously and unexpectedly.

- Safety, quality, or image is threatened or damaged.

- Legal or ethical problems of significant proportions arise.

- Management impropriety is discovered.

We never hear about the tampering with Tylenol bottles a few years ago without the phrase "Tylenol Crisis" added to it. Many crises are public: The Exxon Valdez oil spill, Pentium chip quality problems, Texaco's racial incidents, Astra Pharmaceutical's sexual harassment problems, and Prudential's

Unofficially...
Don't accept "crisis" because someone is yelling it from the rooftops. If everything is a crisis, then nothing is a crisis. Step back and analyze what's happened to decide if the situation is really as bad as others claim.

unethical insurance sales tactics constitute just a short list of "crises" to hit the front pages over the recent years.

A crisis is not an emergency. An emergency occurs when someone has had a heart attack or there's fire raging in the hallway. Emergencies require immediate action with little time for analysis. In most cases, contingent actions are in place to deal with emergencies, precisely because they don't allow the luxury of gradual response at the time. So sprinkler systems turn on, 911 is dialed, and someone initiates CPR.

In a crisis, ironically, you do have the benefit of some analytical time and careful response. If you're informed that a client has decided that they're leaving for the competition, it's unlikely that an immediate phone call from you would be as effective as a measured, thoughtful response. If a woman is claiming that she was sexually harassed by one of your subordinates, speed is important in acknowledging and reacting to the claim, but deliberation is important in weighing the facts and the evidence. Emergencies require immediate action. Crises require planned responses.

When a crisis arises, use the following template to calm yourself and those around you. Remember that others will be apt to follow your lead, and if you head for the hills a stampede with ensue.

1. Do not panic. Seldom are things as bad as they seem and, even if they are, panic simply freezes your analytic abilities and stymies actions. Remember perspective: In all likelihood the crisis will not end existence as we know it.

2. Separate facts from opinion and emotion. Paraphrase reporter Dan Rather's famous

question of President Nixon: "What do we
know, and when did we learn it?" Ask of anyone providing information: "What's your evidence of that?"

3. Involve others who have a bearing on the resolution, despite rank or reporting relationships.
A secretary who talked to the customer every
day could be vital, but the vice president of
sales who never knew the customer could be
irrelevant (or a hindrance). Create a prover-
bial "SWAT" team to react.

4. Determine who's in charge. Is it you? Should it
be someone else? Who will make the final decisions as the matter unfolds further?

5. Determine what a successful resolution would
mean. That will vary. It could be a customer
regained, or substitutes sent into a territory
abandoned by your defecting staff, or the
media printing a correct version of events, or a
manager removed from the premises and provided with counsel. Not many crises can be
"undone," so decide early what an effective resolution and return to normalcy would mean.

6. Launch your plan and monitor it. Crises aren't
scripted, so early actions may not be effective
or may raise still more issues. Stay with the situation until the crisis becomes simply another
manageable issue.

Example: Your Canadian staff, a field manager
and four associates, have sent in resignations by
e-mail and are apparently setting up their own operation to compete against your company, aiming at
taking as many current clients with them as they
can. You verify this by reading the e-mails, and you

Timesaver
In a crisis,
immediately
determine if
human life or
health is at risk.
If so, that is the
sole priority until
resolution. If
not, then you
can take more
time determining
priorities.

call the Montreal office to learn from the office manager that, while her staff remains and the office is open, none of the professionals have been heard from since yesterday.

You involve your other regional managers and call your three largest Canadian customers. None of the three has heard anything out of the ordinary as of this morning. Your regional team manager decides that the priorities are the following, and that you will serve as the crisis leader:

- Retain all Canadian customers.

- Immediately provide temporary professional staff.

- Prevent erosion of leads and loss of market share in the future.

- Permanently replace departing staff.

- Honestly and rapidly inform rest of organization of actions.

Bright Idea
Crises can't be anticipated, but they can be planned for in some ways. Consider a crisis response team, involving field, home office, public relations, and financial representation. Once assembled to respond, the team can determine who else is needed situationally for that crisis.

One of your marketing people calls every Canadian customer to tell them candidly what's happened, and to assure them that the Montreal office is still there to serve them. The Montreal office staff is instructed about how to forward client calls and requests. The manager of the New England region, who has worked in Canada, is sent to Montreal to take charge, and he takes five people from around the U.S. who have Canadian experience, two of whom speak French. You call the legal department to begin investigating unfair competitive practices and a possible restraining order, and you pursue with public relations the advisability of a newspaper ad in several Canadian markets to explain what's occurred. The PR people also put out an internal memo informing employees of what's taken place and what the response had been. Finally, human resources alerts the Canadian recruiters to begin an immediate search for replacement professionals. Locks and codes are changed at the Montreal office.

Within 24 hours the crisis has become a severe but manageable problem. There has been minimal disruption and rumor. On the longer term, human resources will investigate how this could have happened without earlier indicators, and what might be done to prevent it in the future.

In crisis management, you have to "clear the decks" and focus on the issue exclusively in the response and planning stages. After that, as plans are implemented and others are executing their responsibilities, you can return to a somewhat more normal routine. But it's critical in formulating the initial response that you concentrate on nothing other than the organization and deployment of your resources to handle the unexpected situation.

Don't handle crises out of your back pocket or casually, or they can become fatal.

Just the facts

- "Necessary evils" should not be tolerated.

- Ego can be healthy, but needs to be subordinated to results.

- Developing others is essential for your own future.

- The finest managers are well-rounded managers.

- Crises will always occur, and can be systematically resolved.

GET THE SCOOP ON...
Why questions are more important than answers
■ Focusing on results ■ Extending your talents
outward ■ Educating yourself ■
Self-actualization

Chapter 17

Post-heroic Management and Self-actualization

If you've read carefully to this point, you probably realize that "power management" is really "empowered management," and the first person to empower is yourself. If you aren't comfortable, confident, and knowledgeable, your employees and work will suffer as well.

The ultimate state of managerial excellence is "post-heroic." By that I mean that the manager is no longer dependent on external sources of power—the numbers of subordinates, size of office, length of title, a personal parking space, a separate dining room, and so on. Instead, the manager is powerful due to three key measures:

- The results generated consistently exceed expectations.

- People—not only subordinates—respect and follow the manager's lead.

■ The manager meets and exceeds his or her
own internalized standards of excellence.

When people are reliant on the approval of others, they place themselves in a constant position of supplication and trying to please, no matter what their title or authority. The "360° assessment" has become the "smile sheet" of our times. (360° assessments are evaluations of performance which are asked of subordinates, peers, superiors, and sometimes customers. "Smile sheets" are those superficial evaluations attendees receive after a presentation or class that ask how well they liked the presenter, the visuals, the room, and the planning. Neither of these devices is especially helpful because they focus on opinion and the biases of the responder rather than the facts of performance and results.)

Insecure people crave the feedback of others. They use it to establish their own worth and merit, and to adjust their behavior for the future. The problem is that some excellent managerial techniques will provoke and disappoint people, causing poor feedback (for example, cutting back expenses, demanding higher performance, enforcing discipline), and some poor techniques create comfort and support (for example, ignoring performance deviations, protection of employees despite the issue, not supporting the organization in "raising the bar"). Consequently, the feedback is often distorted, discouraging proper behavior and reinforcing poor behavior.

Confident people, however, create their own, internalized measures, which revolve around how much they grow, improve, and meet higher and higher standards of performance. These measures are not based on popularity or others' positive

Watch Out!
Feedback is not, in and of itself, accurate, simply because it comes from another person. Look for patterns in feedback from disparate sources, which can indicate accuracy. Ignore isolated feedback, especially if unsolicited. It's rarely intended to help you.

assessments (though they are often congruent with them). Such personalized measures of success can be called "self-mastery."

Self-mastery occurs for the relatively few managers whose behaviors, skills, knowledge, and experience have progressed to the point where they can set their own goals for growth and success. They take the viewpoints of others into consideration—no one wants to ignore the boss, for example—but they synthesize what they hear and create their own goals from their own analysis. True self-mastery enables managers to disregard clearly incorrect or biased feedback, whether it be mistakenly critical or falsely favorable.

The ancient adage "consider the source" is highly appropriate when you're provided with feedback. Self-mastery allows you to determine which feedback, positive or negative, makes sense, and which to ignore. Sometimes your actions are merely images in the eye of the beholder. After a presentation to 50 people, one woman approached me to tell me that I used language in a neutral and impressive way, never relying solely on male pronouns. Two minutes later another woman told me that I was too sexist in my demeanor, since I recognized questions from males more than from females.

What was true? Probably neither, since both women simply had a personal agenda they wanted to push at every possible opportunity. None of the other women who approached me commented on anything but the content of my remarks. I had not solicited feedback on the nature of my language or gender neutrality, the feedback was unsolicited, and there was no pattern. I had the self-mastery to ignore it, not worry about it, not expend energy or time on it, and move on.

Why questions are more important than answers

Great managers ask great questions. They don't pretend to have all the answers. In fact, in most cases of indecision or uncertainty, there are only three conditions that apply:

■ We have a factual response that we can substantiate.

  Example: "I understand your point about customers leaving us because there are no permanent service people assigned, but the fact is that customers work with no more than two different reps, turnover among reps is below 4 percent, and we've had this system in place for at least 7 years without the customer attrition we're experiencing now. So I doubt that we can cite the rep system as the cause."

■ We have an opinion, based on our experience and judgment.

  Example: "I don't know what's caused the high customer attrition this year, but I suspect that we might want to look at the difference between what the customer is promised at the sale and what is really delivered subsequently. Shortly before the attrition rose, we cut our installation force by 25 percent, and it could be that both speed of installation and resolution of problems occurring right after installation are not being addressed as quickly as our sales force is accustomed to promising."

■ We simply don't know.

  Example: "The attrition is our major problem right now, and I don't even have a good guess.

Let's launch a formal problem-solving effort and find out what's causing it."

Managers are not expected to be omnipotent, only honest. Post-heroic managers, as knowledgeable as they might be, are even more powerful when they ask the right questions, for these reasons:

Heroic Managers:	Post-heroic Managers:
Try to be all-knowing	Try to guide and coach
Desire dependence on them	Foster empowerment
Place premium on being "right"	Value being successful
Demand respect	Earn respect
Crave external reinforcement	Utilize internal standards
Must demonstrate success	Support others' success
Must be seen as "strong"	Are satisfied being human

We've said before that you simply can't learn while you're talking. That's why good questioning will help you to learn so much, because it results in other people doing the talking while you can listen. Look around you in meetings and informal discussions: The outstanding managers at any level are not the ones who immediately take center stage and bark orders or generate information. They are the ones who ask a few initial questions, then sit back, listen, and reflect, until such time as they need to ask a few more questions or are ready to provide some response.

Here are examples of two differing responses to the same situation, the first "heroic" and directive, and the second "post-heroic" and questioning:

Example #1:

SUBORDINATE: "We're going to have to provide the field force with laptop computers as soon as we can arrange it. I have some quotes here."

Timesaver
The most important question of all may be "why." Questions which begin with "why" delve into the core of the situation, and help to stay away from degree, intent, timing, and some other peripheral information for the moment. By itself, it constitutes a powerful response to a demand or recommendation.

MGR: "That's impossible. There is no budget. We've discussed this in the past."

SUBORDINATE: "The competition is using them to provide customers with quotes right at the point of first contact. We're still reliant on a day's delay from home office. We're taking a beating."

MGR: "Home office promised a response by phone while the salesperson is sitting with the prospect."

SUBORDINATE: "Well, that isn't working. Just this morning we lost the Sears contract, which was a major part of our projections for this quarter and which seemed highly likely."

MGR: "That's awful. Get the salesperson on the phone for a conference call. Get the price unit's manager down here to explain why we're not getting on-the-spot phone responses. Leave those laptop quotes on my desk, and send an e-mail to purchasing to find out if they can get us a deal in volume better than this. Oh, and get the budget figures and make some recommendations as to where we can find laptop money if we have to. My advice is to look at cutting off-site training for the rest of the year."

Example #2:

SUBORDINATE: "We're going to have to provide the field force with laptop computers as soon as we can arrange it. I have some quotes here."

MGR: "Why?"

SUBORDINATE: "The competition is using them to provide customers with quotes right at the point of first contact. We're still reliant on a day's delay from home office. We're taking a beating."

MGR: "What makes you say that?"

SUBORDINATE: "Just this morning we lost the Sears contract, which was a major part of our projections for this quarter and which seemed highly likely."

MGR: "Haven't there been numerous meetings with the Sears buyer that included several different pricing schemes?"

SUBORDINATE: "Yes."

MGR: "Then how could a lack of laptops be responsible for our losing it?"

SUBORDINATE: "Well, the customer apparently wanted a revised quote this morning, which caught us by surprise."

MGR: "Did we actually lose the contract?"

SUBORDINATE: "I'm not positive."

MGR: "Look, find the sales rep who was there and find out exactly what happened. Let's make sure we protect this sale and give her all the support that she needs. Do you have any other facts about the lack of laptops causing sales problems?"

SUBORDINATE: "No, but I believe it is a hindrance."

MGR: "Get back to me when you have some facts. Right now, follow up with the Sears rep."

These two conversations take quite a different spin, and have radically different outcomes. Yet they are not uncommon. The same subordinate concerns and responses caused the first manager to blast into action, while the second asked a few questions to clarify and simplify the situation. And this is with a concerned, nonmalicious subordinate. Sometimes recommendations are made with personal agendas, self-serving motives, and even malice as their underpinnings.

A few good questions never require much time, but can save you a great deal of time in terms of inappropriate actions, wrong directions, and spinning wheels. Bolting into action may be the sign of a hero, but it's also the sign of poor leadership when you don't know which direction to charge off in and

Unofficially...
Managers are not paid to take action. They are paid to get results. Consequently, the best results are often achieved by *not* taking action that may be antithetical to the desired results. Asking good questions is the best way to avoid inappropriate actions.

choose one at random. You may just be fighting your own troops.

Focusing on results

Empowered managers focus on results. Ends influence means. Tactics are subordinate to goals.

A manager's vision should always be on the goal, no matter how many alternatives may be available, because some of the alternatives will lead to the wrong destination, or will be unnecessarily circuitous. While we need to ensure that the alternative is accurate and working as promised, no alternative is worth anything if it fails to arrive at our goal. Yet that is what often happens.

The "quality industry" has sometimes subverted what happens to be a very fine idea, which is simply to set, measure, and meet (or exceed) the highest possible quality standards. Yet when quality bureaucracies are created, the means sometimes take precedence over the ends.

When Florida Power & Light won a major national quality award several years ago, the appropriate banners and press releases were soon in the air. But when a new CEO replaced his retired predecessor, he dismantled the formal quality "machinery" (the departments, forms, internal awards, and so on) because he found that winning the award had become an organizational end in and of itself, and that serving the customers and the rate payers had become subordinate to it. He knew that no amount of awards were sufficient if the customer was not happy and not served well, and no absence of awards could detract from happy, well-served customers. He had his priorities in the correct order.

As you can see in the figure below, some alternatives don't lead to the goal, as straightforward, clear,

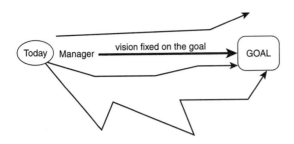

and attractive as they may appear. Others lead to the goal rapidly and accurately, although there may be some risk involved. Still others meander before they arrive, costing time and energy, although they may entail less risk.

Winning a quality award is clear, and the mechanisms and measures for doing so are documented and detailed. The problem is that winning the award is not necessarily a part of the organization's vision or its goals. Similarly, you may often be in a position of having to focus the vision of others, because they are determined to pursue action and alternatives, irrespective of the ultimate end point.

Here are some of the differences between alternative-generated (tasks, inputs) and results-oriented (outcomes, results) approaches:

Alternative focus	Results focus
Seeks assurance on "how"	Seeks assurance on "what"
Tends to favor tried and true	Welcomes new routes to reach goals
Driven from today's position	Driven by tomorrow's position
Conservative	Exploratory and creative
Focus on details	Focus on larger picture
Repairs and fixes alternative	Abandons alternative if necessary
Pride is on execution	Pride is on accomplishment of ends

> 66
> It is not economical to go to bed early to save candles if the result is twins.
> —Old Chinese proverb
> 99

The objectives and measures you establish for your employees should always revolve around this outcome-based philosophy. "Answering the phone promptly" does no good if the response is rude, the ensuing instructions are wrong, or the call is then put on hold.

"Promptly direct the caller to the right destination within 60 seconds."

This focus on results is important because our day can otherwise become mired in the "how to" of business, and our perspectives can be distorted because people tend to panic when a tactic misfires, even though the strategy is still intact and safe. A disconnected call is a problem, but a customer defecting is a calamity. If all problems are desperate, then we tend to lose our focus and our sense of perspective. We overreact to everything, and tend to lump together both the minor and the potentially fatal.

Some of the best managers I've seen use goals as a daily template. Instead of merely focusing on activities—which most "planning systems" and personal calendars actually foster by providing for timed activities, meetings, and the like—they create daily objectives to be met (as well as weekly, monthly, and quarterly objectives).

Here's the difference:

Typical calendar or planner entries:

- 9:30 Meet with supervisors
- 10:30 Call Acme stores client
- Lunch with boss (staff meeting)
- 2:00 Review progress on Smith's performance problems
- 3:30 Complete reorganization report summary

Results-oriented day:

- Gain consensus with supervisors on new staffing plan
- Listen to supervisors' needs for next quarter
- Ensure that Acme buyer is delighted with our service
- Obtain next quarter's guarantee from Acme
- Get input from colleagues on reorganization proposal
- Prompt boss to commit to bonuses I'm recommending
- Obtain Smith's agreement to reach goal by May 1 or transfer out
- Complete reorganization report using colleagues' inputs

Which day has the most excitement, the most focus, and the most promise? Yet it's the same day and the same array of people and issues, but arranged toward results and not merely on "presence" or task completion.

Results-focused managers are not only better at achieving goals, they also tend to have more fun and more stimulation, simply by organizing their time and focus on results.

Extending your talents outward

Edgar Schein, the noted author on consulting, said once that if you ever really want to understand something, try to change it. I like to paraphrase that advice by saying, "try to teach it."

You have the potential to "reach out" to others, both inside and outside the organization's walls. We all remember our great teachers—I can name every one of my great grammar school teachers 30 years

Bright Idea
Look at your personal planner, PDA, or desk calendar for the next week. Reinterpret everything around results and outcomes. Eliminate, adjust, and add as needed. You'll find your time better spent and better enjoyed. If an assistant books your time, educate your assistant to use the same new parameters.

later, but some of my mediocre undergraduate professors are already lost to history. What I've learned is that outstanding teachers make an impact, not only on those they touch, but also on their own futures.

There are several ways to "reach out":

- Teach programs formally within the organization
- Informally teach as a mentor within the organization
- Teach in an educational institution
- Teach in an informal community program

Teaching formally within the organization

Almost every organization has a range of programs delivered by internal trainers, staff members, or external consultants. These range from "front line supervision," to "time management," to "leadership." Some of the programs are orientations for new employees, and some are refreshers for veterans as the organization changes and evolves.

Managers from within the ranks bring a strong dose of credibility and pragmatic experience to what can otherwise be conceptual and theoretical exercises. (It's one thing to discuss how to deal with performance problems, it's another to hear from someone who did so yesterday.) Some organizations solicit management participation, others have to be approached with the idea.

Volunteer for a brief portion of a curriculum—say, 45 minutes or an hour—that won't be overly burdensome on your time (or the program's) but will enable you to interact based on what you know well. Many of these sessions take the form of a question-and-answer arrangement, so that the participants can ask what they need to know, but since they won't always know what they need to know, you should always have something prepared to present (see Chapter 14 of presentation skills).

If you keep it focused, simple, well-prepared, and open to questions, you will learn a great deal about:

- What kind of people the company is hiring and what their needs are.

- The relevance (or lack) of the material they are being presented.

- The perspective they have about work and about the organization.

- What needs to be done on the job to make them productive.

As a managerial visitor to these sessions you'll gain some prestige, be seen as helping others, and learn a lot. And if you prepare well and have a good time, you'll be appreciated as one of the highlights of the program. That's not a bad return on an hour's investment once or twice a month.

Informally teach as a mentor

In our surveys of personal success in organizations of all types, the single most important source cited for promotion and advancement is having a mentor (or sponsor, or coach). Usually, mentors are not direct superiors, although that sometimes occurs. But usually mentors are superiors in other areas who have formally or informally taken on the responsibility of serving as a sounding board and coach for a high-potential individual. (Some organizations have instituted formal mentoring programs, not leaving it to chance, in order to maximize a diverse mix of mentors and mentorees.)

Bright Idea
If you want to create a teaching presentation or other instructional material, start with the end result and work backwards. Don't ask "What should I present?" but rather, "What should they learn?" This guarantees relevancy and an economy of effort.

Mentoring is always about a one-on-one relationship where the person being counseled brings his or her issues to the discussion and asks for guidance. Ideally, these issues are about pragmatic, current events that provide a "real time" opportunity to explore, act, and react to the results. Outstanding mentors don't superimpose their own values or provide specific regimens, but rather allow the other person to find his or her own way, discover his or her own abilities, and apply his or her own talents.

For example, if a mentoree is offered a job that provides for advancement but also requires a geographic move that isn't very attractive, the mentor shouldn't comment, "Don't be a fool. Take the position. We've all had to do that to succeed here." Instead, a more useful discussion is engendered by, "Well, tell me about your personal as well as your professional goals, and then compare them to what you see as the positives and negatives of this move."

Mentorees should never be in a position of claiming, "This wouldn't have happened to me if I hadn't listened to you!" They should be saying, "I'm thankful for your help in guiding me through this so I could make a well-informed and clear decision."

There are two ways to form mentoring relationships.

Unofficially...
Subordinating ego is more important than ever in successful mentoring. Don't take it as a personal challenge that your mentoree has to be more successful than others. Be an accessible guide and counselor, but don't intervene and don't allow your own persona to become attached to the dynamic.

1. Be sensitive when you are approached by others for advice and reaction. Make yourself accessible. Invite them to come back to you after the event has occurred or a new approach has been attempted, and discuss the aftermath. Make sure that this doesn't have to occur in public—a cubicle, glass office, cafeteria, and other public places might not be ideal for confidence. A closed conference room or private office might be more comfortable.

2. Make it known to human resources that you'd be interested in serving as a mentor. If there is a formalized program, you can gain inclusion, and if there are informal opportunities you can be considered.

Usually, once you've served as a mentor, word gets around. It's usually most effective to bear two things in mind once you've become comfortable in the role:

■ You cannot mentor many people at once; in fact, one is usually sufficient before time demands weaken the experience.

■ Try to mentor people who do not look like you do for maximum learning for both parties. If you are a white male, consider deliberately mentoring a minority female, for example. (There are concerns in some areas about male/female mentoring relationships, given current legal fears about harassment. If you're serious and intelligent, there are ways to deal with such fear, such as meetings in more public venues and a clearly defined mentoring relationship.)

How successful is mentoring? If you think about it, you've probably had a couple over the years in one place or another who helped you tremendously and who, themselves, are even more successful today.

Teach in an educational institution

If your job does not require excessive travel, or if you can control the travel, you should consider teaching a course in your general community for any of the following:

■ University or college

■ Community college

■ Trade or professional school

Bright Idea
Teaching credits always look impressive on your résumé, whether for internal use or in search of a new job. Higher educational teaching "credentials" are of tremendous benefit, above and beyond one's personal learning, and even if gained during only a brief span.

More people are attending degree-granting schools of one type or another today than at any other time in our history. Consequently, schools of all types have proliferated. You can teach a course or part of a course without a Ph.D. or formally joining the faculty in many instances. Some of the choices include:

- Evening sessions, typically meeting one night a week.

- Advanced programs for adults, meeting on weekends.

- Contributor to a regular professor's course as your time permits.

- Programs conducted over the Internet or by teleconference.

The best way to do this is to write directly to the institution's president, stressing that you're interested in doing this as a service, not as a paying position (though some schools will insist on payments due to union contracts), that your schedule may offer some constraints but your experience provides for a rare benefit, and you would like to discuss the options available. Most educational institutions don't like to turn away such volunteers, and you should be referred to the head of the proper school or department (which is why you want to start with the president).

I've taught graduate programs for MBA and Ph.D. candidates over entire semesters, served as a guest lecturer for full-time professors' undergraduate classes, provided demonstrations in how to interview at trade schools, and served as a commencement speaker. I've learned a great deal each time.

As your experience grows in these institutions, your ability to increase or upgrade your exposure becomes far easier. Inevitably, I'm graciously received by the administration and the faculty who feel that active businesspeople bring the "real world" into the classroom, which is so often missing in a student's academic experiences.

Teach in an informal community program

Another aspect of community teaching lies in the extension programs and nonmatriculated fields of study. Universities often offer courses in everything from business accounting to conflict resolution to gardening, in programs that utilize the university's facilities during "off" hours. (These programs are immensely popular within the institution because they generate significant revenues.)

Similarly, local governments offer programs, usually sponsored by the recreation department or chamber of commerce. Volunteer and civic organizations such as the Red Cross or United Way sponsor adult-learning experiences. There are also for-profit, private companies, such as the Learning Annex, that sponsor events on a regular basis.

All of these offer you the opportunity to teach, interact, hone your skills, and learn what's of importance to others. Since you are always teaching people, you will constantly acquire and sharpen skills useful with those you manage—other people.

Educating yourself

Perhaps the greatest challenge that is incumbent on you is to continually educate yourself. Unfortunately, the old saw about having 14 years of experience, but actually experiencing the same year 14 times over, is absolutely true in the cases of many managers.

Education was less important as the post–World War II business world developed, with its emphasis on a military hierarchy providing direct orders to subordinates at specific times. Since customers had fewer options, be they cars, televisions, or toasters, and much of society was regulated—including banking, transportation, and power—consumers were less likely to compare or complain. If managers learned the relatively simple tasks of their subordinates, whose jobs they had probably held at some point anyway, and knew the operations manual, and did what they were told, that manager was probably in line for promotion when his or her turn came, and was definitely set for life in the organization's retirement plan.

Since then, the workplace has been transformed by the knowledge worker, instantaneous communications, computerization, diverse customers and workforces, global business, the end of the Cold War, deregulation, and a raft of other changes that once would have required a millennium to absorb. But the modern workplace has absorbed them within about 35 years. (The average citizen of the 16th century—a time of exploration, the Renaissance, and great cultural change—processed less information in an entire lifetime than a person today does in simply reading a single edition of the *Sunday New York Times*.)

The result today is that no amount of formal, pre-determined, and conventional learning is sufficient for the modern manager. Much of our learning is oriented toward today or, worse, yesterday, instead of tomorrow. Much more of it is obsolete, with as short a time span as 5 years. (The 3M company demands, strategically, that 25 percent of its

Timesaver
Any book, magazine, newspaper, newsletter, or other source of information that is piled up and hasn't been read for 90 days ought to be tossed out, and anything older than 6 months demands that your subscription be terminated. By definition, it is not relevant information for you.

revenues are generated from products that did not exist 5 years prior. That's how that organization tries to ensure that it continues to look forward for its own survival and positioning.)

So, what's been choreographed for your learning will simply not be sufficient. You have to be constantly aware and sensitive to learning opportunities that you can avail yourself of or create for yourself. These will have the advantage of being contemporary, relevant, and personalized. But you are the only one who can do this. Relying on the organization, or even on institutions of higher learning, is misguided. (Even MBA graduates are finding they've either learned financial approaches that aren't as applicable as when they began their studies, or that they've missed key learning, such as interpersonal skills. Even "bedrock" curricula at major schools such as Harvard and Yale are now under scrutiny.)

Your best sources for pursuing contemporary and ongoing learning include:

- Serving as a mentor
- Obtaining a mentor
- Teaching others in some capacity
- Job variation, rotation, new assignments
- Cross-functional organizational teams
- Trips abroad, professional or personal (preferably both)
- Massive reading on a wide variety of topics
- Writing for publications or for personal enjoyment
- Pertinent seminars, symposia, and conferences
- Trade association involvement

■ Civic and social organizational involvement

■ Professional association leadership positions

■ Working with youth in some capacity

Bright Idea
Choose any single author, in addition to your diverse reading of others, and read everything that he or she has written. Understand an author's entire body of work. You'll be able to understand other authors even better through this device.

The point is not to engage in all of these activities, but rather to select some that you can do continuously (for example, reading), some that are situational (for example, a given task force), and others that are a part of your personal or professional life (for example, coaching a team or chairing a trade association committee).

A word about massive reading. The wider you read, the more your world view and intellectual firepower will increase. That's not based on reading everything in one area, but in reading across many areas. Many top managers and professionals have maintained that they have learned as much from fiction as from nonfiction, for example. It's no accident that both Peter Drucker and John Updike write both fiction and nonfiction. The opportunity to read is omnipresent, whether in the evening, on airplanes, waiting for an appointment, or carving out time to do so. I can always tell a well-read person just by listening to them briefly.

If you read, for example, the top three books on the *New York Times* best-seller list for both fiction and nonfiction, you'll be able to talk to almost anyone about anything. I simply don't know of a more inexpensive, accessible source of learning for managers in organizational life. It shouldn't be ignored and ought to be exploited.

Self-actualization

Abraham Maslow, a well regarded psychologist, created two lasting mental images for the organizational world. One was a famous aphorism: If the only tool you have is a hammer, you tend to see every problem as a nail. His point, of course, is that you can't allow yourself to be a solution in search of a problem, and that you need to have a wide variety of tools—and know how to use each when appropriate—if you are to stand out in the world of management.

His other near-mythic point was his famous "hierarchy of needs," which postulated that organizational life isn't much different from life itself, in that humankind first requires physical safety, then security, then relationships, and so on up to the highest level on Maslow's scale, which was "self-actualization" (sometimes referred to as "self-realization"). There are debunkers of Maslow's theory, certainly as it applies to people in organizations, but his concept of self-actualization is an interesting one and an apt place to end this book.

Self-actualization as I intend it here, is not about greed, self-aggrandizement, or personal power (and neither was it for Maslow). To me, self-actualization is the opportunity for the individual to express talents and explore new areas in the environment. It may entail something as exotic as travel to Borneo or taking up abstract painting, or it may mean simply accepting work responsibilities you were not prepared to accept before.

The ability to explore and express one's talents is heightened by a greater sense of "self," which means a confidence about one's abilities, the wherewithal to engage in activities outside of one's normal "comfort zone," the capability to recover quickly from setbacks, and the willingness to continue to attempt to build one's personal and professional competence.

Bright Idea
Before you put this book away, thumb through it and choose one key area in which you can improve or make a difference tomorrow. Write it in your calendar or put a note on your desk to make it happen. No matter what else happens, make sure you accomplish this. From here, no one can stop you . . .

Power (empowered) managers are able to do this more readily than others because they have developed skill sets, behaviors, and experiences conducive to self-actualization. But such an exploration does not occur automatically. You have to ascend to that level of being, to that level of contribution, to that level of desire.

Life (and work, which is a part of life) is not about perfection, it is about success. Failure is seldom fatal and even success is never final. It's courage that counts.

Be bold in your plans. Take prudent risk. Treat your job as an end to other means, which include your personal development, the happiness of your loved ones, and positive relationships with friends. Developing into a strong and confident manager has commensurate effects on the kind of person you are because the two are inextricably entwined. People who are self-actualizing are inevitably superior managers, and superior managers are inevitably those with the best opportunity to self-actualize.

The world of work is a noble calling. Providing constructive products, services, and relationships to customers, members, clients, and other beneficiaries is a wonderful pursuit. We can all constantly get better at it and, in so doing, better our own lot, as well.

The techniques in this book are meant to assist you in climbing toward self-actualization and maintaining it for the rest of your life. Remember that merely a 1 percent improvement every day will double your effectiveness in just 70 days.

The best time to start is right now.

Resources for Power Managers

American Management Association
1601 Broadway
New York, NY 10019
212/586-8100
Publishes the excellent *Management Review*, has a fine research library service, and provides seminars, books, and even meeting space.

American Society of Association Executives
1757 I St. NW
Washington, DC 20005-1168
202/626-2723
If you are a manager in an association, or are looking for an association appropriate for your profession and interests, this may be a logical starting point.

National Trade and Professional Associations of the United States
Columbia Books, Inc.
1212 Washington Ave., Suite 330
Washington, DC 20005
202/898-0662
Another excellent source to find professional associations related to your profession or specialty, how to join, location of conferences, local chapters, etc.

The Yearbook of Experts, Authorities, and Spokespersons
Broadcast Interview Source
2233 Wisconsin Ave. NW
Washington, DC 20007
202/333-4904
A good source to find consultants, speakers, trainers, facilitators, and others who may be appropriate for your developmental plans and staff needs.

Communispond
300 Park Ave.
New York, NY 10022
212/486-2300
Individual or group participation to hone speaking and presentation skills, whether in meetings or with the media.

Writer's Digest Books
9933 Alliance Rd.
Cincinnati, OH 45242
513/531-2690
Books and magazines for those who want to publish. May be useful if you'd like to achieve greater visibility through print, or you're called on to contribute in the course of your work.

Annotated Books for the Power Manager

Ackoff, Russell L., *The Art of Problem Solving: Accompanied by Ackoff's Fables,* John Wiley & Sons, New York, 1978.

An entertaining yet pithy look at why most problem solving fails dismally (and only raises still more problems).

Bennis, Warren, *The Unconscious Conspiracy: Why Leaders Can't Lead,* AMACOM, New York, 1976.

His seminal work on leadership, from which all of his other works devolve. Read the original.

Bridges, William, *Managing Transitions: Make the Most of Change,* Addison Wesley, Reading (MA), 1991.

One of the best writers on dissecting change, helping people through it, and exploiting the outcomes.

Drucker, Peter, *Management Challenges for the 21st Century,* HarperBusiness, New York, 1999.

Contemporary insights from the greatest management thinker of all time, still going strong.

Drucker, Peter, *Managing in Turbulent Times,* Harper & Row, New York, 1980.

Words still true and advice still on-target over two decades after it was written.

Jay, Antony, *Management and Machiavelli: An Inquiry into the Politics of Corporate Life,* Bantam Books, New York, 1968.

Rereleased on numerous occasions, the author makes a compelling case that the more we know about organizations, the less we understand.

McKinnon, Wayne, *Complete Guide to E-Mail,* Ryshell Books, Nepean, Ontario, 1999.

If we're going to use it we might as well get good at it, and McKinnon provides more than you'll ever need to know.

Miller, Anne, *Presentation Jazz: How to Make Your Sales Presentations Sing,* AMACOM, New York, 1998.

Guidelines for the all-important internal presentations and customer presentations from a veteran sales trainer and consultant.

Morrisey, George, *Morrisey on Planning* (three-part series), Jossey-Bass, San Francisco, 1996.

These three short books on short-range and long-range planning and strategy are a superb primer for the planning-challenged manager.

Nonaka, Ikujiro, and Takeuchi, Hirotaka, *The Knowledge-Creating Company: How Japanese Companies Create the Dynamics of Innovation,* Oxford, New York, 1995.

The only book I've found that makes "knowledge management" a pragmatic management tool and not another flavor of the month.

Sampson, Anthony, *Company Man: The Rise and Fall of Corporate Life,* Times Business, New York, 1995.
A nonclichéd book about the future of business, demonstrating that old structures will have to change or else.

Weiss, Alan, *Good Enough Isn't Enough: Nine Challenges for Companies that Choose to Be Great,* AMACOM, New York, 1999.
The author's analysis and insights for success in the 21st century, based on his consulting work around the world.

Weiss, Alan, *Managing for Peak Performance: A Guide to the Power (and Pitfalls) of Personal Style,* Summit Consulting Group, East Greenwich, Rhode Island, 1992 (originally published by HarperCollins).
A guide to personal characteristics that can lead to success or failure, and how to manage one's own behavior as well as that of others.

Weiss, Alan, *Our Emperors Have No Clothes,* Summit Consulting Group, East Greenwich, Rhode Island, 1995 (originally published by Career Press).
The follies of the executive suite, and how downsizing and layoffs are inevitably the fallout of executive errors.

Wheatley, Margaret, *Leadership and the New Science: Learning about Organization from an Orderly Universe,* Berrett-Koehler, San Francisco, 1992.
Sometimes abstruse and often esoteric, a nonetheless thoughtful exploration of chaos and the lack thereof, in nature and in business.

Wild, Russell, *Games Bosses Play,* Contemporary
    Books, Chicago, 1997.
A humorous but accurate view of deadly and toxic
bosses, their habits, and what you can do to avoid
fatal injury.

A

Accountability, for conflict resolution, 68–69

Acquiring leadership style, 251–52

Active leadership, 230

Adaptive actions, 163–65, 180, 181

Alcohol consumption, 11–12

Alternatives
as component of decisions, 183
conflict about, 48–51
evaluating, 198–200
generating, 196–98

Alternatives variable, in leadership situations, 244

American Airlines, 143

American Association of Retired People (AARP), 154

American Management Association, 391

American Psychological Association, 110

American Psychological Society, 110

American Society of Association Executives, 391

Amorphous issues, 225

Analogies, 126
in presentations, 302

Anticipating, 163, 208, 209, 211
what may go wrong, 208–10

Apple Computer, 280

Apple Computer Company, 101

Assertiveness, 98, 104, 106–7, 109

Assumptions, separating facts from, 66

Attention to detail, 105–9

Attitude, poor performance and, 83, 84

Audience involvement, at presentations, 313–18

Autocratic leadership style, 236–37, 245, 251

B

Behavioral interviewing, 110–12

Behaviors
  assessing and adjusting your own, 112–15
  basic measures of, 104–10
    assertiveness, 104
    attention to detail, 105–9
    persuasiveness, 105
    tolerance for repetition, 105
  changing, 107–8
  empowerment and rewarding, 36
  skills distinguished from, 99–100
  variables that affect, 97–98

Best balanced choice, 202–3

"Big stick" approach, 5–7, 14

Binary decisions, 196

Binary questions, 128

Bipolar depression, 63–64

Blame, finding causes versus, 163–75

Boeing, 278

Boredom (ennui), 112, 113

Boundaries, developing empowered employees and, 31–32

C

Cafeterias, environmental interference with communication in, 119

Carey Limousine, 189–90

Carlyle, Thomas, 363

"Carrot and stick" approach, 5–7, 14

Causes, finding, 163–75

Change(s)
  affecting distinctions of problem area, identifying, 170–73
  developing possible causes from the, 173
  myth that people resist, 19–20
Changing behaviors, 107–8
Chrysler, 280
Circular discussions, ending, 332–33
Coaching, 80–89
  defined, 80
  by employees themselves, 83
  process of, 81–83
Cognitive interference with communication, 121–24
Comfort zones
  changing behaviors and, 107–8, 110, 112, 113
  communication and, 124–25
Commitment to the decision, 234–35
Commitment variable, in leadership situations, 244
Communication, 117–34

cognitive interference with, 121–24
comfort zones and, 124–25
conflict resolution and, 66–67
differences in styles of, 124–26
environmental interference with, 119–21
negotiation and, 253
power managers' excellence in, 356–59
testing incoming, 121
testing outgoing, 123–28
Communispond, 392
Competition, subordination of ego and, 350
Compromise, negotiation and, 253, 254
Conflict
  as almost always temporary, 64–65
  defusing hostility and, 52–55
  forms of, 48–51

Conflict, *(cont.)*
  personality, 52,
    55–64
    with depressed
      employees,
      63–64
    with egoists, 60
    "it's not me"
      personality
      disorder and,
      56–57
    with neurotic
      employees,
      57–58
    with politician
      employees,
      59–60
    with psychotic
      employees,
      62–63
  resolving, 64
    keeping the
      conflict non-
      emotional,
      65–66
    maintaining
      frequent
      communica-
      tions chan-
      nels, 66–67
    at meetings,
      322, 333
    separating fact
      from assump-
      tion, 66
    testing with
      third parties,
      67–68

Confrontation, poor
    performance
    and fear of, 75
Consensus
  as leadership style,
    239–40, 245, 252
  meetings and, 322
Consultants, gener-
    ating alternatives
    and, 197
Contingent actions,
    163, 165,
    211–16, 218, 219
Corrective actions,
    162, 163, 180,
    181, 209–10
Costs, negotiating
    about value
    versus, 269–70
Counseling
  defined, 81
  process of, 83–89
Crisis management,
    363–67
Cultural barriers,
    overcoming, 334
Customers
  negotiating with,
    265–70
  primary focus on,
    359–61

D
Day 1 problems,
    177–78
Decision chain,
    187–203

best balanced choice, 202–3

establishing "musts" and "wants," 193–96

establishing objectives and, 190–91

evaluating alternatives, 198

generating alternatives, 196–98

identifying resource restraints and expected results, 191–93

risk assessment, 200–202

Decision making, 183–203. *See also* Decision chain; Leadership

avoiding and escaping traps in, 184–87

failing to stay the course, 187

following the rut, 184–85

listening to the last or loudest voice, 185

lousing up the timing, 186–87

permitting a single factor to turn the tide, 185–86

components of decisions, 183–84

empowerment and, 35

quality in, 234

Defenses, emotional, 78

Demographic changes, as source of innovation, 153–55

Demonstration, in presentations, 303

Depressed employees, personality conflicts with, 63–64

Describing the parameters, identification of problems and, 167–69

Detail, attention to, 105–9

Deviation from standard, identification of problems and, 165–67

Distinctions about the problem area, 169–70

Downsizings, 73
Drowsiness, 112

E

Educating yourself, 385–88
Education, continual, 37
Ego
    subordinating, 36–37
    subordination of, to organizational needs, 349–50
Egoists, personality conflicts with, 60–62
Emerson, Ralph Waldo, 299
Empowerment, 27–45
    defined, 27
    as effective management tool, 28–29
    rules for, 34–37
    steps in developing empowered employees, 31
Enlightened self-interest, 10–12, 19
Ennui (boredom), 112, 113
Enthusiasm, 4, 11
Environment, behaviors and, 98

Environmental interference with communication, 119–21
Ethical standards, 109
Ethics, 348–49
Eustress, 298
Exemplars, choosing and supporting, 23
Exemplars (role models), 345, 346–47
Expectations, decision making and, 193
Experience, generating alternatives and, 197
Expertise, 232
Extroverts, 128
Eye contact, at presentations, 308–9

F

Facts, in presentations, 301
Failure
    freedom to fail, 29
    unexpected, as source of innovation, 144–45
Failure work, 28
Falling asleep on the job, 112

Fear as mover, not motivator, 5–7
Features and benefits, results and outcomes versus, 266–67
FedEx, 146
Feedback, 370
  coaching and, 82, 83
  empowerment and, 35
  overreaction to, 113
  unwillingness to respond to, 113
Feuds, 65, 69
Fleet Bank, 30
Ford Motor Company, 144–45
Freedom to fail, 29
Future job, probability of success in, 103–4

G
Gates, Bill, 3
General Motors, 145
Gestures, at presentations, 310–11
Goals
  empowerment employees and, 36
  integration of ethics and values into, 348–49
Goals variable, in leadership situations, 244
Gravity, 220
Group leadership style, 238–39, 252
Growth, 221
  as source of innovation, 149–51
Grudges, 65

H
Hallways, environmental interference with communication in, 119–20
Harvard Law School, 278
Hereditary factors, behaviors and, 98
Hewlett-Packard, 285
Hierarchical power, 231
Honesty, 24
Hostility, defusing, 52
Human resources, poor performance and inadequate oversight over, 75
Humor, in presentations, 302

Hypothesis, problem
solving and,
164–65, 169–73
developing
possible causes
from the
changes, 173
identifying
changes affect-
ing distinctions,
170–73
identifying distinc-
tions of the
problem area,
169–70

I

Iaccoca, Lee,
144–45, 280
Identification of
problems,
164–69
actual deviation
from standard
and, 165–67
describing the
parameters and,
167–69
hypothesis and,
169–73
Illustration, in
presentations,
303
"In crowd"
approach,
7–10
Influence,
13–16

Information vari-
able, in leader-
ship situations,
243
Informed, keeping
people, 23–24
Innovation, 141–42,
352–53
empowerment
and, 35–36
sources of, 143–57
changes in
industry
and/or mar-
ket structure,
148–49
demographic
changes,
153–55
high growth,
149–51
new knowl-
edge, 156–57
perception
change,
155–56
process weak-
ness, 145–46
technologies,
151–52
unexpected
events,
147–48
unexpected
failure,
144–45
unexpected
success,
143–44

Inquiring leadership mode, 237, 243

Interests, reciprocity of, 16–19, 29

Interim actions, monitoring the progress of plans and, 218–20

Interviewing, behavioral, 110–12

Introverts, 128

"It's not me" personality disorder, 56–57

J

Japan, 124–25

Jobs, Stephen, 101

Journey to the future, 20, 21

K

Kepner, Charles, 162

Knowledge transfer, as role of meetings, 323

Kosovo, war in, 276

L

Leadership and Decision Making (Vroom and Yetton), 234

Leadership decision making, key factors in, 234–36

Leadership (leadership styles), 229–52

acquiring, 251–52

active, 230

autocratic, 236–37, 251

consensus, 239–40, 245, 252

dynamics of, 240–43

by example, 230

factors in determining appropriateness of, 234–36

group, 238–39, 252

inquiring, 237, 243

one-on-one, 237–38, 252

variables in leadership situations, 243–52

Legal issues, poor performance and, 74

Letters, writing, 357–59

Letting go, 22–23

Leveraging the talents of others, 37–40

Listening, 126–27
  empowerment and, 35
  to the last or loudest voice, as decision trap, 185
  negotiating and, 258–59
  reflective, 129–31

M

Mager, Robert, 84
Managers
  as role models, 345, 346–47
  traits of memorable, 346
    communication and interpersonal abilities, 356–59
    crisis management skills, 363–67
    development of subordinates, 353–54
    innovation and raising of standards, 352–53
    integration of ethics and values into business goals, 348–49
    living a complete life, 361–63
    positive role model, 345, 346–47
    primary focus on customer, 359–61
    prudent risk taking, 355–56
    sharing credit and accepting blame, 350–52
    subordination of ego to organizational needs, 349–50
Mandatory objectives, 194
Manic depression, 63–64
Maslow, Abraham, 388–89
Maturity, 109
3M Corporation, 144
Measurable objectives, 194
Meetings, 321–42
  avoiding unproductive, 336–38
  conflict resolution and, 66–67

firmness in running, 329–31
functions of, 321–26
getting the most out of participation in, 338–42
high nervous energy at, 112
power techniques for, 331–36
  ending circular discussions, 332–33
  maintaining high energy, 334–36
  overcoming cultural barriers, 334
  stopping road hogs, 331–32
results-oriented agendas for, 326–29
Mehrabbian, Albert, 298–99
Memos, writing, 357–59
Mentor, teaching as a, 381–83
Merck & Co., 45, 119, 129, 130, 157, 281
Metaphors, 126

Mileposts, monitoring the progress of plans and, 215–18
Money, 4
Mustang, 145
Musts, in negotiations, 255–59
"Musts," establishing "wants" and, 193–96

N

National Trade and Professional Associations of the United States, 392
Negotiation(s), 253–73
conducting effective, 258–61
with customers, 265–70
  costs versus value, 269–70
  easy-to-accommodate issues, 267–68
  features and benefits versus results and outcomes, 266–67
defined, 253

Negotiation(s),
(cont.)
   flow of, 270–73
   meetings and, 322
   musts and wants
      in, 255–59
   tough issues and,
      261–63
   tough responses
      and, 264–65
Nervous energy, 112
Neurotic employees,
   personality con-
   flicts with, 57–58
Normative pressure,
   7
"Numbers prob-
   lem," 47–48

O
Objectives
   aligning corporate
      and individual,
      287–93
   as component of
      decisions, 183
   conflict about,
      48–51
   decision making
      and establishing,
      190–91
   establishing
      "musts" and
      "wants," 193–96
Obscene language,
   86

Observable behav-
   ior, performance
   evaluation and,
   76
One-on-one leader-
   ship, 237–38
Open-door policy,
   permanent, 223
Opinion, separating
   fact from, 179
Outcomes, features
   and benefits ver-
   sus results and,
   266–67
Ownership, 210,
   212, 241, 244,
   251
   meetings and,
      322

P
Parameters, describ-
   ing, identifica-
   tion of problems
   and, 167–69
Parking lots, envi-
   ronmental inter-
   ference with
   communication
   in, 119–20
Participation vari-
   able, in leader-
   ship situations,
   244
Passivity, 98
Patience, 105, 107

Pavlovian conditioning, 3

Peer pressure, 7–9, 12

People problems, 175–77

Perception change, as source of innovation, 155

Performance evaluation, 74
    critical nature of, 89–90
    effective, 89–94
    observable behavior as focus of, 76–77
    as substitute for raises and benefits, 75

Permanent actions, monitoring the progress of plans and, 218–20

Personality conflicts, 52, 55–64
    with egoists, 60
    "it's not me" personality disorder and, 56–57
    with neurotic employees, 57–58
    with politician employees, 59–60

with psychotic employees, 62–63

Personality disorders. *See also* Personality conflicts
    "it's not me," 56–57

Personality types, psychobabble about, 79

Persuasiveness, 105, 107, 109

Plans (planning), 139, 162, 205–26
    anticipating what may go wrong and, 208–10
    contingent actions and, 213–14
    identifying steps in, 206–8
    monitoring progress of, 214–20
        permanent and interim actions, 218–20
        triggers and mileposts, 215–18
    protective actions and, 210–13
    situation appraisal and, 220–26
    steps in, 206–8

Plan statements, 206–7

Playing field, developing empowered employees and creating the, 31

Politician employees, personality conflicts with, 59

Politicking, 223

Poor performance, 73–94
coaching and counseling to deal with, 80–89
steps in dealing with, 79

Positive world view, 4

Post-heroic management, 369–71

Post-It Notes, 144

Power
hierarchical, 231
to punish, 232, 233
referent, 232–34
to reward, 231–33

Powerless people, 28

Power techniques
for meetings, 331–36
ending circular discussions, 332–33
maintaining high energy, 334–36

overcoming cultural barriers, 334
stopping road hogs, 331–32

Presentations, 297–319, 339
audience involvement at, 313–18
common problems at, 318–19
"dress rehearsal" for, 307–8
ending, 317–18
ending of, 305–7
key points in, 303
keys to professional, 297–98
personal demeanor for, 307–11
preparing for, 298–307
"hooks" or "grabbers" in, 301–3
organizing your remarks, 300–307
understanding the audience, 300
speaking at, 311–13
visual aids and handouts, 305
visual aids at, 318

Preventive actions, 163, 165, 210–16, 218, 219
Priorities, setting, 220–26
Problem solving, 139–42
  approaches to, 162–63
  art of, 178–81
  day 1 problems, 177–78
  finding causes and, 163–75
    hypothesis, 169–73
    validation, 173–75
  identification of problems and, 164–69
    actual deviation from standard and, 165–67
    describing the parameters and, 167–69
    hypothesis and, 169–73
  people problems, 175–77
Process, conflict and, 48
Process weakness, as source of innovation, 145–46

Prohibition, 11
Promises, 24
Promotions
  probability of success in future job and, 103–4
  for wrong people, 100–104
Protective actions, 210–13
Provocative questioning, encouraging others to speak by, 128–29
Psychobabble, avoiding, 76–80
Psychotic employees, personality conflicts with, 62–63
Punish, power to, 232, 233

Q
Quality, in decision making, 234
Quality variable, in leadership situations, 243
Questions. See also Interviewing
  as more important than answers, 372–76
  at presentations, 314–16

Questions, *(cont.)*
  provocative,
    encouraging
    others to speak
    with, 128–29
  turn-around,
    131–34

R

Rational Manager,
    The (Kepner and
    Tregoe), 162
"Reaching out" to
    others, 379–85
Reading with com-
    prehension,
    356
Realistic objectives,
    194
Reciprocity of inter-
    ests, 16–19, 29
Recognition, in
    presentations,
    302
Recognition of per-
    formance, meet-
    ings and, 322
Referent power,
    232–34
Reflective listening,
    129–31
Repetition, toler-
    ance for, 105,
    109
Resource restraints,
    decision making
    and, 191–93

Restaurants, envi-
    ronmental
    interference
    with communi-
    cation in, 119
Rest rooms, environ-
    mental inter-
    ference with
    communication
    in, 120
Results
  features and bene-
    fits versus out-
    comes and,
    266–67
  focusing on,
    376–79
Results expectations,
    decision making
    and, 193
Reward, power to,
    231–33
Rewarding behav-
    iors, empower-
    ment and, 36
Rhetorical ques-
    tions, in presen-
    tations, 302
Risks, as component
    of decisions, 184
Risk(s), assessing,
    200–202
Role models (exem-
    plars), managers
    as, 345, 346–47
Rut, following the,
    as decision trap,
    184–85

S

Schein, Edgar, 379
Scientific management, 73
Scully, John, 101
Sears, 278, 280
Self-actualization, 388–90
Self-esteem
  cycle of motivation and, 40–45
  empowerment and, 34
Self-interest(s)
  determining others' rational, 17–19
  enlightened, 10–12, 19
  influence and, 13–16
  reciprocity of interests and, 16–19
Self-mastery, 371
Separation technique, 223–26
Silences, 126
Situational leadership, 234
Situation appraisal, 220–26
Skills
  application of, 43
  behaviors distinguished from, 99–100

building, 42–43
developing
  empowered employees and, 32–33
  problems with, 84
  self-esteem and, 42–44
"Smile sheets," 370
Smiling, at presentations, 308
Smith, Fred, 146
Smoking, 11–12
Speaking
  encouraging others to speak, 127–34
    provocative questioning, 128
    reflective listening, 129–31
    turn-around questions, 131–34
  at presentations, 311–13
Statistics, in presentations, 301
Stereotyping, 47
Strategy
  defined, 280
  formulation of, 282–83
  implementation of, 283–87

Strategy, *(cont.)*
 manager's role in, 281–83
 tactics versus, 275–80
Stress
 inducers of, 21–22
 presentations and, 298
Structure variable, in leadership situations, 244
Subordinates
 development of, 353–54
 negotiating and, 258
Subordinating ego, 36–37
Success, unexpected, as source of innovation, 143–44
Success trap, 37
Supportive systems, developing empowered employees and, 34

T
Tactics, 275
 defined, 280
Taylorism, 73
Teachable moment, 42

Teaching, 379–85
 in an educational institution, 383–85
 in an informal community program, 385
 formally within the organization, 380–81
 informally, as a mentor, 381–83
Temporary employees, empowerment of, 33–34
Texas Instruments, 29–30
Third parties, conflict resolution and, 67–68
360° assessments, 370
Time management, 222
Timing, 235
 decision making and, 186–87
Tolerance for repetition, 105, 109
Training, poor performance and, 74
Tregoe, Benjamin, 162
Triggers, monitoring the progress plans and, 215–18

Turn-around questions, 131–34
Tylenol, 145

U

Unexpected events, as source of innovation, 147
Unexpected failure, as source of innovation, 144–45
Unexpected success, as source of innovation, 143–44

V

Validation, problem solving and, 165, 173–75
Value, negotiating about costs versus, 269–70
Values, 348–49
  strategy and, 281–82
Velocity, 220–21
Vendettas, 65, 69
Victories
  empowerment of employees and, 36
  self-esteem and, 41, 43

Vision
  empowerment employees and, 36
  strategy and, 282
Visual aids
  at meetings, 335
  at presentations, 305, 316–18
Voice, for presentations, 311–13
Volstead Act, 11
Vroom, Victor, 234

W

Wants, in negotiations, 255–59
"Wants," establishing "musts" and, 193–96
Whining, 223
Willingness, developing empowered employees and, 33
Writer's Digest Books, 392
Writing memos and letters, 357–59

Y–Z

Yearbook of Experts, Authorities, and Spokespersons, 392
Yetton, Phillip, 234

The *Unofficial Guide*™ Reader Questionnaire

If you would like to express your opinion about power managing or this guide, please complete this questionnaire and mail it to:

The *Unofficial Guide*™ Reader Questionnaire
IDG Lifestyle Group
1633 Broadway, floor 7
New York, NY 10019-6785

Gender: ___ M   ___ F

Age: ___ Under 30   ___ 31–40   ___ 41–50
___ Over 50

Education: ___ High school   ___ College
___ Graduate/Professional

What is your occupation?

_____

How did you hear about this guide?
___ Friend or relative
___ Newspaper, magazine, or Internet
___ Radio or TV
___ Recommended at bookstore
___ Recommended by librarian
___ Picked it up on my own
___ Familiar with the *Unofficial Guide*™ travel series

Did you go to the bookstore specifically for a book on power managing?   Yes ___   No ___

Have you used any other *Unofficial Guides*™?
Yes ___   No ___

If Yes, which ones?

_____
_____
_____

What other book(s) on power managing have you purchased? _____

_____

_____

Was this book:

___ more helpful than other(s)

___ less helpful than other(s)

Do you think this book was worth its price?

Yes ___ No ___

Did this book cover all topics related to power managing adequately?

Yes ___ No ___

Please explain your answer:

_____

_____

_____

Were there any specific sections in this book that were of particular help to you? Yes ___ No ___

Please explain your answer:

_____

_____

_____

On a scale of 1 to 10, with 10 being the best rating, how would you rate this guide? ___

What other titles would you like to see published in the *Unofficial Guide*™ series?

_____

_____

Are Unofficial Guides™ **readily available in your area?** Yes ___ No ___

Other comments:

_____

_____

_____

_____

Get the inside scoop...with the *Unofficial Guides*™!

Health and Fitness

The Unofficial Guide to Alternative Medicine
ISBN: 0-02-862526-9 Price: $15.95

The Unofficial Guide to Conquering Impotence
ISBN: 0-02-862870-5 Price: $15.95

The Unofficial Guide to Coping with Menopause
ISBN: 0-02-862694-x Price: $15.95

The Unofficial Guide to Cosmetic Surgery
ISBN: 0-02-862522-6 Price: $15.95

The Unofficial Guide to Dieting Safely
ISBN: 0-02-862521-8 Price: $15.95

The Unofficial Guide to Having a Baby
ISBN: 0-02-862695-8 Price: $15.95

The Unofficial Guide to Living with Diabetes
ISBN: 0-02-862919-1 Price: $15.95

The Unofficial Guide to Overcoming Arthritis
ISBN: 0-02-862714-8 Price: $15.95

The Unofficial Guide to Overcoming Infertility
ISBN: 0-02-862916-7 Price: $15.95

Career Planning

The Unofficial Guide to Acing the Interview
ISBN: 0-02-862924-8 Price: $15.95

The Unofficial Guide to Earning What You Deserve
ISBN: 0-02-862523-4 Price: $15.95

The Unofficial Guide to Hiring and Firing People
ISBN: 0-02-862523-4 Price: $15.95

Business and Personal Finance

The Unofficial Guide to Investing
ISBN: 0-02-862458-0 Price: $15.95

The Unofficial Guide to Investing in Mutual Funds
ISBN: 0-02-862920-5 Price: $15.95

The Unofficial Guide to Managing Your Personal Finances
ISBN: 0-02-862921-3 Price: $15.95

The Unofficial Guide to Starting a Small Business
ISBN: 0-02-862525-0 Price: $15.95

Home and Automotive

The Unofficial Guide to Buying a Home
ISBN: 0-02-862461-0 Price: $15.95

The Unofficial Guide to Buying or Leasing a Car
ISBN: 0-02-862524-2 Price: $15.95

The Unofficial Guide to Hiring Contractors
ISBN: 0-02-862460-2 Price: $15.95

Family and Relationships

The Unofficial Guide to Childcare
ISBN: 0-02-862457-2 Price: $15.95

The Unofficial Guide to Dating Again
ISBN: 0-02-862454-8 Price: $15.95

The Unofficial Guide to Divorce
ISBN: 0-02-862455-6 Price: $15.95

The Unofficial Guide to Eldercare
ISBN: 0-02-862456-4 Price: $15.95

The Unofficial Guide to Planning Your Wedding
ISBN: 0-02-862459-9 Price: $15.95

Hobbies and Recreation

The Unofficial Guide to Finding Rare Antiques
ISBN: 0-02-862922-1 Price: $15.95

The Unofficial Guide to Casino Gambling
ISBN: 0-02-862917-5 Price: $15.95

All books in the *Unofficial Guide* series are available at your local bookseller, or by calling 1-800-428-5331.